Mary of Nazareth
Myth or History?

Mary of Nazareth

by Bonaventura Rinaldi

THE NEWMAN PRESS

Myth or History?

Translated by Mary F. Ingoldsby

WESTMINSTER, MARYLAND 1966

MARY OF NAZARETH—MYTH OR HISTORY? is a translation of the Italian *Maria di Nazareth—Mito o Storia?* by Bonaventura Rinaldi, first published by Massimo, Corso di Porta Romana, 122, Milano. Copyright © Massimo, Milano, 1962

Nihil Obstat: Very Rev. Msgr. Caroll E. Satterfield
Censor Librorum

Imprimatur: His Eminence Lawrence Cardinal Shehan
Archbishop of Baltimore
August 22, 1966

Preface

IN ORDER to justify the publication of this new Marian work which I have the pleasure of introducing to its readers—and I hope they will be numerous—only one thing is required, namely, that the book be read entirely from the first page to the last. I feel sure that anyone who takes the trouble to read it will be aware at once that in the mass of Marian writings which flood the market the work that we here present is to be distinguished from all the rest and has claim to a special place of honor.

The book is outstanding, in the first place, for the originality of its treatment of the Marian problem. What might appear from a superficial viewpoint as no more than a myth proves to be a divine echo of the deepest human aspirations—the yearning after tenderness, purity, and love, of which the Virgin Mother is the supreme expression, the most vivid reflection, in turn, of the infinite tenderness, purity, and goodness of God.

Thus we arrive at the root and essence of Mariology and of its profound *raison d'être* in the vast and fertile field of theological knowledge and culture.

Another powerful echo of this deep human yearning after tenderness, purity, and love is to be found in the myths of the ancient oriental peoples, the Babylonians, the Canaanites (particularly the Ugarities), and the Egyptians.

The book stands out, in the second place, for its vast and deep learning, both profane and sacred, that is brought into harmonious union. As an eloquent indication of this we have the widely varying sources of information and the abundant quotations and notes.

It is remarkable, in the third place, for its dexterity and brilliance and, not infrequently, the geniality of its form and expression, together with the concise logic of its reasoning.

Certainly there are not many books like this one. It is a book which Marian literature did not yet possess and of which the need was felt.

On reaching the end the reader will be convinced that Mariology, far from being a mere appendage of Christology, as K. Barth would have it, is, on the contrary, the fairest and most sweetly-scented flower of the science of Christ, King and Center of all hearts.

FATHER GABRIEL M. ROSCHINI
Dean of the Marianum Theological Faculty

Author's Introduction

THE HUMAN heart has always known an insatiable longing for affection. Anne Frank writes in her diary: "In spite of all my theories and however much trouble I take, each day I miss having a real mother who understands me." [1] These words were written by a fourteen-year-old girl on Christmas Eve, 1943. The young girl was beginning to awaken to life and its problems. Little did she realize, though, that her heart's desire had already been adequately answered in the Christmas mystery of the Virgin Mother with her child.

C. Baudelaire, at forty, felt an intense need of maternal caresses and therefore wrote to his mother: "I would like to have a little courage and a few caresses. I do not know what I would not give to spend a few days with you, with the only being to whom my life is attached. Who knows if I shall be able again some day to open my whole heart to you, the heart you have never appreciated or known! I write this without hesitation, knowing it to be true. If you find a reproach in what I write, be aware that this in no way changes either my admiration for your great heart or my gratitude. You have always sacrificed yourself. You have a real genius for sacrifice. I do not know what I would not give to see you and embrace you. I implore peace; give me peace, love and a little affection." [2]

The author of *Les Fleurs du Mal* was inclined to believe on that particular May 6, 1861, that May is just an ordinary month like the rest, that it is not the symbol of renewed life. Mythology had already bedecked the queen of May with flowers, because she was to represent Cybele, the great mother.[3]

Was it not therefore fitting that this month of flowers should be dedicated to Mary of Nazareth, to the one who is no myth, but a historical fact? Dedicated, that is to say, to a revelation of God who wishes to save us through the tears and the smile of Mary?

*   *   *

From an aesthetical point of view, nothing could be more appropriate. But the point which troubles us today is a very different one. No unbeliever doubts that, from the aesthetical viewpoint, Catholicism and particularly Mariology is a wonderful world. But they anxiously ask the Catholic to show them the difference between Cybele and Mary, between myth and history.

Non-Catholics who love the history of religion are inclined to identify myths with Mariology. To them Mary is a continuation of the myth that has always painted the Great Mother in vivid tints.[4]

While admitting that the crowds who sang the praises of Mary in Ephesus were descended from those who had once sung to Artemis, we ask ourselves if the image of Mary is raised up by divine hands or by the mere human desire to venerate the Mother? Is Mary just a human utterance or is she also and above all a divine utterance?

The pages which follow will show substantially, in an evident way, whether Mary is simply a myth or a historical fact from which springs forth a faith that enables us to penetrate into the innermost depths of God's being, to discover the all-tender and loving Father.

Mariology does not contradict myth, which is the imaginary personification of human longings, but it renders it historical in what is most human, because revelation is the answer to the questionings of man's mind and heart.

To demonstrate that myth and history are not contradictory is a formidable task, one to which we bring a few suggestions that to us appear substantial.

These will lead us to conclude that God has responded to the human thirst for tenderness, reserving the Mother as his final gift (John 19, 26). For it seems that only in a maternal embrace can we fully understand that God is a Father.

We hope in this way to demonstrate that the essence of Mariology tallies perfectly with the essence of God and of theology.

    ❖   ❖   ❖

If we accept Alain's intuition that maternal love is the model of all love (stressed by Fulton Sheen in his book on the Most Blessed Virgin *The World's First Love*),[5] we ask ourselves if this affirmation does not contradict the indisputable biblical dogma that Christ as the Word of the Father's love is the first and supreme love in the universe.

We begin by penetrating into the ancient mythical world and into the existentialist world of today, and we conclude that undoubtedly mythology and psychology agree that the Mother is the first love, born of tenderness and irradiated by the maternal smile.

In the second chapter we enter into the Old Testament where God, in the most solemn moments of history, manifests himself as merciful tenderness, as saving love, and an inebriating smile. We naturally ask ourselves whether the maternal world and the divine world are in opposition, or if one suggests the other.

We find that God's tenderness appears precisely in these more sublime moments, expressing his merciful love in the figure of the Mother treading under foot the Serpent, the Son of Death (Gen. 3), and showing that he wishes women to be known as "tenderness," as a living symbol of the Lord who loves again (Os. 2, 2-25).

Especially in the books written after the Babylonian exile (536-100 B.C.) do we find a more spontaneous effusion of maternity and tenderness, summed up in the expression: "As a mother comforts her son, so will I comfort you; in Jerusalem you shall find your comfort" (Isa. 66, 13).

Against this admirable background Mary of Nazareth appears with Jesus. In the first Gospels, those of Matthew and Mark, and in the Pauline Epistles we find an atmosphere filled with the tenderness (2 Cor. 1, 3) and love of the redeeming God (Rom. 5, 5 ff.). But when we go to the Gospels of Luke and John we notice a decisive clarification of revelation. Luke adopts the concepts of the Lord's grace and tenderness (6, 36) applying them to Christ: "the grace of God in him." Mary becomes the "redeemed" or the one who is full of grace par excellence through the Son of God who has become her own child.

With Mary's redemption all mankind is to have once more the life-bearing Mother. John is to tell us in fact that the most human gift of the dying Christ was Mary: "Behold thy mother" (19, 27).

Thus revelation, centered in Christ the Eternal Word of the Father, confers a supernatural consecration on the myth of the Mother.

❋   ❋   ❋

When we offered this book to the public for the first time two years ago, it was with a certain uneasiness, because it seemed that we were saying something too new. Hence we employed too rapid a style in speaking of Our Lady.

In presenting this work today to the American public, we have the pleasure of remarking that the dogmatic Constitution *De Ecclesia* promulgated by the Second Vatican Council adopts a similar moderate mode of expression centered in trinitarian theology.

It begins, first of all, with "The most merciful God . . . the Father of all mercies." Our own work, in fact, has as its impetus the triple idea of God as tenderness, mercy, and love, expressed in grace and kindness.

In relation to the Father, Mary is the "well-beloved Daughter"; in relation to the Son, she is "the Mother . . . above all others and in a singular way the generous associate and humble handmaid of the Lord" while in relation to the Holy Spirit, she is "the Temple."

Our whole mariological conception moves on this basis. It is not split up into a number of theses, as though Mary at the Nativity were to become the Mother of Jesus, on Calvary the Co-Redemptrix, in heaven the Mediatrix and our Mother. No! Mary is all this at every moment of her life, but in an ever more perfect way:

"Predestined from eternity, by that decree of divine providence which determined the Incarnation of the Word, to be the Mother of God, the Blessed Virgin was on this earth the Virgin Mother of the Redeemer, and above all others and in a singular way the generous associate and humble handmaid of the Lord. She conceived, brought forth and nourished Christ, she presented him to the Father in the temple, and was united with him by compassion as he died on the cross. In this singular way she cooperated by her obedience, faith, hope and burning charity in the work of the Savior in giving back supernatural life to souls. Wherefore she is our mother in the order of grace.

"This maternity of Mary in the order of grace began with the consent she gave in faith at the Annunciation and which she sustained without wavering at the cross, and lasts until the eternal fulfillment of all the elect. Taken up to heaven, she did not lay aside this salvific duty, but by her constant intercession continued to bring us the gifts of eternal salvation. By her maternal charity she cares for the brethren of her Son, who still journey on earth surrounded by dangers and difficulties, until they are led into the happiness of their true home" (*De Ecclesia*, pp. 61-62).

Another characteristic of our study is a sound evaluation of the filial sentiment of mankind toward Mary. The Supreme Pontiff, Paul VI, emphasizes as follows the feeling of filial devotion to Mary on the part of the Christian people:

"We are fortunate, brethren and children, in having been educated at the school of Holy Church in this veneration of the Mother of God, and we know almost by way of an irrefutable experience that this cult which we wish to be interior, personal, human and truly holy, does not by any means prevent us from recognizing the unique, transcendent, divine source of truth, of life, of grace, Jesus Christ. It conducts us to him, it binds us to him, it unites us to him as to the only Holy One, our only Lord and most high Master and Redeemer" (*Osservatore Romano*, Feb. 3, 1965).

In quoting Sacred Scripture, especially the Old Testament (Gen. 3, 15 and Isa. 7, 14), we have allowed the ancient manuscript to carry us spontaneously, without any compulsion, to the Mother of the Savior "prophetically foreshadowed in the promise" (*De Ecclesia*, p. 55).

Finally, let us point out the frequent insistence of the Council upon the words *mother* and *maternal,* as the keystone of our Mariology. The two theses on the Co-Redemptrix and the Mediatrix should be read in order to remark how we have dwelt insistently on this aspect, convinced that if God is the Father of mercy, Mary cannot be other than the Mother according to grace which flows from the heart of God.

These pages are intended to be a tribute of gratitude to our venerated teachers of the Pontifical Institute Angelicum in Rome, who taught us to see all things in the light of God, as well as to the professors of the Pontifical Biblical Institute, who with great competence showed us how God stepped into history through his word, written in the Sacred Book.

Nor can we forget the humble sons of St. Francis, professors of the Pontifical Institute Franciscanum in Jerusalem, who conducted us through the desolate expanses of Palestine to touch with the heart, rather than the hand, the fact that Christianity is no myth but is written in human history, in letters of blood, the blood of the all-tender and loving Son of God.

We heartily thank professors P. M. Zerwick, Monsignor E. Galbiati, and Father Silverio Zedda for their valuable advice. Similarly, we wish to thank Father Giacomo Pesce who very unselfishly took much of his time from the re-editing of his *Mariale* in order that the present work might be worthy of the great Mother of God.

We wish to express our gratitude in a particular way to Monsignor Battista Peruzzo, Archbishop of Agrigento (Sicily), for his paternal encouragement toward the publication of this Marian work, as well as to Father G. Roschini who condescended to read it word for word and who, as well as offering valuable advice which we carried out to the letter, introduced us to a public desirous of penetrating into the marvels of the Marian world.

We hope their labors will have contributed toward drying Mary's tears, so that this weary society of our day may receive the Mother's comforting smile.

Several improvements have been made in the English edition. These have been introduced with a view to rendering the vocabulary clearer, especially where the Egyptian language is concerned. We have also outlined more precisely the synthesis of each chapter and of the entire book, completing the definition of the myth and its relation to revelation, although we do not claim to have treated the question exhaustively.

In this laborious work of revision we have been greatly aided by the suggestions made by R. Laurentin, H. Cazelles, L. M. Dewailly, and M. Peinador, who not only stressed originality in the work but offered us some very wise counsel. To these and to all our friends and colleagues who by word of mouth or in writing have assisted us in emphasizing the true countenance of Mary, we offer our hearty thanks.

FATHER BONAVENTURA RINALDI, C.P.

TURIN, February 27, 1965
Feast of St. Gabriel of Our Lady of Sorrows

◄{ NOTES }►

1. Anne Frank, *The Diary of a Young Girl* (New York: Pocket Books, Inc., 1959), p. 110.
2. *Lettere alla Madre,* translation by B. Dal Fabbro (Bompiani: 1945), pp. 171-179.
3. E. O. James, *Le Culte de la Déesse-Mère* (Paris: 1960), pp. 204-208. (*The Cult of the Mother-Goddess* [New York: Barnes and Noble, 1961]).
4. James, *ibid.,* pp. 219-245. The author, a student of the history of religions, is of the opinion that the worship of Mother-Church has taken the place of worship of the mother-goddess. It was only in the twelfth century that the cult of *Mater Ecclesia* gave rise to Marian worship. G. Van der Leeuw in *Religion in Essence and Manifestation,* also holds that we pass from myth, from the veneration of Cybele, Diana, and the rest, to Marian worship, without any intermediate revelation which raises Mariology to another level, that of divine revelation. Cf. also F. Heiler, "Marienverehrung," in *RGG* (1960), IV, 763-764.
5. Fulton Sheen, *The World's First Love* (New York: Doubleday, 1953).

{ }

List of Abbreviations

IN QUOTING reviews and books we have employed either the abbreviation currently used or else we have written the title in full. Nevertheless, for the sake of clarity, we mention here some of the works to which frequent reference is made in this book, adding our own opinion of these.

ANET   *Ancient Near Eastern Texts,* edited by James B. Pritchard (Princeton: Princeton University Press, 1955). A vast collection of texts taken from oriental literature.

ATD   *Das Alte Testament Deutsch.* Edited by Volkmar Herntrich and Artur Weiser. Protestant edition of the Old Testament, comprising 25 volumes, moderate and important from the ascetical viewpoint.

Beauvoir   *Le Deuxième Sexe* (Paris: Gallimard), Vol. I, Ed. 103; Vol. II, Ed. 94 (*The Second Sex* [New York: Knopf, 1953]). Atheistic, existentialist conception of women. Discerning style with occasional intuitions of a certain value.

Buytendijk *La Femme* (Paris: Desclée de Brouwer, 1954), Ed. 1. Catholic synthesis of phenomenology of women by a Dutch doctor who is not opposed to existential phenomenology.

BZ   *Biblische Zeitschrift.* German-speaking Catholic's biblical review, with extensive contributions on biblical literary problems.

Deutsch   *The Psychology of Women:* a Psychoanalytic Interpretation: Vol. I, Girlhood; Vol. II, Motherhood (New York: Grune and Stratton, 1946). The authoress is a disciple of Freud although she tones down the latter's extreme conclusions.

Eliade   *The History of Religions* (Chicago: University of Chicago, 1959). We quote this work according to paragraphs. The author tends in a moderate way toward a rationalism which denies Christian revelation.

LThK   *Lexicon für Theologie und Kirche,* edited by J. Hoefer and C. Rahner, Ed. II, 1957, Vol. IX, 1064. The most updated Catholic encyclopedia of scriptural, theological, and ecumenical questions.

Kampmann   *Anthropologische Grundlagen ganzheitlicher Frauenbildung,* Vol. I, 1947, Ed. II; Vol. II, 1947. Published at Paderborn. A true Catholic encyclopedia on the physiology and psychology of women.

NRTh   *Nouvelle Revue Théologique,* University of Louvain Catholic theological review. A fine open-mindedness in regard to modern problems without any claim to infallibility.

RGG   *Die Religion in Geschichte und Gegenwart,* edited by Kurt Galling, in 6 vols. Ed. III (Tübingen: J. C. B. Mohr, 1957-1962). Celebrated dictionary of theology and the history of religion, published by German Protestants. This is a true mine of information on the present-day Protestant view of the world. Although articles on a rationalistic basis are not lacking, the orthodox Protestant conception dominates, in conformity with the Reformation mentality.

SBJ   *La Sainte Bible de Jerusalem.* The Holy Bible translated into French under the direction of the Jerusalem Biblical Institute (Paris: Les Editions du Cerf, 1956). Moderate annotation, harmonious in style, and of dense content.

SBM   *La Sacra Bibbia,* edited by Msgr. S. Garofalo, in 3 vols. (Marietti, 1961). Translation into Italian from the original with appropriate explanatory notes with the collaboration of foremost Italian exegetes.

TWNT   *Theologisches Wörterbuch zum Neuen Testament,* edited by G. Kittel, G. Friedrich, W. Kohlhammer (Stuttgart: Vol. I, 1933, Vol. II, 1964). A very rich Protestant biblical dictionary from the linguistic viewpoint, moderately influenced by Reformation dogma.

{ }

Contents

Mary of Nazareth
Myth or History?

{1}

Myth and Mariology

I. INTRODUCTION: VARIOUS CONCEPTS OF MYTH

Anyone who sets out to write about Marian history and dogma cannot, we feel, overlook mythology. It is sufficient to read the Bible from Genesis to the Apocalypse to be convinced that God did not reject myths absolutely, but that he redeemed them.

The outstanding mythical figure is the wonderful woman with her child struggling against a serpent, an imaginative concept reflected in other myths of a woman treading a serpent under foot, or giving birth to a child in a mythical virginal halo, or of the birth of a divine child who is to vanquish the dragon and overcome death.

With the ancient myth we have the modern one, called the psychological, existential myth. This myth is less imaginative, less heroic, and less extroverted. It is deeper and more palpitating, taken from real life.

We can express it as follows: every man dreams of his own mother as the most beautiful among women, without the slightest blemish and resplendent with the finest virtues.

Here also the Bible is far from suppressing such a poetic mythical instinct toward the Mother. Indeed, it is to be remarked that this instinct appears more and more distinctly the nearer we approach the fullness of revelation. If we read, for instance, the prophetic and sapiential books of the last six centuries before Christ, such as Isaia

49, 15; 63, 7-15; 66, 13, and Proverbs 8, 22-36, we shall be convinced that divine tenderness is shown under the symbol of maternal love.

The New Testament also, with its gospel of the Annunciation to Mary and the words addressed by Christ crucified to his Mother, completes this evolution toward the maternity of God.

Naturally, much discussion is possible and necessary before we decide in what measure the maternal enters into revelation and to what extent the mother image is to be found in ancient and modern non-biblical literature which has a vital relation with the Bible.

However, the anxiety of modern philosophers who fear the intrusion into religion of what is human and even more so of what is maternal, seems to us to be an exaggeration.

There is, it is true, serious danger of reducing the divine to the human level, but the Christian is nevertheless convinced that the Incarnation has quality extolled by Holy Scripture.

In a word, the believer must accept God as he presents himself. For the believer Holy Scripture in its entirety is the word of God, and it is no less divine today when, in the light of ancient mythical literature, it appears very human and material.

The unbeliever will find it very hard to accept a maternal God when he proclaims the very existence of God to be an absurdity. However, he will have to confess with the later Sartre that he has created and shut himself up in a world of anarchical and individualistic "imposture" that systematically rejects the "God of tenderness."

It is not by chance that the vast literature of Sartre and his followers lacks the tenderness of the Mother, just as the smile is missing from Pascal's genius.

But the open-minded unbeliever can establish that the Bible contains passages distinctly divine and supernatural, which render the very humanity and maternity of God objectively and rationally acceptable. He can be convinced that the epic or psychological myth deserves our assent because it is guaranteed by the infallible word of God.

1. The Marxist Concept

The myth is defined as a mere projection of the human mind and heart that has no real or objective counterpart. Simone de Beauvoir devotes special attention to the Woman in mythology in her book *The Second Sex*. But the conclusion is a pessimistic one, namely, that all that has been written about woman is mere myth, because the true woman has never existed since she has never been allowed to act.[1a]

This is to deny completely the first principle of Mariology; it is to deny nature and womanhood.

We do not wish to become involved in the philosophical, existential field. We shall see, however, that four thousand years of history teach us something; they do not allow us to believe that the world begins with ourselves.

I consider that an internationally famous psychoanalyst saw things more clearly when she wrote: "While we recognize the importance of social factors, we assume that certain feminine psychic mainfestations are constant and are subject to cultural influence only to the extent that now one and now another of their aspects is intensified. The primeval feminine Automoë, the fertile Demeter, the motherless Pallas Athene, the androgynous Amazon, all are creations of mythologic fantasy; yet they seem to have really existed in all societies. These prototypes of the feminine psyche recur constantly, always the same, yet always different, according to their culture, their race, and their degree of historical development in their society. The façade may change, but the feminine care remains unchanged throughout all storms." [2]

Now, what is the significance of this nucleus or essence of woman in creation and in revelation? Neither the Marxist conception nor that of psychoanalysis has taken the trouble to furnish an answer.

2. *The Rationalistic Concept*

This concept acknowledges the existence of God, but denies him any extraordinary intervention in history, not because he cannot, but because he does not wish to intervene. History is just a continual interrogation to which there is no reply. The myth is nothing more than the projection of human anxiety.

The Mother with the Redeemer in her arms has always been a sweet and agreeable dream of the human heart. Mary is a purely human utterance, a myth.

Van der Leeuw, a friend of R. Bultmann, affirms in volume one of his book *Religion in Essence and Manifestation:* "Believing that behind Power he decries the outlines of a Form, man recognizes therein the features of his own mother; his loneliness when confronted with Power thus transforms itself into the intimate relationship to the mother.... Woman and the soil are in fact associated in the religious sense: woman is the plowed field, the field a fertile woman. ... Like the tilled field, she too is the bearer of life, and like it she conceives and gives birth. ... Demeter and Isis are mothers; Mary, their successor, is mother and maiden. But despite the ideal of virginity, the church was just as little able to dispense with the mother's form as was later Buddhism in the case of Kwanyin in China and Kwannon in Japan. It is true that side by side with the mother, Mary, who has borrowed her form and even her attributes from the mothers of the Mediterranean basin, Christianity recognized another mother also, the Church. . . . Thus we can understand how, in the history of mankind, one form never completely supplants the other; and the form of the mother lives on in religion because it is alive in our hearts. . . ." [3]

Naturally, by these fine expressions Van der Leeuw does not intend to go beyond the mother myth and a vague sentimentalism which associates Isis, Demeter, and Mary beneath the same aura of a vague and enchanting maternity. Eliade follows the same line. He quotes Homer: " 'Concerning Earth, mother of all I sing,' we read in the Homeric *Hymn to Earth*, 'firm earth, eldest of the Gods, that nourishes all the things in the world. . . . Thine it is to give or to take life from mortal men' (1 ff.; trans. A. Lang, *Homeric Hymns*, p. 246). And in the *Choephori* Aeschylus celebrated the earth 'who bringeth all things to birth, reareth them, and receiveth them again in her womb' " (127-128; trans. Verrall, "*Cheophori*," p. 214). . . .

"An Indian prophet, Smohalla, chief of the Wanapum tribe, refused to till the ground. He held that it was a sin to mutilate and tear up the earth, mother of all. He added: 'You ask me to plow the ground! Shall I take up a knife and tear my mother's bosom? Then when I die she will not take me to her bosom to rest. You ask me to dig for stone! Shall I dig under her skin for her bones? Then when I die, I cannot enter her body to be born again. You ask me to cut grass and make hay and sell it, and be rich like the white men! But how dare I cut off my mother's hair. . . .

"As we have seen, the myths and rites of the Earth-Mother chiefly express ideas of fecundity and abundance. These are religious ideas, for what the various aspects of universal fertility reveal is, in sum, the mystery of generation, of creation, of life." [4]

Earthly love for the Mother is shown by some curious rites, as, for example the practice of laying the sick and agonized on the ground, so that Mother Earth may heal them; of placing newborn babes on the ground or on the waters so that these may protect them, as we read of Atlas, Perseus, Sargon and Moses; or of burying the sinner so that he may come forth a second time from the maternal womb. It is not without reason that a twelfth-century hymn calls Mary "untilled ground which brings forth fruit" (terra non arabilis quae fructum parturit).

These are wonderful myths! We can agree with the author that they are not a mere imaginative projection of a natural event, because they already contain something religious and supernatural, but we cannot fully accept the myth that hates time and space, forcing itself upon history and swallowing it up, "for the myth, like a work of art, is an act of autonomous creation on the part of the spirit and revelation comes about by means of this creative act."

The conclusion here is the perfect rationalistic concept which holds that history is explained by the myth and not the myth by history, as we believe.

Even the Protestant of today replies energetically that Christ crucified is too covered with blood to be confused with a myth. But Protestants have not yet found the true justification of Mary's history.[5]

Without being unfaithful to truth, it is necessary to understand that if it is easy to see history in the man Christ, it is less easy to render historical the sentiments of a mother that echo so deeply in man that he is not even aware that they come from above.

We shall see, though, what a historical, objective, and unequivocal significance Mariology has in the New Testament. In mythology and in the Old Testament, on the contrary, a sense of vagueness is so predominant that these cannot compete with the history of Mary.

3. The Catholic Concept

The Catholic proceeds cautiously where mythology is concerned, both in dealing with the Old Testament where myth is to be found only partially, and from the point of view of literary style.

Thus, regarding the first eleven chapters of Genesis, the Catholic maintains that if, on the one hand, we cannot consider them as history in the modern sense, or even according to the classical concept,[6] on the other hand, they cannot be dismissed as mere mythology. This is so not only because they treat of the longing of the human heart for tenderness and love, but because God reveals himself in them, speaking to us and promising us that there will be a mother.

Such caution may cause the impulsive exegete to lose his patience, feeling that he is hindered. But a wise rule of scientific prudence teaches us (after the destruction of so many myths built up by human pseudo-science and demolished by the latest archaeological discoveries) [7] that it is not reasonable for the Church to entrust its most sacrosanct truths to private intuition.

It fears the tendency to mythicize the Bible, and it encourages those who are so inclined to discover God and his history even in the myth.

St. Paul did this when he commenced to speak of the mythical altar to the "unknown god," and he finished by manifesting the known God of revelation, Christ.

Thus every woman, and in a particular way every mother, in mythology is like an invocation to God to send the Mother. God, with infinite and loving condescension, answers, first, by promising her solemnly in the Old Testament, and subsequently by causing her to appear in the New Covenant, in Mary of Nazareth who surpasses all human expectations.

For the sake of greater clarity we add a definition of the myth, after which we shall enter into the relation between myth and Bible, terminating with the "history of Mary of Nazareth."

This, in fact, is the substance of the first three chapters of our book.

(a) DEFINITION OF THE MYTH

From among a multitude of definitions of the myth we choose to mention that of N. Turchi which appears in the Italian *Enciclopedia Cattolica:* "In its more general acceptation and in its psychological source the myth is the animation of natural and life phenomena, due to that primordial and intuitive form of human perception by which man projects himself into things, that is, animates and personifies them, endowing them with a character and attitudes suggested by his imagination. It is, in short, *an imaginative representation of reality* spontaneously outlined by the mental apparatus. This conception excludes, at the outset, all intellectual elaboration and any attempt at interpretation of the myth. . . .

"On the contrary, when we consider the myth from the point of view of its meaning and of its specific value, in conformity with the elements offered by the mythology of various peoples, it can be defined as a narration of the deeds performed by divine figures who act outside the limits of space and time: *a narration which is the spontaneous explanation of certain physical phenomena* or of *certain laws,* customs and traditions of the social organization. . . ."

A. Anwander dramatizes as follows the definition of

the myth: "If we consider the things that are dearest to the human heart, such as love, life, etc., we realize that these soon become the true object of the myth that seeks to define them. But in vain, because these realities elude all definition. The word itself (the *logos*) which attempts amid the vagaries of the myth to reach the essence of things, strips it of its deep religious significance, often reducing it to falsehood without reaching its true soul." [8]

We moderns, on the contrary, see the myth as more akin to an image or a symbol. But the myth is something more than an image or symbol. "The pure myth is concrete, the product of the vital meeting between the living man and living reality; it is creation and creature, profound as the world and the afterlife, but obscure, ambiguous, insidious as the enigma of the Sphinx, having no solution." [8a]

Divine revelation does not impoverish the myth, nor does it circle around it like the human word, seeking in vain to enter into the heart and essence of things. It reaches the soul of the myth. It redeems it along with the human word, so as to build in man's heart the marvels of grace.

However, unlike the human word which is mere speculation, revelation is related to history. Prior to the myths about F. Barbarossa and Bismarck, facts regarding these men were recorded in history. This remark must always be borne in mind by anyone who adopts the fragile nomenclature—which we ourselves continually avoid in this work—that describes Christianity as "the myth from above," as opposed to "the myth from below." That is to say that Christianity is a superhuman fact that has entered into our human history to indicate the direction we must take to reach salvation. Thus man, feeling that the "myth from above" corresponds perfectly to the "myth from below"— which it even defines clearly and the expectations of which it greatly surpasses—accepts God who knows how to make himself understood by man.

Dr. A. Anwander, in a recent book dealing with myths also treats the question in a subtle manner.[9] He emphasizes, in the first place, that the myth is rooted in the essence of human thought and sentiment, being abundantly used in mysticism, art, and philosophy. And what of revelation? Here we must deplore the fact that the confused treatment by the existentialist and rationalist R. Bultmann has greatly compromised the peaceful solution of the problem that is really nothing more than the relation between nature and supernature. Returning to the nomenclature favored by Dr. Anwander, revelation is the myth from above in contrast with the myth from below which springs from man. He shows how this myth is engrafted onto what is human, so that it can be explained how the Bible and revelation give great prominence to the terms *Adam, son of man, anthropos,* which we find frequently applied to Christ.

Finally, "the myth must be redeemed, but it is not unacceptable. No physicist or astronomer, no philosopher or theologian, not even the biblical scholar or the mystic can reject it, no one can recklessly undervalue it." [10]

It appears to us that the professor from Munich University has hit the nail on the head. The myth is rooted in human nature and to reject it completely is to smother man's nature.

But what is human must be understood in its dynamic sense and, let us say, in its dramatic sense. Its primordial manner of thinking, hearing, and speaking strikes intuitively and confusedly its true object, namely, its happiness. This innate desire can err later on by attributing too much importance to things that it hears and sees. But the root is always sound and can therefore be saved.

God chooses to graft the divine onto the human, infusing into it a supernatural rhythm that is at the same time profoundly human and unmistakably divine.

Historically God did not reveal himself to man in general, but to the Hebrew people living between the fourteenth century before Christ and the first century after Christ, who had human ties with the other peoples of the eastern Mediterranean.

He therefore redeemed not only what is noblest and dearest to the human heart but also the Eastern spirit and the Hebrew race. Finally, if we were asked what God sublimated and what he rejected, we should reply that he rejected all error, all pantheism, all overestimation of the human, and every diminution of the divine. But he saved the deepest exigencies of the heart, of the Oriental mentality, and of the progeny of Abraham, Isaac, and Jacob.

The most practical means of seeing how God redeemed the myth is to study individual myths and their comparison with the biblical accounts that are expressed in the same literary style. But care must be taken not to degrade the myth in order to extol the supernatural character of the Bible or to lower the Bible to the level of the myth.

The former tendency denies the incarnation of the Bible, the latter its supernatural character, two unfortunate exaggerations equally to be avoided.

We ourselves, in summarizing all these remarks, define the myth (the myth from below) as *the imaginative personification of the most deeply felt human needs, as an answer to the innermost anxiety of man.*

Besides the myth there is something deeply rooted in the heart of man. In our case it is to be the primordial need of maternal tenderness.

This unsatisfied desire has caused the human imagination to create for itself the ideal mother. She naturally does not exist, but is the echo which results—confusedly it is true—from a deep desire of the heart.

The example of Anne Frank with which our book commences will convince us of the correctness of our approach to the myth.

Writing on that memorable Christmas Eve she complains: "However much trouble I take, each day I miss having a real mother who understands me. That is why with everything I do and write I think of the 'Mumsie' that I want to be for my children later on. The 'Mumsie' who doesn't take everything that is said in general conversation so seriously, but who does take what *I* say seriously. I have noticed, though I can't explain how, that the word 'Mumsie' tells you everything. Do you know what I've found? To give me the feeling of calling Mummy something which sounds like 'Mumsie' I often call her 'Mum'; then from that comes 'Mums': the incomplete 'Mumsie' as it were, whom I would so love to honor with the extra 'ie.'" [11]

In this ingenuous description we find the mother myth gushing forth from the human heart. Apparently an undefined thing, in reality it is something welling up from the innermost recesses of the soul.

It is that something which can never exist by human power alone, but of which the imagination dreams, *the mother who causes the entire rainbow of fond maternal tenderness to shine forth in the most perfect manner.*

Finally, it is *the essence or heart of the Woman experienced in all its living expressiveness and projected onto the mythical altars consecrated to the Mother.*

(b) MYTH AND REVELATION

Those who wish to enter into this question should read the powerful article by A. Voegtle.[12] For the purpose of our own work we like to recall the article by F. Porporato.[13] The author affirms with due prudence that mythical expressions and images are not excluded from the

Bible; but, purified of what is imaginary and exaggerated, they can be utilized in communicating the divine message to man.

Among other examples he mentions the mythical figure of the god Mot (Death) which is not completely rejected but is stripped of mythicism and of the crown of divinity and used to indicate the terrible power of death:

"The breakers of death have surrounded me, the floods of Belial have made me afraid" (2 Kings, 22, 5; Psalm 17, 5).

It can therefore be established that myth and the Bible are not absolutely exclusive of each other.

But nevertheless they are not to be confused nor mistaken one for the other. Why? Here lies the colossal problem.

Some prefer to speak of a merely external reclothing, but the example just quoted tells us that there is a closer connection between myth and Bible. To speak of a mere external reclothing would be to discredit mythology without appreciating the value of the true soul God gave it, and which human phantasy has not succeeded in corrupting completely.

On the contrary, those who accept our definition of the myth as being the personification of innermost human needs can easily understand that God takes up the divine seed that he had placed in the human heart and which myth had tried to suffocate, and causes it to germinate by a supernatural action until it brings forth the ripe fruit of Christ.

In Holy Scripture, then, God would consecrate anew the creation which had been profaned in the myth. He would purify it and elevate it to a higher plane, a supernatural one.

Holy Scripture, therefore, does not kill the myth, but it removes its vagueness and lack of precision, bringing once more to the surface, amid the discourses of human mythical poetry, the spark of divine revelation which God placed in the heart of man at the dawn of human history, when Adam and Eve fell so miserably.

This spark of divine revelation, this soul of the myth revived and redeemed, we shall call in this first chapter of our book the heart and essence of woman, who endeavors to escape the insidious Serpent and to give life to her child in a sweet halo of virginal purity.

Thus there appears in Babylon the tender wife of Utnapishtim (he who has found life and immortality), who is to help Gilgamesh to reach eternal youth or life. The sweet figure of this woman appears all the more attractive beside the atrocious Tiamat who, in league with the Serpent, injects death into the hearts of her children.

Among the Canaanites the figure of the warlike Anath stands out, desirous of defending her life and essence from the seven-headed serpent. It is to be a titanic struggle, ending with the total defeat of the god Death (Mot), so that the flood of life which Baal brings to men may flow freely.

Life is to be symbolized more perfectly by Nikkal, who generates life in a sweet halo of virginal youth.

The same reality is expressed in another form by the birth of the son of Keret, who was wrapped in the veils of divinity.

In Egypt, too, though under different mythical forms, the same reality is represented, that of life ensnared by the serpent Apophis who triumphs in the god Re and in his son, the Pharaoh. Isis is the mother who wishes to penetrate into Re's heart to learn his name and reveal it to her son, the Pharaoh.

"Isis is the Lady of Life who rules over nature, the foundress of civilization, the benefactress of men. Good rulers are at her service, and the Greek queens who come from Egypt are venerated as dispensers of happiness. Fortunate the one who works for her, the Pharaoh's mother, the spouse of Osiris-Serapis" [14]

All these are myths that are often confused and even atrocious and immoral, but they contain fragments of truth, such as the need to save the Mother because she brings forth life.

Although they are all myths and therefore fantastic creations, when read in the light of the Bible, they remind us of human values which God has not annihilated but has purified and sanctified, that man might feel himself to be understood by his God.

So, while separated from the Bible, man continues to express himself in myths, into which he projects his yearning for salvation. The believer in the divine message feels that his yearning has already received an answer.

This is the recent case in a psalm discovered at Qumran which reminds us of the Apocalypse (Chapter 12):

"Save now the soul from every danger . . . which I have been made to see.
They place my soul in a boat in the midst of the sea's depths.
Indeed, as a fortified city when the enemy approaches calls on its brethren to share its anguish, so it is also with the pregnant woman expecting her first child. . . . Indeed, through the mouth of death has the male child been brought forth and by the pains of Sheol is he expelled from the maternal womb.
Now the viper, pregnant, is in pain, and the mouth of the pit suffers at the birth of all creatures of terror . . . across the abyss voices are to be heard and the great doors of Sheol are to open to admit the creature of the viper. But the doors of the pit will close before the unweaned babe, and the bolts of the world will be drawn before all the spirits of the viper." [15]

What a difference between this myth written perhaps toward the year A.D. 115, in which the desired Messias is still expected, and the twelfth chapter of the Apocalypse in which, although in apocalyptic language, the clear-cut figures of a son and his mother appear, against whom the red dragon is powerless!

God alone can have placed them there, so that in the dense vegetation of human poetry the divine fruit of the Mother with her Child might flourish!

But before looking up to heaven to see the *Woman clothed with the sun,* we must descend among the myths created by the mind of man to observe how man left to himself seeks in vain to save the Mother who, in her tenderness, is the expression of the merciful tenderness of God.

At the same time we shall meet with the literary forms which are to re-echo later in the Bible, although sublimated because God has sanctified all that was wholesome in man.

The appendix dealing with the essence of man according to modern psychology will serve to provide a better frame for the vague mythical figures. It will convince us that if God wills to be defined as the God of grace and tender love, Mary with Christ our Redeemer is the most human and divine expression of this concept.

II. BABYLONIA

About the eighteenth century before Christ, Abraham left Babylonia in obedience to the divine command which was revealed to him:

> "Leave your country, your kinsfolk
>   and your father's house,
>   for the land which I will show you;
> I will make a great nation of you.
> I will bless you and make your name great,
>   so that you shall be a blessing" (Gen. 12, 1 ff.).

But his thoughts are often to return to his own land, to the ancient traditions, and even to the horrible myths of his native country.

Having selected him to be the father of the Chosen People, God will not completely destroy the man of Babylonia. He will merely cause him to follow another path, because he wishes to build the world not upon the too humanistic policy of the Tower of Babel but upon the Jewish people who are continually on the march.

We shall quote two texts alone which seem to us to be of capital importance, since they are taken from two cuneiform tablets which serve as a background to the biblical facts of the Deluge (Gen. 7-8) and the Creation (Gen. 1-2).

1. The Dual Concept of Woman

In the wide-open spaces of sunny Babylonia two very distinct female figures appear during the eighteenth century before Christ. The first is the *tender* wife of Utnapishtim, the god who has found life and is able to bestow it on man. The other is the fierce Tiamat, the *inhuman* mother who plots the ruin of her children.

The gentle Siduri, Utnapishtim's wife, is to induce her husband to grant the prodigious plant of eternal youth to the hero Gilgamesh who sets out in search of life. The hero is despoiled of this divine plant by the Serpent when he plunges into the refreshing waters, little dreaming that it is precisely in the depths of the sea that the Tempter lurks.

The tale is preserved on the eleventh tablet of the *Epic of Gilgamesh*. Toward the end of the narrative we read that Gilgamesh has fallen asleep:

> Utnapishtim says to her, to his spouse:
> "Behold this hero who seeks life!

Sleep fans him like a mist."
His spouse says to him!
"Touch him that the man may remain awake,
That he may return safe on the way whence he came . . .
Gilgamesh has come hither, toiling and straining,
What wilt thou give him that he may return to his land?"
At that, Gilgamesh raised up his pole
To bring the boat right to the shore.
Utnapishtim says to him:
"Gilgamesh, thou hast come hither, toiling and straining.
What shall I give thee that thou mayst return to thy land?
I will disclose a hidden thing,
And a secret of the gods I will tell thee:
This plant, like the buckthorn is. . . .
Its thorns will prick thy hands just as does the rose.
If thy hands obtain the plant, thou wilt find new life. . . ."
Gilgamesh saw a well whose water was cool.
He went down into it to bathe in the water.
A serpent snuffed the fragrance of the plant;
It came up from the water and carried off the plant.
Going back it shed its slough.[16]

Very different is the description of Tiamat who amasses weapons and begets monsters and serpents:

. . . sharp of tooth, unsparing of fang,
With venom for blood she has filled their bodies.
Roaring dragons she has clothed with terror,
Has crowned them with halos, making them like gods,
So that he who beholds them shall perish abjectly,
And that, with their bodies reared up, none might turn
    them back.
She has set up the Viper, the Dragon . . . the Great-Lion,
    the Dragon-Fly, the Centaur—
Bearing weapons that spare none, fearless in battle.[17]

The end is even more tragic. The great mother, vanquished, is severed in two and thus gives origin to heaven and earth.[18]

It would more have served our purpose to quote the

texts in which Gilgamesh speaks to his mother Ninsun, the goddess who knows all things. Or else the other text which shows us Gilgamesh swearing by the life of his mother to enter into the land of the living:

"By the life of Ninsun, my mother who gave birth to me,
    of pure Lugalbanda my father,
May I become as one who sits to be wondered at on the
    knees of Ninsun, my mother who gave birth to me. . . .
By the life (of Ninsun) my mother who gave birth to me
    (of pure Lugalbanda my father),
In the 'land' verily I have known thy dwelling . . .
After he himself had finished off for him the seventh,
    he approached his chamber,
. . . . the 'snake of the wine-quay' in his wall,
Like one pressing a kiss he slapped his cheek.
Huwawa, (his) teeth shook, he warded off Gilgamesh:
'To Utu I would say a word: O Utu, a mother who gave
    birth to me I know not, a father who reared me I
    know not.
In the 'land' thou didst give birth to me, thou dost rear me.' " [19]

The account of Siduri, however, appears to us to be more flexible. While it narrates the same tale of the desire to reach immortality, a desire which is unfulfilled because of Gilgamesh's imprudence, nevertheless the youthful Siduri appears to us to offer a better picture of woman's cooperation in the acquisition of life. Not without reason does Siduri occupy such an important place in Babylonian literature, as Albright has clearly shown.[20]

In face of these myths our purpose is not so much to observe the enormous difference between the Babylonian concept of creation and the Hebrew one, as to stress the dual concept of woman, full of tenderness and grace, or bloodthirsty and atrocious. The Serpent, on the contrary, is always the treacherous one and to form an alliance with him is to associate with the realm of death.

2. Woman in the Service of the Temple

The concept of a virgin mother seems, on the contrary, to be lacking in Babylonia. But the subjection of woman to a rule placing her at the service of the temple is highly developed. In the *Code of Hammurabi* (*CH*), king of the Babylonians in the seventeenth and eighteenth centuries before Christ, we find a most extensive nomenclature in this regard. We have the priestess, the consecrated, the cloistered, the holy, the conventual.[21] It is not possible to determine the value of these terms. Nevertheless, they appear to bring too much of what is human into the temple for these institutions to be confused with the biblical ones, which decidedly reject all consecration of human corruption.

III. UGARIT

Abraham's successors always made efforts to obey the precept of their father, which forbade them to intermingle with the Canaanite people in Palestine.

Rebecca said to Isaac: "I am disgusted with life because of the Hethite women; if Jacob should marry a Hethite woman like these, a native of the land, what would life mean to me?" (Gen. 27, 46). And she sent Jacob into Babylonia to her brother Laban to take Rachel as his wife.

Despite this segregation from the neighboring peoples, the Jews appear to be sons of their new land more than they would wish to be. Biblical traditions have characteristics that are more distinctly Canaanite than Babylonian.

Among the Canaanites special mention should be made of the Ugaritic people. Although living along the shores of northern Lebanon, these people had penetrated with their traditions into the very heart of Palestine. In the thirteenth century they were annihilated by the peoples of the sea, but their traditions survived, even among the sons of Isaac and Jacob, continually exposed to the temptation to adore Baal and Ashtoreth.[22]

1. Anath and the Serpent

Foremost among the Ugaritic myths is that of Anath and Baal. The gods are divided into two camps. The celestial gods are headed by Baal, the god of rain and wind. At his side is Anath, his sister and spouse.

Anath is an ambitious woman who boasts that she knows the *Light which neither men nor gods know.* She is bloodthirsty and delights in wallowing in the blood of slain soldiers.

In the opposite camp, that of the gods of earth, Astarte or Asherah, their mother, is particularly active. Among these gods are Gapn and Ugar and the seven-headed serpent.

One day Ugar and Gapn arrive as messengers of the earthly gods. The furious Anath mistakes them for rebels and cries:

> "Why come Gapn and Ugar,
> What enemy's risen 'gainst Baal,
> What foe 'gainst the Rider of Clouds?
> Crushed I not El's Belov'd Yamm?
> Destroyed I not El's Flood Rabbim?
> Did I not, pray, muzzle the Dragon?
> I did crush the crooked serpent,
> Shalyat the seven-headed.
> I did crush El's Belov'd Ar. . . . (Mot) [23]

The young men assure the clairvoyant goddess that no rebellion has broken out against her brother.

But despite the apparent truce, the struggle continues implacably. While the mother of the earthly gods is praying to Thor, the creator, the god of mercy, in favor of the children of the sea, Baal and Anath arrive on the scene. Asherah becomes violently agitated and bursts forth in protests:

> "Why does Baal come?
> Why cometh the Virgin Anath?
> These two trample upon me and upon my children." [24]

Baal, at the end of the titanic struggle, obtains the victory and becomes lord of the earth:

> "Baal seizes the sons of Asherah.
> Rabbim he strikes in the back.
> Dokyamm he strikes with a bludgeon . . . he falls to
>   the earth.
> Baal mounts his throne of kingship." [25]

Much remains obscure in this literature, but the general idea is clear, a question of two worlds in open conflict. There are feigned friendships, but in reality, implacable enmities.

The Serpent is not so much the symbol of fecundity [26] as of the being who darts forth from the realm of Death (Mot) to snatch the kingdom from the heavenly gods, while the woman endeavors to save her essence from infernal treachery, crushing the head of the Dragon, the son of Death (Mot).

2. The Virgin Mother

Ugaritic literature, in addition to its mythological epics, has some dramas of incomparable lyricism. The most harmonious song is that for the marriage of Nikkal, goddess of the moon, already known to the Babylonians by the name of Ningal:

> "I will sing to Nikkal and Ib,
>   The king of summer Hrhb.
>   When the sun is setting and the moon rises,

The virgin will give birth to a child.
Behold the young woman will beget a son.
Answer: by her love, by her flesh she is of my blood." [27]

The connection between virgin (*btlt*) and young woman (*glmt*) is evident, as appears, moreover, in Scripture, which calls Rebecca at the same time virgin, young woman, and girl.

This clothing of maternity in a nimbus of virginity is softer, even though the harsh human reality causes the halo to vanish, unless God should intervene to change the course of human events by his divine power.

3. *The Arrival of Her First-born Child*

In the Elegy of Keret, the Ugaritic Job, we find a song for the birth of the first child. The famous king has lost his wife and all his children. It seems as if death has definitely prevailed. While he weeps in his desolation, the birth of a son and heir is announced to him from heaven. Exultantly he exclaims:

"Give me Lady Hurriya,
The fair, thy first-begotten;
Whose fairness is like Anath's fairness
Whose beauty like Ashtoreth's beauty;
Whose eyeballs are the pureness of lapis,
Whose pupils the gleam of jet. . . .
And let her bear offspring to Keret
And a lad to the Servant of El." [28]

Lady Hurriya is the girl-wife who brings forth the divine child, the victor over Death.

This combination of maiden and wife, however, is expressed more clearly in the following passage:

"The woman thou takest, O Keret,
The woman thou takest into thy house,
The maid thou bringest into thy court,
Shall bear seven sons unto thee." [29]

The need of divinizing the first-born is human. It reveals the insatiable longing of the human heart for a son who is never to die, that is, who will never be subject to the god Death (Mot), while the halo of youth and virginity reveal the aspiration of the human heart toward an ideal mother who is never to be withered by old age!

We ask ourselves, then, what is the connection between the myth of Anath and the Serpent and the Woman who vanquishes the Serpent in Gen. 3, 16 ff.? Or between the Ugaritic hymn to the virgin mother and Isaia 7, 14: "The virgin shall be with child, and bear a son"? Or between the birth of the son of Keret and that of the prodigious child in Isaia 9-11: *"Puer natus est nobis . . ."*?

It seems to us that they have something in common as regards style. But in Ugaritic the surrounding of maternity with the soft halo of virginity is a mere myth that is never fulfilled in prosaic human reality. On the contrary, we see in Isaia 7, 14 that God promises to cause a mother to appear who will remain at the same time a virgin. Such, at least, is the infallible interpretation in Matthew (1, 22-23), which is to give us assurance of it. The myth of the virgin mother, unrealizable by human power alone, becomes a reality through the supernatural intervention of God who, in sheer mercy, responds to the yearnings of the human heart.

Meanwhile the immortal Son is to be divinely promised in Isaia 9-11 and is to appear in our history from heaven (Titus 2, 11; 3, 5: "The grace and the kindness of God our Savior has appeared . . . according to his mercy").

But let us not confuse Our Lady of Lebanon, who still dominates that Christian oasis in the midst of a Mohammedan world, with the mythical figures of Anath and Asherah. The latter are archaeological figures which we rediscover by digging among the dead, whereas Mary is a living person who by her smile lifts us up to God, to the immortal Son (Rom. 9, 5).

Let us listen to the warning written on the tomb of Hiram (eleventh century before Christ): "Do not descend further among the tombs, because Death is to be found there!"

The mythical god Mot (Death) is indeed to be found in the bowels of the earth, while the God of life is up above, close to the Mother.

IV. EGYPT

In the days of Jacob the Hebrews went down into Egypt.

It can never be repeated often enough that at least the original nucleus of the Pentateuch, indeed a substantial part of it, dates back to Moses, a man who was educated at the Egyptian court. Traces of Egyptian culture are to be recognized in Chapters 32-34 of Exodus, which tell us of the name and the essence of God.

On the banks of the Nile a civilization grew up that certainly surpassed that of the Canaanites and the Babylonians. To be convinced of this it is sufficient to visit the Cairo museum and to observe the austere contour of the pyramids.

Even a brief reading of the papyri leaves us amazed at the grandeur of Egyptian myths. We shall refer to only a few that relate to our subject.

1. The Serpent Myth

The most grandiose myth is that which tells of the god Re, supreme deity and creator of all things, who vanquishes the dragon Apophis. We select some of the more significant passages:

> "He is one fallen to the flame, Apophis with a knife on his head.
> He cannot see, and his name is no more in this land.
> I have commanded that a curse be cast upon him; I have
>   consumed his bones;
> I have annihilated his soul in the course of every day. . . .
> Re is triumphant over thee, Apophis!
> Horus is triumphant over his enemy!
> Pharaoh,—life, prosperity, health,—is triumphant over
>   his enemies!" [30]

Observe how the Pharaoh, or Horus, vanquishes his enemies in imitation of Re who conquered the supreme Enemy, the Dragon.

2. *The Woman and the Serpent*

More graceful and naive is the description of Isis' astuteness in finding out the name or essence of the god Re. The goddess causes the supreme god to be stricken by a serpent; Re, after much reticence, is obliged to reveal his name if he wishes to be restored to health.

Now Isis was a clever woman. Her heart was craftier than a million men; she was more beautiful than a million gods. There was nothing which she did not know in heaven and earth, like Re, who made the content of the earth.

The goddess decided to learn the name of the august god.

(While Re, the great god, is delirious from the fever occasioned by the serpent's poisonous sting, Isis asks):

"Tell me thy name, my divine father, for a person lives with whose name one recites."

"I am he who made heaven and earth, who knotted together the mountains and created what is thereon. . . . I am he who made the heavens and the mysteries of the two horizons, so that the soul of the gods might be placed therein. I am he who opened his eyes, so that light might come into being, who closed his eyes, so that darkness might come into being, in conformance with whose command the Nile flows but whose name the gods have not learned. I am he who made the hours, so that days might come into being. I am he who opened the year and created the river. I am he who made the living fire, in order to bring into being the work of the palace. I am Khepri in the morning, Re at noon, and Atum who is in the evening."

But the poison was not checked in its course and the great god did not recover.

Then Isis said: "Thy name is not really among these which thou has told me. If thou tellest it to me, the poison will come forth, for a person whose name is pronounced lives."

The poison burned with a burning. It was more powerful than flame or fire.

Then the majesty of Re said: "Let thy ears be given to me, my daughter Isis, that my name may come forth from my body into thy body. . . . If there should take place a first issuing from my heart, tell it to thy son Horus, after thou hast threatened him with an oath of the god and hast placed the god in his eyes."

"Flow forth, scorpion poison! Come forth from Re, O Eye of Horus! Come forth from the burning god at my spell! Behold, the great god has divulged his name, and Re is living, the poison is dead, through the speech of Isis the Great, the Mistress of the Gods, who knows Re by his own name." [31]

In reading this myth, rather than being amused at the ingenuousness of Re and the completely feminine ability of Isis, we should stress the magic power of the mother, who desires to know the name or essence of God in order to reveal it to her son, the Pharaoh or Horus.

Very different is to be the skill of Moses in trying to discover the name of the true God; he has the capacity of humble prayer heard by God (Ex. 33, 12-23).

But something of the Isis myth has penetrated into the soul of Moses—perhaps through the stories related by the Pharaoh's tender daughter who rescued him from the waters. It is the longing to know God's name.

3. *Isis the Mother*

In Isis we meet the Mother par excellence. She reappears under the most varying names, but in reality she is always the Mother, with her son Horus by her side (he who knows the name of Re, conqueror of the Dragon), his forehead encircled by a double crown, in his hands the papyrus sceptre and the rounded cross, symbol of life.[32]

Isis, as the Pharaoh's mother and as mother of the whole Egyptian race, is to conquer with Egyptian forces the whole of Palestine, the East, Greece, and Rome.[33]

To this day the visitor to the Palestine coast at Ascalon can see Isis with her child Horus: cold stone, perhaps, or rather a symbol of the human heart which has always desired the Mother and has consecrated altars to the "Unknown Mother," who neither by naive astuteness nor by familiarity with the Serpent could reveal to her children the true name of God, the tender and loving Father.

Thus, in Egypt we have the eternal Enemy, the Dragon, and the astute Mother who wishes to introduce us to the heart, the essence, the name of God.

It is ever the discerning tenderness of a mother that leads us to God.

4. *Prediction of the Birth of a Prophetical Son*

Cheops, the great builder of the pyramid that bears his name, died in 2700 B.C. Weighed on the scales of justice (Maat) he is found to be just and worthy to enter into the secret chambers of the pyramids. But he does not yet know the sacred number indispensable for entry into the kingdom of the hereafter. Who is to reveal it to him? The firstborn of the triplets of Reddjedet, wife of Re's priest.

The text is preserved in *Libro dei Racconti*. A. Gardiner offers us the original text with an adequate translation, which we give below, with the addition of some Egyptian words which will help us to understand the Egyptian mentality and to learn the most probable etymology of the names *Moses* and *Mary*.[34]

Then said the (king) Cheops, the deceased: (What about) the saying thou knowest the number of the secret chambers of the sanctuary of Thoth? And Djedi said: So it pleases thee, I know (*rh*) not the number thereof, O Sovereign, my lord, but I know (*rh*) the place where it is. And His Majesty said: Where is it? And Djedi said: O Sovereign, my lord, behold it is not I who will fetch it for thee. And His Majesty said: Who will fetch it for me? And Djedi said: The eldest of three children who are in the womb of Reddjedet will fetch it for thee. And His Maesty said: Indeed I should like it! (*mr.i*). (But as regards) what thou hast said, who is this Reddjedet? And Djedi said: She is the wife of a priest of Re, lord of Sakhebu, who is pregnant (*iur.ti*) of three children belonging to Re, lord of Sakhebu; and he has said about them (?) that they shall exercise this beneficent office throughout the entire land; and the eldest of them shall be high priest in Heliopolis. Thereupon His Majesty grew sad in his heart because of it. And Djedi said: What is this mood, O Sovereign, my lord? Is it on account of these three children I spoke of? Next your son, next his son, and next one of them! And His Majesty said: At what moment will she give birth (*ms.s*), Reddjedet? (And Djedi said:) She will give birth on the fifteenth day of the first month of Winter.

We remark especially the eagerness to know (*rh*) which is innate in the Egyptian soul and which we have already found in the story of Isis. In the latter it is a question of knowing the name (*rn*), while in the present case it is the number (*tnu*). In both instances we have the human longing to discern the truth which leads to happiness.

More interesting still is the comparison between the prediction of the birth of Reddjedet's son and of Ismael, son of Agar. While the Egyptian slave is escaping from the anger of her mistress Sara, the angel of God addresses her thus:

"You are with child, and shall bear a son; you shall call him Ismael, because the Lord has heard of your humiliation. He shall be a wild ass of a man, his hand against everyone, and everyone's hand against him; he shall dwell apart, opposing all his kinsmen." She named the Lord who spoke to her: "You are the God of vision"; for she said: "Have I really seen God and remained alive after my vision?" (Gen. 16, 11 ff).

To Samson's mother, too, the angel says:

"Though you are barren and have had no children, yet you will conceive and bear a son. Now, then, be careful to take no wine or strong drink and to eat nothing unclean. As for the son you will conceive and bear, no razor shall touch his head, for this boy is to be consecrated to God from the womb. It is he who will begin the deliverance of Israel from the power of the Philistines" (Judg. 13, 3-5).

These passages have in common the foretelling of the birth of a prophetical son whose glorious future is predicted. Note, however, that in the Bible God speaks directly to the future mothers, while in Egyptian literature the colloquy takes place between the gods and the man. Moreover, Agar and the mother of Samson lack the mythical aura and the innate vagueness of the Egyptian text and they appear as living women. Agar, victim of Sara's jealousy, flees in search of a cradle in which to lay her newborn babe. Samson's mother, full of faith in the Lord, is confident that if he has revealed himself, it is not in order to kill, but to save.

These preannouncements bring us close to the New Testament in which the angel of the Lord explains to Joseph: "Do not be afraid, Joseph, son of David, to take to thee Mary thy wife, for that which is begotten in her is of the Holy Spirit. And she shall bring forth a son, and thou shalt call his name Jesus; for he shall save his people from their sins" (Matt. 1, 20).

In the Annunciation scene also we hear:

"Do not be afraid, Mary, for thou hast found grace with God. Behold, thou shalt conceive in thy womb and shalt bring forth a son; and thou shalt call his name Jesus. He shall be great, and shall be called the Son of the Most High; and the Lord God will give him the throne of David his father, and he shall be king over the house of Jacob forever; and of his kingdom there shall be no end" (Luke 1, 30 ff.).

From the context we are aware that these two episodes, although recalling the Old Testament, indicate a marvelous entry of God into the history which is his, an entrance into history that upsets the normal order and causes stupefied man to turn aside to adore the Son, while the Mother is not to fail in her resolution of virginal consecration to God although she tastes the joy of having a child call her "Mother"!

Names themselves, so deeply significant as to indicate the quintessence of a person, will direct us in our search for the indications of God who penetrates by degrees, in a supernatural manner, into human events.

Thus the name "Moses" which means "son" or "he is born" (*ms*), is to have many contemporaries: Thut-Mose (1480-1435 B.C.), and Ahmose. But the great Hebrew legislator is to break away from the myths of the gods Thoth, father of Thut-Mose, and Luno, father of Ahmose, to describe himself as saved from the waters by the Lord (Ex. 2, 10). The Messias, on the contrary, is not to be saved, but is the Savior, Jesus.

The name "Mary" also had its roots in myth. In fact, it originally meant "beloved (*mrt*) from Amon." In the Egyptian Museum in Turin is to be found the tomb of Mary (*mrt*), the wife of a fourteenth-century government official named Cha.

Moses [1] sister is to receive the same name, but at once it is added that she will be the prophetess of the Lord, who invites the Hebrew women to sing the praises of God the Savior (Ex. 15, 21).

The greatest woman of all is also to be called Mary and is to be the Mother of the Savior, Jesus, the High Priest and the new Moses.

Here the myth is not suppressed, but is stripped of its ingenuousness and rendered divine in the Old Testament through God's saving action, while its power is derived from the history of Jesus that is set in motion by the supernatural intervention of the Father.

CONCLUSION: MYTHS, SCATTERED SPARKS OF PRIMITIVE REVOLUTION

In the East we hear everywhere of the Serpent and the Woman.

The Serpent is the eternal Tempter, while the Woman, if she allies herself with him, cannot but poison human existence. Tiamat, Anath, and Isis enter too easily into alliance with the Serpent and the Snake.

But both the gentle wife of Utnapishtim and the redeemable Anath and Isis are able to assume the true aspect of the Mother. Theirs is a bizarre maternity, if you wish, from which, however, stem rays of tenderness.

What is God to do in face of this world? Is he to destroy it mercilessly, to show his omnipotence, or is he to gather up every germ of human goodness, every spark of love preserved in the human heart, to make of these a masterpiece?

History teaches us that God has condemned evil, sin, the Serpent, and all alliance with him, but that everything good and redeemable has been preserved and sublimated.

God did not create a second time. He rebuilt and renewed his shattered work, because he never destroys anything he has created and never regrets anything he has done.

The sin of man will not force him to change his divine plans but will afford him an opportunity of showing that his bountiful giving contains tenderness and love, the donation of himself to ungrateful and sinful man.

Thus the myths concerning the virgin Mother and her battle with the Serpent, son of Death, are merely indications of a primitive revelation which God himself is to reanimate by his divine word in Genesis 3, 15, where we are reminded that when we fell in Adam, God promised the Mother as the expression of his tenderness and his pardon.

APPENDIX: THE ESSENCE OF WOMAN.

Before entering decisively into the Bible, we must mention the essence of woman according to modern psychology, which will give us a better understanding of the mother figure in the Old Testament, foreshadowing the greatest mother of all, Mary of Nazareth.

Especially will this lead us to understand or at least to have an inclination as to the deep relation between the essence of woman and the essence of God. Mariology merely personalizes this essence, saying: here it is not a question of just any woman at all, but of the historical figure of Mary; here it is not a question of any god, but of the Father who enters into history through his Son, the Word, in the loving emanation of his Divine Spirit.

Thus is easily explained the fact that the problem of woman, next to the problem of God, is the object of the most widespread and most widely discussed literature.[35]

We moderns have declared war so mercilessly on the myth that we no longer want to hear it mentioned.

Yet we are immersed in myth. Baeumler writes shrewdly: "A single glance at the face of a modern man or woman in the streets of Berlin, Paris, or London is sufficient to convince us that today the cult of Aphrodite is the one for which the cults of Zeus and Appollo must prepare the way. In the midst of a late and decadent civilization new temples are raised up to Isis and Astarte, to those maternal deities of the East who were served by means of orgies and intemperance, accompanied by sentiments of wild abandonment to enjoyment. The fascinating female is the idol of our times and with painted lips she goes about the European cities just as she once went about in Babylonia." [36] Even today the mythical island does not mean an earthly paradise, but rather love, freedom, rest and relaxation, vacations and dreams of faraway places. This is reflected in the novel, on the screen, and in the imaginations of many men.[37]

We must admit, though, our love for the myths of our own time: technical progress, space achievement, and especially the psychological myth. We know what a cult C. G. Jung made of the latter.

In the introduction to his study of Greek mythology, C. Kerenyi affirms that psychology is more in harmony with our times. He accepts Thomas Mann's happy expression: "Mythological interest is so much a part of psychology, just as psychological interest is deeply rooted in all poetical activity." [38]

It will be well, therefore, to pass from the pre-Christian mythical world to the modern one, which finds better expression in the psychological sciences, a necessary adjunct to the literature of modern existentialism.

While granting to Simone de Beauvoir that new social structures require new accidental manifestations of woman's vitality, we believe that the historical evidence of four thousand years permits us to sketch a sort of definition of woman, as follows: *Woman is the human person, corporally mother, spiritually the gift of love, finding expression in kindness, grace, and tenderness.*

1. She Is a Human Person

This is a general primordial decision which prevents us from lowering her to inferior rank, from forcing her into the sphere of mere sex and attributing to her what is ordinarily called *sex appeal*. The term was coined a few decades ago in reference to the actress Jean Harlow, but it had already appeared very clearly in Ugarit.[39]

2. Corporeally Mother

Agreement on this point is so universal that is unnecessary to insist further upon it. We stress, though, the term body (*corpo*-reality), since in it palpitates the organ of tenderness, the maternal bosom, called by the Greeks *oictirmôn* and by the Hebrews *rhm*.[40] See, for example, "*tenderness*" in the vocabulary at the end of this book.

3. Spiritually Love and Donation

We wish to indicate the fluid spiritual element which vivifies this body. It is love colored by sentiment, emotivity, cordiality, sensitiveness, intimacy, solicitude (*souci*). It is love which expands in order to receive and which reawakens in order to give itself.[41]

In his book *Les Idées et les Âges*, Alain has some wonderful passages on maternal love: "Filial devotion comes first in order of time. The love of a mother is first in perfection. We must use these two loves which are similar as our model. . . . Insisting thus on this venerated image of the Virgin Mother, by whose intercession all love must reach its highest end, we have a means of thinking humanly of the things above without refusing to think physiologically. . . . Maternal love, celebrated, venerated, and perfected in every human collectivity, adored to a supreme extent, enlightens us more fully. Because it is true that mother and child are for a long time one and the same being, maternal love is therefore the model for all love. Because, says Descartes, what is our first and our oldest love if not that of the blood enriched by good nourishment, by pure air, by pleasant warmth, in fact by all that favors nutrition? The oldest language of love, speaking especially to itself, consists in this movement, this tendency, this intimate consent, this delightful agreement of the vital organs yearning for good milk. The first hymn of love is this hymn to maternal milk, sung by the whole body of the infant who receives and welcomes this precious nourishment. This first keen desire to suck is from the physiological point of view the first and the true pattern of all enthusiasm in the world. . . . I am well aware, and I shall explain this amply, that nothing is more violent, more exasperating, more brutal than sexual attraction and that in man, by reason of the terrible mental activity attached to this red-hot spur, this instinct is truly disturbing, painful, shameful and wicked. So this savage love must be saved by a return to the first charm and fidelity of the oldest love." [42]

This sublime poetry leads us undoubtedly to love for Mary, called by Fulton Sheen *The World's First Love!*

We still have to solve the problem, though, as to how maternal love not only does not contradict divine love, the supreme love, but leads us to it, so that the heart of the Mother becomes the mirror in which we find the reflection of God.

4. She Expresses Herself in Kindness, Grace, and Tenderness

Observe the word *express* which is intended to indicate the appearance in the body of the deepest reality of the feminine soul, namely, love.

But let us add at once the characteristics of this love. It is not a turbid love which deprives of liberty, but a kind love that reawakens it. A kindness which while being demanded of all, is particularly required in the woman.

Kindness is not to be confused with diplomacy, which is something artificial and inauthentic. This kindness is as gracious and spontaneous as a smile.

There is particular charm in a smile. It is born of tenderness, is the typical expression of a mother, and falls like the dew which restores and revives all things, giving them new color. It appears to be the only thing capable of causing life to blossom again.

Albert Camus has described very well this atmosphere of smiling tenderness in his novel *The Plague*.

While Tarrou is dying, Madame Rieux draws near to him. "Tarrou had had his eyes shut for some time. Sweat had plastered his hair on his stubborn forehead. Madame Rieux sighed, and he opened his eyes. He saw the gentle face bent over him and, athwart the surge of fever, that steadfast smile took form again. But at once the eyes closed. . . .

"Tarrou's head was turned toward Madame Rieux, who was sitting close beside the bed, her hands folded on her lap; in the dim light of the room she seemed no more than a darker patch of shadow. Tarrou was gazing at her so intently that, putting a finger to her lips, Madame Rieux rose and switched off the bedside lamp. Behind the curtains the light was growing and presently, when the sick man's face grew visible, Madame Rieux could see his eyes still intent upon her. Bending over the bed, she smoothed out the bolster and, as she straightened up, she laid her hand for a moment on his moist, tangled hair. Then she heard a muffled voice, which semed to come from far away, murmur: 'Thank you,' and all was well now. By the time she was back in her chair Tarrou had shut his eyes, and despite the sealed mouth, a faint smile seemed to hover on the wasted face." [43]

Why this maternal gesture of placing a hand on the sick man's head as if he had become a child again to be caressed by his mother? Why the smile on his face? Does he contemplate during the night his mother's face? Is it not the mother, by her tenderness and kindness, who causes life to blossom again and the smile to appear on the lips of the dying Tarrou?

In vain would we seek similar descriptions in Sartre and Pascal, two geniuses devoid of smiles and tenderness! We must add, with Charles Moeller, that Tarrou's death, rendered peaceful by this earthly mother, is a mystery. Beyond the mortal and tangible expression, it could be said that Tarrou's peace is inexplicable, unless we admit that in this dialogue, through these simple folk, we reach a transcendent love, that of the Mother! "I should say, that of the Virgin Mary." [44]

But Camus, like all atheists, cannot believe in the supernatural reality. He can apply to himself what he writes concerning Doctor Rieux and his relations with his mother: "At that moment he knew what his mother was thinking, and that she loved him. But he knew too, that to love someone means relatively little; or rather, that love is never strong enough to find words befitting it. Thus he and his mother would always love each other silently. And one day she—or he—would die, without ever, all their life long, having gone farther than this by way of making their affection known." [45]

Thus the existentialist novelist, who had cancelled from his vocabulary the word *charity* because it was too commonly used, died an atheist without having understood in full the value of tenderness which is the first and deepest colloquy between creatures, between mother and son.

But he had touched something which is not communicated by words but by smiles!

When tenderness enters in, kindness loses its softness, and grace is no longer a smile that dazzles but a penetrating ray of God's loving gaze turned upon the parched land of the human soul.[46]

If such is the essence of woman and if the Bible chooses the words grace and kindness, tenderness, and love to indicate the essence of God, how can we be surprised that God has chosen a woman to be the historical symbol of Redemption?

Here, though, we must not play with fancy, the mythicizing faculty, but we must read the Bible which relates the marvelous history of God's revelation of himself in his Word, who reposes in the arms of a Mother.

LOOKING BACK

In the first chapter we started from the Marxist concept, of which existentialism according to Jean Paul Sartre is the most active nucleus, and we allowed ourselves certain reservations regarding the concept of Simone de Beauvoir, who maintains that woman has never existed.

The rationalistic concept represented by Van der Leeuw and M. Eliade has convinced us that woman as mother has always reigned supreme. At this point man asks, "How is this?" And the answer comes: "Because the Mother is truly the *world's first love.*"

The Christian asks in return: "And is this primordial sentiment contrary to revelation which affirms that God is the first and supreme love?"

In this first chapter we have limited ourselves to proving that the love of the Woman and the Mother penetrates into the heart of Babylonian, Ugaritic, and Egyptian literature. A few simple comparisons with biblical texts convince us of the necessity of due appreciation of the *humanum* in the myths concerning the mother, revealing a certain similarity, but not denying the supernatural element which distinguishes the Bible from non-biblical writings.

Not until the second chapter will we see in greater detail how the myth is made fruitful in a supernatural manner by the divine Word.

The appendix on the psychology of woman is intended to clarify in modern existentialistic terms that which myths express with phantasy. This penetration into the quintessence of the woman as grace, tenderness, and love poses a serious problem. Is there a connection between the God of grace, tenderness, and love and the woman?

In order to reply we must observe the progressive course that God gives to the Old Testament and to the New, a course which renders ever more evident the role of the woman in the history of salvation.

This is what we shall endeavor to deal with in the next two chapters, taking care to illustrate how the Old Testament opens up more and more clearly the view of mother as the mirror in which God is reflected.

But it is only in the New Testament that we shall be able to see how God rests in the maternal embrace and how on the cross alone the dying Christ leaves to us, as his parting gift, the Mother.

SUMMARY OF CHAPTER ONE:

THE author is seeking the essence of woman which is veiled in the myth, though not intrinsically corrupted. This essence was always attacked by the Serpent allied with Death (the god Mot). Where does the third part (Ugarit) come in, to which the author attaches so much importance? Frequently the essence of the woman does not appear clearly, but is veiled by mythical figures and symbols. Such is Anath who has the light of life from Baal (Text 51, IV, 40-45), an admirable combination of the concepts "word" (*thm*), "wisdom" (*hkmt*), and "life" (*hyt*) (*Anath* III, 20-25; V, 35-40), and who must defend it against the Serpent who is in league with the god Mot.

On the other hand, the songs to the Mother, surrounded by the mythical aura of virginity, and the songs to her first-born are hymns to the victory of life over death.

Above all, the study of these figures introduces us to the atmosphere of the literary style of Genesis 3, 15 and Isaia 7-11, where the clearest prophecies of salvation through Mary are to be found.

∜ NOTES ⊱

1. *Cf.* R. Jolivet, *Sartre ou la Théologie de l'Absurde* (Paris: Librairie Arthème Fayard, 1965).

1a. Simone de Beauvoir, *Le Deuxième sexe* (Paris: 1949), p. 392 (*The Second Sex* [New York: Knopf, 1953]), which follows along the same lines as L. Feuerbach's, *The Essence of Christianity* (Gloucester: Peter Smith, 1958), in which the author passes from Marian considerations of the Montfortian type to the crudest atheism. Contrary to such a concept are both the ancient writers (cf. P. de Ambroggi, *Le Lettere Pastorali* [Turin: 1962], pp. 44-45) and the modern (M. Eliade, *The Sacred and the Profane* [New York: Harper, 1961]; Van der Leeuw, *op. cit.*, pp. 404-407, who throws into relief a certain objectivity inherent in the myth.)

2. H. Deutsch, *The Psychology of Woman* (New York: Grune and Stratton, 1946), I, 386.

3. G. Van der Leeuw, *Religion in Essence and Manifestation* (New York: Harper & Row, 1963), I, 91, 95, 98, 100.

4. M. Eliade, *The Sacred and The Profane* (New York: Harper Torchbooks, 1961), pp. 138, 189, 147.

5. S. Mowinckel-R. Bultmann, *Mythos und Mythologie,* in *RGG,* 1960, IV, 1272-1282. The former writer observes: "The myth does not necessarily conflict with history." As regards the second article,

literally re-edited in the second edition and said to be unsurpassed, the severe criticism of G. Staehlin in *TWNT*, IV, 798-803 is recalled: "The central symbol of the Gospel is the cross, which represents a harsh and perfectly historical reality. This symbol cannot be incorporated in and subordinated to myth, because this would be to deprive the *Verbum Crucis* of meaning. The cross be separated neither from the person who bore it nor from its historical setting. Without Christ on Golgotha, the cross becomes an empty myth, a senseless sign, a pagan symbol."

We observe with pleasure that the same Protestant author begins to suspect that in John 19, 27 there may be something more than a mere private relationship between Mary and John; but in his comment on Apocalypse 12 he sustains that we have returned to pure myth (cf. *RGG*, 1960, IV, 747-748).

6. Cf. *Enchiridium Biblicum*, Ed. 3, No. 581.

7. W. F. Albright, *The Archaeology of Palestine* (London: 1956), pp. 238-249.

8. A. Anwander, *Wörterbuch der Religion* (Würzburg: 1962), article "Mythus."

8a. *Ibid.*

9. A. Anwander, *Zum Problem des Mythus* (Würzburg: 1964), pp. 106-117.

10. *Ibid.*, p. 117.

11. Anne Frank, *loc. cit.*, p. 110.

12. A. Voegtle, "Mito e rivelazione," *Problemi e Orientamenti di Theologia Dommatica* (Milan: 1957), I, 823 ff.

13. F. Pororato, "Miti e Ispirazione Biblica," in *Civiltà Cattolica*, February-March, 1941.

14. K. Schefold, *L'Art Greca* (Garzanti: 1962), pp. 173-175.

15. 1*QH*, 3, 6-18 *passim*.

16. *ANET*, pp. 95-96.

17. *ANET*, pp. 66 ff.

18. W. F. Albright, *Recent Discoveries in Bible Lands* (New York: 1955), pp. 61-65: "The continual effort to reconcile Genesis with science is as futile as the search for perpetual motion."

Von Rad, *Gesammelte Studien zum A. T.* (Munich: 1958), p. 146: "I can conclude that it is impossible to bring together the Old Testament world of faith and the mere history of religions."

The same idea has the support of H. Gunkel, quoted by H. Cazelles in *Introduction à la Bible* (Desclée, 1959), pp. 325 ff.

19. *ANET*, p. 49.

20. M. Eliade, *op. cit.*, par. 105.

21. In the *Code of Hammurabi* there is special mention of this in pars. 144-146 and 178-182. The corresponding words in Accadian are: *entum* (priestess), *naditum* (consecrated), *sikrum* (cloistered), *nadit gagim* (conventual), *gadishtum* (holy woman). Without a doubt there

are shades of meaning here which at present it is not possible to determine. (Cf. *ANET* in the paragraphs mentioned).

22. Cf. I Kings, 7, 4. For a philological analysis cf. O. Eissfeldt's, article "Asherah and Astarte" in *RGG*. 1957, I, 637. As regards the identification of the two deities we ourselves are inclined toward the opinion of Mayer in *LThK*, 1957, I, 918, 958.

23. *Anath* III, 33-47. The comparison of the Ugaritic text with Genesis 3, 15 ff. is most interesting. Although there is a similarity between the two scenes and the two women, from the philological point of view the only word we have in common is enmity (*'ib*). The greatest difference lies in the continual mention of crushing (*mhsh*)— four times in relation to *kl*— to destroy, and of trampling under foot (*mhs*), and yet the biblical *shuf* (to ensnare, to trample on, to crush) never appears, which is even more puzzling because it does not appear in other parts of the Bible nor in the literature of the epoch.

Mhs, on the contrary, appears fifteen times in the Old Testament and indicates a rather severe blow, sufficient to produce even abortion (cf. in Accadian the *Code of Hammurabi*, pars. 202-213).

Is it possible to pass from *mhsh* to *shuf* by means of *mhs?* Not even when we compare the Ugaritic text 67, I, 1-3, which agrees excellently with Isa. 27, 1-2 and with Ps. 74, 13, where the Dragon and the Serpent are mentioned, do we see that in the biblical texts *mhs* is missing. For this reason philology does not allow us to associate Ugarit with Gen. 3, 15.

24. Text, 51, II, 21-24.

25. Text, 49, V, 1-5. In the latter two texts strike (*mhsh*) and trample on (*mhs*) appear to us to be synonymous. Cf. also *Anath* III, 43.

26. We have abundant evidence to show that the Serpent indicates fecundity. Cf. Albright, *Archaeology*, illustrations on pp. 97 and 107: here it is represented in the form of a woman with the lily and the Serpent; E. Wright, *Biblical Archaeology* (London: 1957), p. 112, interprets the lily as sex appeal and the Serpent as the symbol of fecundity. Strange to say, the goddess who is represented as a sacred prostitute was called holy (*qdsh*).

Cf. Zev Vilnay, *Israel Guide* (Jerusalem: 1960), figs. 472, 487, 578. The first of these represents Ashtoreth with the lily and the sign of life, the rounded Egyptian cross; the second, Anath, likewise with this cross; the third is a standard which was perhaps borne in processions, the image of the goddess surrounded by serpents. The author recalls Num. 21, 8.

27. Text 77, 1-9: *Tld btl* (*T/hl glmt bn . . .*).

Besides the combination of virgin and maiden, already present in the Old Testament where Rebecca is called at the same time virgin, young woman, and girl (Gen. 24, 16, 43, 54), the emphatic introduction of Isa. 7, 14 is worthy of consideration: "Behold the maid . . ."

The association is suggested also by A. Felin in *Introduction à la Bible*, p. 509.

28. *ANET*, p. 144.

29. *ANET*, p. 146. In the antecedent text the combination of maiden and wife was dubious, because it is not certain if it is the same wife who has already borne children. In the present text the two expressions seem synonymous.

30. Cf. translation in *ANET*, pp. 6-7. Perhaps the study of the Egyptian text can furnish an answer to the questions which the Ugaritic leaves unsolved.

31. *ANET*, pp. 21-14.

32. James, *op. cit.*, pp. 65-68.

33. G. Riciotti, *Paul The Apostle* (Milwaukee: Bruce, 1961), nos. 14, 37, 72.

34. A. Gardiner, *Egyptian Grammar* (New York: Oxford University Press, 1957), par. 511.

35. T. Kampmann, *Anthropologische Grundlagen ganzheitlicher Frauenbildung* (Paderborn: 1947), p. 75.

36. Baeumler, *Der Mythos von Orient und Okzident* (1926), pp. 291-293.

37. M. Eliade, cf. *op. cit.*, par. 165.

38. C. Kerenyi, *Die Mythologie der Griechen* (Zürich: 1951).

39. E. Wright, *op. cit.*, p. 112.

40. F. I. Buytendijk, *La Femme* (Desclée, 1954), pp. 361-363; T. Kampmann, pp. 152-153; H. Deutsch, II, 3-57; Beauvoir, II, 290-344.

41. "The girl becomes a woman at the moment in which she recognizes that in her body and soul she is a gift" (Radeski, *Die Welt in der Tasche*, p. 50). "The personality of the woman is entirely contained in love" (O. Schneider, *Die Macht der Frau* [Salzburg: 1938], p. 113); Simone de Beauvoir defines woman as "a great lover"; Kampmann, as "the genius of love" (Rizzoli Edition, p. 126).

42. Alain, *Les Idées et les Âges* (Paris: 1927), pp. 9-11.

43. Albert Camus, *The Plague* (New York: Knopf, 1949), pp. 258, 259.

44. Charles Moeller, *Littérature du XX Siècle et Christianisme*, I, 72.

45. Camus, *op. cit.*, p. 262.

46. As regards kindness: "Every social group appreciates a particular form of kindness, but in every case this fundamental quality is required in the woman" (Buytendijk, p. 13).

As regards the theme woman and grace, cf. R. Guardini, *Mutter des Herrn* (Würzburg: 1955), pp. 76-77; concerning grace and the smile, cf. Guitton, *La Vierge Marie* (Paris: 1949), p. 260; *Madonna* (New York: Tudor, 1962).

As regards tenderness: *"it is the characteristic expression* of the maternal vocation."* (Buytendijk, p. 366: "Maternal love is the direct affective expression of the positive relation between mother and child; its principal characteristic is tenderness."

We shall see how ancient literature agrees excellently with modern discoveries in psychology. Cf. Chap. 2, n. 12.

Hebrew literature, without being as clear as the Accadian or the Ugaritic, has preserved a telling phrase. In the Song of Deborah we have the wives of the victor replying to his mother, saying that perhaps he delays in coming because he is dividing up the booty, namely, the women: "They must be dividing the spoil they took: there must be a damsel or two for each man" (Judg. 5, 30).

{2}

The Divine Promise of Mary in the Old Testament

I. INTRODUCTION: TRANSITION FROM MYTH-OLOGY TO THE OLD TESTAMENT

In between mythology and the history of Mary we have the Old Testament.

It is no myth, but nevertheless it does not entirely reject mythology:

"On that day, the Lord will punish with his sword that is cruel, great, and strong, leviathan the fleeing serpent, leviathan the coiled serpent; and he will slay the dragon that is in the sea" (Isa. 27, 1-2).

"You crushed the heads of Leviathan, and made food of him for the dolphins" (Ps. 73, 14).[1]

Here it becomes clear that the myth cannot wander at will, that it has been given a specific purpose, namely that of indicating that all terrestrial and demoniac powers are at God's disposal and that he uses them in dealing with his elect.

Let us take some further examples from Egyptian literature. The sky is represented as a woman who touches the earth with her hands and feet, encircling it with her body bent in the form of a bow. In the Egyptian Museum in Turin she is depicted in precisely this embracing attitude.

Elsewhere the vault of heaven is represented as a cow. The sun, her calf, passes beneath her in search of milk. The goddess Hathor, the Egyptian Juno who assists at childbirth, is also personified in the effigy of a cow.

The sky is also portrayed as an immense expanse of water over which the sun passes by day, or else as a vast sheet of copper resting on the pillars of the earth's poles.

The first two representations are excluded decidedly from the Bible since they are pantheistic, but the latter ones have some evident connection with the early chapters of Genesis.

It can be seen, therefore, how the sacred text rejects, modifies, and consecrates the myths in accordance with the inspiration of a superior mind.

But we do not yet venture to call the Old Testament history, because too often the manner in which God is to accomplish our salvation is not clearly seen in it.

The gaze of the Old Testament is entirely fixed on the future, which is to reveal wonderful things to us. It is the divine promise, the shadow which is to reveal its true face only in the New Testament.

The Gospel is not only the fulfillment of the Old Testament, but also the revelation of its soul and spirituality, which has freed itself with difficulty from human additions so as to appear in all its fullness.

The Old Testament is not a photograph of the person who is to appear in the New Testament, but it is a continual preparatory focusing of the camera, until, in the time established by the Father, in the "fullness of time," the clear image of the Word is to appear (Gal. 4, 4). After the death of the Son we enter on a new era together with the Mother. This is the period of *commemoration,* under the guidance of the Son's own Spirit.

In order to understand this second chapter of our book the reader must bear in mind continually that we are seeking one thing alone: *the essence of God,* which always appears in a setting of sorrow and sin.

Sometimes God expresses his name clearly as he did to Moses on the mountain (Ex. 32-34). On other occasions the divine essence is clothed in the tenderness of a woman and a mother (Os. 1-2; Isa. 49; 66). Especially in the peak moments of human history does God manifest himself in the resplendent figure of a mother with her son (Gen. 3; Isa. 7). This is the course we shall follow in our second chapter.

II. THE ORIGINAL SIN OF MANKIND (GEN. 1-3)

In passing from Oriental literature to the Bible, we observe at once a great difference: in the myths we have a tiresome prolixity, paradoxical conceptions, ingenuous and surprising situations; in the Bible all proceeds in a measured and calm manner. Ordinarily it is God who speaks, revealing the true meaning of things. Man merely observes the wonderful works of God and praises him.

In the first three chapters of Genesis we have the revelation of the profound religious meaning which permeates the whole of creation, with particular attention given to the role of the woman at the beginning of human history and the part she is to play in the future.

Naturally we must not expect these first three chapters of the Bible to give us an accurate history of creation. This would imply postponing the composition of the Bible for over four thousand years. God spoke several thousand years ago and his word is embodied in the mentality of that era. What mentality is this?

1. The Unity of All Created Things (Chapter 1)

God created the entire universe: the starry sky that charms the nocturnal shepherd; and the earth which seems prepared for the coming of man who is to rule over it.

But when God created man, he pondered and took counsel with himself and decided:

"Let us make mankind in our image and likeness; and let them have dominion over the fish of the sea, the birds of the air, the cattle, over all the wild animals and every creature that crawls on the earth." God created man in his image. In the image of God he created him. Male and female he created them. Then God blessed them and said to them, "Be fruitful and multiply fill the earth and subdue it" (1, 26-28).

From this solemn, unequivocal passage it clearly appears that God created all things, but that the entire creation is merely the royal palace prepared for mankind, for man and woman.

Man is the *image* of God! To us of the West an image is something abstract and ideal, but to the Greek and Oriental mentality it is something concrete and real. The Hebrew term *slm* recalls immediately the shadow or the statue. Thus man is the shadow of God, the figure which represents him in the created world.

When a people rebelled against their prince or king they broke his statue to pieces. This was a symbol of the destruction of the royal power and of the royal person.

Only those who think back to these Oriental usages can fully understand the first chapter of Genesis: man created in the image of God, who is to appear unveiled in Christ.

2. The Dual Personality in Mankind (Chapter 2)

It would seem that God does not favor mass production. Each human person has his own characteristics, fitting in, however, to one of the two types, man and woman, of which mankind is comprised.

The Bible, which is the work not only of one God but of a number of men, is to treat this primordial problem too. The author who cooperates with God is a man of refined and poetic feeling. He is interested in the dialogue, the speech, and response to it, rather than in the unity of the whole.

Man feels himself to be alone in Eden, conscious of the warning: "From the tree of the knowledge of good and evil you must not eat; for the day you eat of it, you must die."

He calls *by name* the subjects of his kingdom, the birds of the air and the beasts of the field, but none of these respond satisfactorily to his call.

In his dejection he falls into a deep, mysterious sleep, like Keret in Ugarit. In sleep—that is, in ecstasy—God is to offer him the one who can respond to him, who springs forth from the depths of his being by God's power, and God then presents her to him. Adam, exultant, exclaims:

"She now is bone of my bone, and flesh of my flesh;
She shall be called Woman, for from man she has been taken."
For this reason a man leaves his father and mother, and clings to his wife, and the two become one flesh.
Both the man and his wife were naked, but they felt no shame
(2, 23-24).

Man's joy here in woman's company is not the spiritual joy found in the Pauline mystical views on marriage (Eph. 5, 25-26); but neither is it immersed in sex as in Ugarit. The final words assure us that their love was untroubled.[2]

3. The Mother (Chapter 3)

Whereas in the second chapter we find the spouse, here it is the mother who particularly emerges. It is an odd coincidence. Just as a child calls out immediately to his mother if he falls,[3] so also mankind, immediately

after the fall, must have felt in a particular way the need
of tenderness as an expression of divine pardon. God responded precisely to this longing. It happened in this
way: the treacherous serpent, enemy of the God of heaven,
begins his colloquy with the woman:

"Did God say: 'You shall not eat of any tree of the garden?'"
The woman answered the serpent, "Of the fruit of all the trees in
the garden we may eat; but 'Of the fruit of the tree in the middle
of the garden,' God said, 'you shall not eat, neither shall you
touch it lest you die.'"
But the serpent said to the woman, "No, you shall not die; for God
knows that when you eat of it, your eyes will be opened and you
will be like God, knowing good and evil." Now the woman saw that
the tree was good for food, pleasing to the eyes, and desirable for
the knowledge it would give. She took of its fruit and ate it, and
also gave some to her husband and he ate (3, 1-7).

Then began the flight from God and the tension between man and woman. God did not abandon his creature,
but sought him out so as to restore to him his gift, although
this was to involve suffering:

"I will put enmity between you and the woman, between your seed
and her seed; she shall crush your head and you shall lie in wait
for her heel."
To the woman he said: "I will make great your distress in child-
bearing; in pain shall you bring forth children; for your husband
shall be your longing, though he have dominion over you."
And to Adam he said, "Because you have listened to your wife,
and have eaten of the tree of which I commanded you not to eat:
Cursed be the ground because of you; in toil shall you eat of it all
the days of your life; thorns and thistles shall it bring forth to you,
and you shall eat the plants of the field. In the sweat of your brow
you shall eat bread, till you return to the ground, since out of it
you were taken; for dust you are and unto dust you shall return."
[And the man called his wife Eve because she was the mother of
all the living] (3, 15-20).

This is an odd conclusion, but a consoling one, for the

divine words are no mere curse, but a foreshadowing of salvation through suffering.

*   *   *

In this text we are not surprised to find the role of the Serpent, the Tempter, the alliance of the Woman with him, and the consequent irruption of the kingdom of Death. Nor does it surprise us to meet with the search for that knowledge which Anath and Isis claimed to possess.

On the contrary, it is difficult to establish exactly whether in this text *the Serpent is the symbol of Death alone, or if he is also the symbol of life* sought elsewhere than in God.

That the Serpent may also be the symbol of life clearly appears not only from Oriental literature and from archaeological discoveries,[4] but also from the Bible itself: because of the murmurings of the Hebrew people, God sent winged serpents or dragons who by their bite caused a vast number of the people to perish. Then Moses interceded for them and salvation appeared when they fixed their gaze on the winged serpent or dragon which Moses raised up as an emblem of salvation. The Serpent in this case was a symbol of Jesus crucified.[5]

But can we argue from this text that Eve rebelled against God and sought maternity elsewhere than in the divine order, seeking it from the Serpent, the implacable enemy of God and of mankind?

Although we have given the title "The Mother" to this last section, and although such a conclusion would render our whole treatment more evocative, we are not yet convinced of this point, because in Anath as in Tiamat and Isis the serpent appears exclusively as "the son of Death" (Mot).

Our conclusion therefore is that the author is speaking

of the Serpent intended to indicate Satan, first enemy of mankind and of God.

We do not exclude the possibility of another implication: that the author also meant to indicate that Eve in her desire for maternity was infatuated by a more human—too human—knowledge and not a supremely divine one. But the evidence in support of this theory is not yet convincing.

Who, then, is the victorious woman?

(a) RATIONALISTIC OPINION (VON RAD)

The rationalists deny that the text contains any messianic foreshadowing and consequently any Marian significance. They consider all to be sufficiently explained in Eve.

We think that this would render it difficult to distinguish the Old Testament from the myths, since it would be to deny to the Old Testament that outlook toward the New Testament which is characteristic of its every page as the shadow and symbol of a more impressive reality to come.

(b) MANY CATHOLICS

Many Catholics hold that the victorious woman cannot be Eve. Undoubtedly their opinion is far from being improbable when we consider that the text speaks of an implacable hatred between the Woman and the Serpent. Such a situation appears almost impossible in regard to Eve.

(c) OTHERS, PARTICULARLY THE EXEGETES

These do not willingly agree on the exclusion of Eve—to whom the title "mother of the living" undoubtedly refers—from the announcement of the victorious woman.[6]

In conclusion, whether one admits that the woman is literally Eve, as a type or symbol of Mary of Nazareth, or whether one goes so far as to retain *that the literal sense calls for Mary*, one thing is now certain: that God at the beginning of human history promised the Mother, so that her tenderness might become a symbol of his merciful forgiveness. But it is only in the "history of Mary of Nazareth" that the Mother's face is to appear distinctly.

III. THE ORIGINAL SIN OF THE HEBREW PEOPLE (EX. 32-34)

It is difficult to find in the Old Testament any colloquies between a woman and God.

It is easy, on the contrary, to find men speaking with God. Think of Noah and of Abraham. Moses, though, is worthy of special mention. God revealed to him his name, Yahweh, "He who is" (Ex. 3, 14).

But Moses received the true revelation of God's essence or name when the Hebrew people adored the golden calf. God wished to exterminate the idolatrous people, but Moses intervened to appease him, and in the end God manifested to him his essence, *tender, kind, full of mercy toward sinners.*

The Hebrews, emigrating from Egypt in the thirteenth century before Christ, followed Moses with enthusiasm. But when the journey had continued for several years, in the midst of untold privations—hunger and thirst, bloody attacks by the Bedouin tribes of the desert—they began to tire of Moses and to experience a nostalgia for their former Egyptian captivity.

One day Moses ascended the mountain to obtain from God the gift of the Law. The people took advantage at once to celebrate a festival. All their gold was brought together and melted. As soon as they had fashioned it into a golden calf, they placed this on a pedestal and danced around it.

God saw all this from the mountain and began to complain to Moses.

1. God Speaks to Moses on Sinai

God announces to him that because of the people's prevarication he intends to destroy Israel. Moses intercedes and appeases him.

"Let me alone, then, that my wrath may blaze up against them to consume them. Then I will make of you a great nation."

But Moses implored the Lord, his God, saying, "Why, O Lord, should your wrath blaze up against your own people, whom you brought out of the land of Egypt with such great power and with so strong a hand? Why should the Egyptians say, 'With evil intent he brought them out, that he might kill them in the mountains and exterminate them from the face of the earth'? Let your blazing wrath die down; relent in punishing your people."

"Remember your servants Abraham, Isaac, and Israel, and how you swore to them by your own self, saying, 'I will make your descendants as numerous as the stars in the sky; and all this land that I promised, I will give your descendants as their perpetual heritage.'"

So the Lord relented in the punishment he had threatened to inflict on his people (Ex. 32, 11-14).

2. Moses Speaks to God in the Camp

Moses, coming down from the mountain, shatters the golden calf and orders the extermination of the transgressors who persevere in their sin. For the others he continues to pray:

. . . Moses said to the people, "You have committed a grave sin. I will go up to the Lord, then; perhaps I may be able to make atonement for your sin." So Moses went back to the Lord and said, "Ah, this people has indeed committed a grave sin in making a god of gold for themselves! If you would only forgive their sin! If you will not, then strike me out of the book that you have written." The Lord answered, "Him only who has sinned against me will I strike out of my book. Now, go and lead the people whither I have told you. My angel will go before you. When it is time for me to punish, I will punish them for their sin."

Thus the Lord smote the people for having had Aaron make the calf for them (Ex. 32, 30-35).

3. Moses Speaks To God in the Tent

In the camp everyone is in grief and mourning because of their sin. Moses continues to intercede, pleading on the grounds of having "found favor":

The Lord used to speak to Moses face to face, as one man speaks to another. . . .

Moses said to the Lord, "You, indeed, are telling me to lead this people on; but you have not let me know whom you will send with me. Yet you have said, 'You are my intimate friend,' and also, 'You have found favor with me.' Now, if I have found favor with you, do let me know your ways so that, in knowing you, I may continue to find favor with you. Then, too, this nation is, after all, your own people."

"I myself," the Lord answered, "will go along, to give you rest." Moses replied, "If you are not going yourself, do not make us go up from here. For how can it be known that we, your people and I, have found favor with you, except by your going with us? Then we, your people and I, will be singled out from every other people on the earth."

The Lord said to Moses, "This request, too, which you have just made, I will carry out, because you have found favor with me and you are my intimate friend."

Then Moses said, "Do let me see your glory!" He answered, "I will make all my beauty pass before you, and in your presence I will pronounce my name, 'Lord'; I who show favors to whom I will, I who grant mercy to whom I will."

"But my face you cannot see, for no man sees me and still lives" (Ex. 33, 11; 12-23).[7]

4. Moses Beholds God on Sinai

Moses ascends the mountain once more with the two tablets of stone, that God may again write the Law upon them. Early in the morning he reaches the summit. Down below on the plain only sand and parched earth are visible, while up above there is freshness and liberty of movement. The kite flies tranquilly in the sky, poised on the wing. Moses is to remember well this scene and to have his people chant:

He found them in a wilderness, a wasteland of howling desert. He shielded them and cared for them, guarding them as the apple of his eye. As an eagle incites its nestlings forth by hovering over its brood, so he spread his wings to receive them and bore them up on his pinions (Deut. 32, 10-11).[8]

In this enchanting setting God appears in the cloud. While God stands before him and shows him his glory, Moses invokes his name:

"The Lord, the Lord, a merciful and gracious God, slow to anger and rich in kindness and fidelity, continuing his kindness for a thousand generations, and forgiving wickedness and crime and sin: yet not declaring the guilty guiltless, but punishing children and grandchildren to the third and fourth generation for their fathers' wickedness!" (Ex. 34, 6-7).

Moses then prays:

"If I find favor with you, O Lord, do come along in our company. This is indeed a stiff-necked people; yet pardon our wickedness and sins, and receive us as your own."
"Here, then," said the Lord, "is the covenant I will make. Before the eyes of all your people I will work such marvels as have never been wrought in any nation anywhere on earth, so that this people among whom you live may see how awe-inspiring are the deeds which I, the Lord, will do at your side" (Ex. 34, 9-10).

Many remarks could be made on the very complicated question of the sources, which appear to be contradictory.

Moses sees God face to face and he cannot see him; the people are pardoned and exterminated, and so forth. Remarks could also be made on the Egyptian atmosphere which pervades the style of writing—to know by name, to write and cancel in the book. But we will limit ourselves to what is essential.

Little by little as we proceed with the reading, we are aware that Moses takes advantage of having "found favor" with God, which permits him to intercede for sinners.

Another important thing to be noted is that the definition of God, of his name and essence is: *tenderness and grace*. This definition is born of the experience which Moses has had in his four colloquies with the God of mercy and salvation.

Finally, God promises in the pact with the people that in the future his face will be distinctly revealed. The Hebrew's gaze is constantly fixed on the future. Moses himself is to die without seeing the Holy Land, because of his sin (Deut. 32, 31). He was not *full of grace* (Cf. Luke 1, 28).

IV. THE KINDNESS AND TENDERNESS OF GOD IN THE PSALMS

The individual prayer of Moses creates, as it were, the atmosphere for the synagogue's social prayer, the Psalms. Let us select a few of the more meaningful.

1. Psalm 102: God Is the Kind and Tender Father

Such seems to me to be the title of this Psalm which is called "God is love," or "the soul in love with God." [9]

Bless the Lord, O my soul; and all my being, bless his holy name. Bless the Lord, O my soul, and forget not all his benefits; [10] he pardons all your iniquities, he heals all your ills.

He redeems your life from destruction, he crowns you with kind-
ness and compassion, he fills your lifetime with good; your youth is
renewed like the eagle's.
The Lord secures justice and the rights of all the oppressed. He has
made known his ways to Moses, and his deeds to the children of
Israel.
Merciful and gracious is the Lord, slow to anger and abounding in
kindness.
He will not always chide, nor does he keep his wrath forever.
Not according to our sins does he deal with us, nor does he requite
us according to our crimes.
For as the heavens are high above the earth, so surpassing is his
kindness to those who fear him.
As far as the east is from the west, so far has he put our transgres-
sions from us.
As a father has compassion on his children, so the Lord has com-
passion on those who fear him. . . .

Here we breathe the air of Sinai, but observe how the
divine anger is confined to a moment, whereas his tenderness knows no bounds.

Tender as a father. Why not as a mother? In the Old
Testament a tendency to masculinize is remarked, in com-
parison with other peoples. It is false, though,—and we
shall see this later on in the present work—to define the
Old Testament as the kingdom of the Father, and the
New Testament as that of the Mother.[11]

Perhaps the reason lies in the poor reputation and role
attributed to woman in the history of Israel: the dancers
around the golden calf, the Moabite seductresses (Num.
25), Bethsabee who leads David to sin, Solomon's wives
who drive him to idolatry, Jezabel who causes the prevarication of the northern kingdom, Athalia who wants to
destroy the dynasty of David. Nonetheless, good examples
of women are not lacking, such as Moses' sister and the
pharaoh's daughter who saves the prophet from the king's
wrath.

We shall see, however, how this unilateral view is to be corrected by the prophets.

2. *Psalms 144-146: Anthology of the Psalms*

An ancient rabbi assures us: "Anyone who recites this prayer (Ps. 144) three times a day can be sure that he is a son of the world to come." In this Psalm also we hear the echo of Moses' prayer:

They discourse of the power of your terrible deeds and declare your greatness.
They publish the fame of your abundant goodness and joyfully sing of your justice.
The Lord is gracious and merciful, slow to anger and of great kindness.
The Lord is good to all and compassionate toward all his works. . . .
The Lord keeps all who love him, but all the wicked he will destroy.

Psalm 145 continues in the same vein:

The Lord gives sight to the blind.
The Lord raises up those that were bowed down.
The Lord protects strangers; the fatherless and the widow he sustains.
The Lord loves the just but the way of the wicked he thwarts.

Note how mercy, justice, and goodness are blended, while tenderness stands out above all. But we must not be deceived by phrases that speak of the universality of divine love, as the final words warn us.

There is a marked difference between Old Testament spirituality and Christian spirituality, which makes the tenderness of God to consist in his grace and kindness toward the *ungrateful* (Luke 6, 35-36); or, as Matthew says, toward the *unjust* (5, 43-48).

Brevity prevents us from examining Psalms 24, 76, 110, 111, 115—all of them vibrant with the same spirituality.

We cannot refrain, though, from quoting a few verses of the *Miserere* (Ps. 50) and the *De profundis* (Ps. 129).

3. *The* Miserere *and the* De Profundis

In the *Miserere* it is not Moses, the just one, who intercedes, but David, the adulterer, on whose account Bethsabee's son is threatened with a horrifying punishment David discovers with horror the abyss of sin into which he has fallen:

Have mercy on me, O God, in your goodness; in the greatness of your compassion wipe out my offense.
Thoroughly wash me from my guilt and of my sin cleanse me.
For I acknowledge my offense, and my sin is before me always:
Against you only have I sinned, and done what is evil in your sight—
that you may be justified in your sentence, vindicated when you condemn.
Indeed, in guilt was I born, and in sin my mother conceived me.

(The Miserere, or Ps. 50)

As in Job 14, 4, a mother appears as the source of weakness and sin. Thus life is considered as impure water issuing from the turbid spring of the maternal womb.

Meanwhile, the human longing continues to rise to God, praying him to send the Mother, the source of life in whose arms we can find repose:

> "The arms of mothers are made of love
> Let children sleep there blissfully"
> (Victor Hugo, *Les Misérables*).

Now the human soul has descended into the worst squalor and it groans as it thinks of the Mother:

If you, O Lord, mark iniquities,
Lord, who can stand?
But with you is forgiveness. . . .
Let Israel wait for the Lord,

For with the Lord is kindness and with him is plenteous redemption;
And he will redeem Israel from all their iniquities.

(The *De Profundis,* or Ps. 129).

Thus the soul, submerged in the abyss of guilt, continues to hope in God. The *De Profundis,* a psalm of hope, infuses into us continually this trust in God.

According to some exegetes, the seventh verse, "Let Israel wait for the Lord," is taken from the psalm which follows, where it has a more suitable context:

"Nay rather, I have stilled and quieted my soul like a weaned child. Like a weaned child on its mother's lap, so is my soul within me. O Israel, hope in the Lord, both now and forever" (Ps. 130, 2).

The peace of this soul which no longer seeks the consolations of God, but only the God of consolations, is admirable when compared to the picture of the child already weaned, who stays tranquilly by his mother's side.

What must be the Christian's trust, knowing as he does that God, the Lord and Savior, appears in Jesus Christ in the arms of his Mother?

When the *De Profundis* is sung at Christmas Vespers, is not the Christian soul more at peace than the pious Jew who is as yet unaware that God is tender as a mother and that the name of that mother is Mary?

V. WOMAN, THE SYMBOL OF DIVINE TENDERNESS (OSEE AND JEREMIA)

Where sin abounds, there God is to be found. He must chastise, because he hates sin, but in the end his love and his tenderness prevail. This is precisely the situation of Samaria and Jerusalem, the two cities who apostatized from God. The divine word pronounced by the prophets

Osee (eighth century B.C.) and Jeremia (sixth century B.C.) is to descend consolingly upon them.

But how is God to carry out his intention of forgiveness? By beginning with the redemption of the woman!

1. Osee (Chapters 1-2 and 11)

The scene occurs somewhere between 745 and 724 B.C., in the capital of the northern kingdom, Samaria. Wealth has brought in its wake corruption, injustice toward the poor, idolatry. God is angry with these degenerate Israelites who have by this time exhausted his divine patience. He wishes therefore to punish them by causing their army to be annihilated in the valley of Jezrael. But at the same time he will call the prophet Osee to fortell that his mercy is to prevail in the end. How is all this to be indicated? God will command his prophet to take as his wife a woman of doubtful reputation, by whom he is to have three children. These, by their names, are to be the living symbols of God's manner of dealing with his people:

So he went and took Gomer, the daughter of Debelain, and she conceived and bore him a son.

Then the Lord said to him: Give him the name Jezrael, for in a little while I will punish the house of Jehu for the bloodshed at Jezrael and bring to an end the kingdom of the house of Israel; on that day I will break the bow of Israel in the valley of Jezrael.

When she conceived again and bore a daughter, the Lord said to him: Give her the name Lo-ruhama; I no longer feel pity for the house of Israel: rather I abhor them utterly.

Yet for the house of Juda I feel pity; I will save them by the Lord, their God, but I will not save them by war, by sword or bow, by horses or horsemen.

After she weaned Lo-ruhama, she conceived and bore a son.

Then the Lord said: Give him the name Lo-ammi, for you are not my people, and I will not be your God. . . .

The number of the Israelites shall be like the sand of the sea,

which can be neither measured nor counted.
Whereas they were called, "Lo-ammi" ["not my people"], they shall be called, "Children of the living God."
Then the people of Juda and of Israel shall be gathered together; they shall appoint for themselves one head and come up from other lands, for great shall be the day of Jezrael.
Say to your brothers, "*Ammi*," ["My people"] and to your sisters, "*Ruhama*" ["tenderness"] (Os. 1, 3-9; 3, 1-3).

It seems to us that this word *tenderness*,[12] which is often lost in the translations, ought to be preserved absolutely. It is the acceptance of a well-documented word reserved for the woman in Ugaritic literature. In Babylonian texts we find traces of it also.

To us the deep religious significance is of particular interest: the woman, by her very nature, is destined to manifest the tenderness of God. Just as tenderness is the natural attitude of the mother toward her child in need of help, so, applied to God, it signifies his natural compassion for the sinner.

Whereas initially the woman was called Lo-ruhama (not-tenderness) (1, 6) because she was to symbolize by her graceless life the wrath of God who would have abandoned Samaria to war and pillage. (Cf. Lam. 4, 10 where it is related that the *tender hands of mothers* went so far as to roast the little bodies of their babies during the siege of Jerusalem in 586 B.C.) Later she was given once more the name of "tenderness" (2, 2), so as to become the palpitating expression of God's pardoning love (2, 25)!

All this, however, is still projected into the future where it is to be taken up and clarified by Luke. Osee can here be called, without doubt, the Luke of the eighth century B.C.

Before leaving Osee it is well to complete our treatment of this prophet with another text which explains the same truth, but from the point of view of love and paternity.

When Israel was a child I loved him, out of Egypt I called my son.
The more I called them, the farther they went from me, sacrificing
to the Baals and burning incense to idols.
Yet it was I who taught Ephraim to walk, who took them in my
arms; I drew them with human cords, with bands of love; I fostered
them like one who raises an infant to his cheeks; yet, though I
stooped to feed my child, they did not know that I was their
healer. . . . [13]
How could I give you up, O Ephraim, or deliver you up, O Israel?
How could I treat you as Adama, or make you like Seboim?
My heart is overwhelmed, my pity is stirred.
I will not give vent to my blazing anger, I will not destroy Ephraim
again; for I am God and not man (11, 1-4; 8-9).

Here it is not clear whether the prophet considers God
to be more maternal or more paternal. We can certainly
accept that at this point Osee be called the John of the
eighth century B.C.

The conclusion is a radical one: God is above every
love that exists, whether it be maternal or paternal.

2. Jeremia (Chapter 31)

It has been said that the soul of Osee is present in
Jeremia [14] and it is true. Indeed, he is to develop more
fully the spirituality of Osee in his soul that was ruled by
implacable hatred and intense love. Jeremia is the lover
of flowers, of the domestic hearth, and he is continually
homesick for the peace of his own Anathoth. When he
rests at Anathoth his longing is for Jerusalem, for the
Temple.

Jeremia is one of those afflicted souls who suffer for a
trifle, who willingly forgo all responsibility. But it is
precisely this man who is called by God.

He preaches in Jerusalem a short time before the terrible Chaldean invasion and destruction, between 626 and
586 B.C. The situation is clear. Juda has apostatized, has

betrayed her God and spouse. Is there to be no more pardon? Yes! Although a husband may not take back his repudiated spouse, God will receive once more the sinful Judaic nation.

If a man sends away his wife and after leaving him she marries another man, does the first husband come back to her? Would not the land be wholly defiled?
But you have sinned with many lovers, and yet you would return to me! says the Lord. . . .
And I thought, after she has done all this she will return to me. But she shall not return. . . .
Juda did not return to me wholeheartedly, but insincerely, says the Lord. . . .
Go, proclaim these words toward the north, and say:
Return, rebel Israel, says the Lord, I will not remain angry with you; for I am merciful, I will not continue my wrath forever (Jer. 3, 1-7; 10; 12).

After thirty chapters of similar reproaches, the prophet leads us to hope. Here is the famous Chapter 31, the canticle of divine love and tenderness, in the atmosphere of the New Covenant. It is a song of consolation, addressed to the inhabitants of Jerusalem, who had witnessed in 597 B.C. (or 586?) the depopulation of the city and the departure of endless streams of their compatriots, deported as slaves to Babylonia.

(a) THE SONG OF ETERNAL LOVE (31, 1-14)

Thus says the Lord: The people that escaped the sword have found favor in the desert.
As Israel comes forward to be given his rest, the Lord appears to him from afar: with age-old love I have loved you; so I have kept my mercy toward you (vv. 2-3).

Joyous cries are therefore to be heard, and nuptial songs and dances. They indicate the joy of the exiles as they return to God who is "Father, and Ephraim his first-born."

(b) THE SONG OF DIVINE TENDERNESS (vv. 14-20)

In the midst of much rejoicing, the plaint of a mother is heard: Rachel weeping for her absent children. God is touched. He consoles the mother and assures her that he too is moved to compassion for the repentant sinner.

In Rama is heard the sound of moaning, of bitter weeping!
Rachel mourns her children, she refuses to be consoled because her children are no more.
Thus says the Lord: Cease your cries of mourning, wipe the tears from your eyes.
The sorrow you have shown shall have its reward, says the Lord, they shall return from the enemy's land.
There is hope for your future, says the Lord; your sons shall return to their own borders.
I hear, I hear Ephraim pleading: You chastised me, and I am chastened; I was an untamed calf.
If you allow me, I will return, for you are the Lord, my God.
I turn in repentance; I have come to myself, I strike my breast;
I blush with shame, I bear the disgrace of my youth.
Is Ephraim not my favored son, the child in whom I delight?
Often as I threaten him, I still remember him with favor; my heart stirs for him, I must show him mercy, says the Lord.

(c) THE SONG OF THE ETERNAL COVENANT
(vv. 22-34)

Israel, as the spouse of God, is invited to return to him. Sublime times are foretold in which: "God has created a new thing upon the earth: the woman must encompass the man with devotion." This will be the era of the New Covenant, when the People of God will return to him:

The days are coming, says the Lord, when I will make a new covenant with the house of Israel and the house of Juda.
It will not be like the covenant I made with their fathers the day

I took them by the hand to lead them forth from the land of Egypt;
for they broke my covenant, and I had to show myself their master,
says the Lord.
But this is the covenant which I will make with the house of Israel
after those days, says the Lord.
I will place my law within them, and write it upon their hearts;
I will be their God and they shall be my people. . . .
For I will forgive their evil-doing and remember their sin no more
(31-34).

Although we admit that the single phrases are difficult
to interpret, we find the context clear: the days are foretold in which there will be a New Covenant, when the
people will be faithful to God in an atmosphere of reciprocal understanding: forgiveness on the part of God, while
men, accepting this pardon, are to enjoy a peace which
surpasses that of this world.

God loves us with an eternal love and is therefore
moved to compassion at the sight of human distress.

The weeping and tenderness of Rachel are reflections
of the tenderness and love of the merciful God.

The prophet of Anathoth had always been struck by
the wickedness of the human heart, which can reject God's
love (Jer. 17, 5-11; 18, 12).

In the thirty-first chapter, on the contrary, the tumult
of the Lord's sentiments is expressed as his avenging justice battles with his tenderness. Which is to triumph? His
tenderness, which, almost forgetful of the bilateral alliance of Sinai, is to make another covenant with man,
infused into the very heart of flesh so that man may no
longer be seduced by idols but may remain faithful to the
merciful God.[15]

Amid much tenderness and grace the maternal figure
of Rachel stands out in marvelous manner, apparently
detached from the context as far as style is concerned, but

not from the divine and human atmosphere of sorrow and love!

VI. THE MOTHER WITH HER CHILD, SYMBOL
OF THE REDEMPTION (ISA. 7-11)

Woman sins, say Osee and Jeremia, but here too the man, as in Genesis, listens willingly to his wife. The laconic expression of Sartre concerning woman's guilt remains always true: "Half victims, half accomplices, like everybody."

Man sins, especially when seated on a throne and holding a sceptre in his hand. In this, Sacred Scripture pardons none, neither David, nor Solomon, nor Achaz, king of Juda (735-715 B.C.).

The story of Achaz' sin is related by Isaia, the noble aristrocratic prophet, and perhaps the only philosopher-prophet.[16] He fits admirably in the eighth century B.C., between Osee and Jeremia. The latter are two exceptional men sensitive to the needs of the people, while Isaia is the learned poet who does not allow himself to be carried away by sentimentalism, but in a few rhythmic phrases places before us historical fact and its deep religious significance.

The chapters which concern us are 7 to 11. Mention is made twice of a mother with her child (7-8) and of two prodigious births (9-11). Indisputably these images emerge among the infinite historical misfortunes occasioned by the sins of the people and their kings. Achaz has formed an alliance with Assyria and therefore draws upon himself the hatred of the kings of Damascus and Samaria, who are declared enemies of the Assyrian king. The two kings are preparing to attack Jerusalem, and it is precisely at this time that God sends the prophet Isaia.

1. The Virgin-Mother (Chapter 7)

This is the central figure. Isaia invites King Achaz to fear neither the Syrian king nor the ruler of Samaria, both of whom are threatening his territory. He invites him to trust in God, indeed, to ask for some sign, anywhere he wishes. King Achaz, sceptical, places his whole trust in his fortifications and therefore replies sarcastically, evading the invitation. Isaia, indignant, exclaims:

Listen, O house of David! Is it not enough for you to weary men, must you also weary my God? Therefore the Lord himself will give you this sign: the virgin shall be with child, and bear a son, and shall name him Emmanuel.

He shall be living on curds and honey by the time he learns to reject the bad and choose the good.

For before the child learns to reject the bad and choose the good, the land of those two kings whom you dread shall be deserted (vv. 13-16).

2. The Non-Virginal Mother, Wife of Isaia (Chapter 8)

In reading the Hebrew Bible, we pass naturally from this prophecy to that of Chapter 8. Here, too, we have a fact which is prodigious although less solemn, placed in the same period and which would seem at first sight to indicate the same thing, except for the fact that the woman in this case is clearly singled out:

The Lord said to me: Take a large cylinder-seal, and inscribe on it in ordinary letters: "Belonging to Maher-shalal-hash-baz."

And I took reliable witnesses, Uria the priest, and Zacharia, son of Barachia.

Then I went to the prophetess and she conceived and bore a son. The Lord said to me: Name him Maher-shalal-hash-baz, for before the child knows how to call his father or mother by name, the wealth of Damascus and the spoil of Samaria shall be carried off by the king of Assyria (vv. 1-4).

3. Birth of the First-born Son (Chapters 9-11)

Galilee, the enemy of Judaea, is invaded by Tiglat-Phalasar III, who comes to the aid of Achaz (732 B.C.). The inhabitants are carried off as slaves. To these men languishing in their squalid prison, the joyful news is announced of the birth of the heir:

The people who walked in darkness have seen a great light. . . .
For a child is born to us, a son is given to us; upon his shoulder dominion rests.
They name him Wonder-Counselor, God-Hero, Father-Forever, Prince of Peace.
His dominion is vast and forever peaceful, from David's throne, and over his kingdom, which he confirms and sustains by judgment and justice both now and forever.
The zeal of the Lord of hosts will do this (9, 1-6).

In the eleventh chapter there is a return to the same prodigious birth, in more or less similar accents:

But a shoot shall sprout from the stump of Jesse, and from his roots a bud shall blossom.
The spirit of the Lord shall rest upon him: a spirit of wisdom and of understanding, a spirit of counsel and of strength, a spirit of knowledge and of fear of the Lord, and his delight shall be the fear of the Lord.
Not by appearance shall he judge, nor by hearsay shall he decide, but he shall judge the poor with justice, and decide aright for the land's afflicted (vv. 1-4).

These chapters, like the songs of the servant of God, have always been a point of contention for the exegetes. Who are these mothers and these children? As in the case of the woman in Genesis, here also we have a triple interpretation.

(a) THE MYTHICAL CONCEPT

Today it is conceded that virgin and maiden are, after all, the same thing in Hebrew and Ugaritic literature [17] without going back as far as the Septuagint. However, the *genus annunciationis* (the manner of the announcement of a birth) teaches us that even if the concepts of virginity and maternity are juxtaposed, they are not for this reason contemporaneous. It means, after all, that she is a virginal maiden, a fine young woman who will find a husband to wed her and will then become a mother. Here are the two texts of major importance:

The virgin will give birth—behold the virgin shall bear a son. . . . Take your wife into your house—bring the maiden to your court— she shall bear you seven sons. (Compare with Ugarit.)

Therefore, there is no supposition of a virgin mother. Isaia 7 can very well be united with Chapter 8. Perhaps the wife of Achaz is indicated.

As regards the child, the one mentioned in Chapters 7 and 8 is the son Isaia and the one in Chapters 9-11 is Ezechia, son of Achaz. The titles attributed to him cause us no surprise. Consider Keret's son to whom divine qualities are attributed. Or, better still, read the epilogue to the *Code of Hammurabi* which describes:

"A perfect king, who caused light to be born, of great talent and vigor, profoundly wise, of strength unequalled, a just king who established justice for the oppressed and the widow." [18]

(b) THE CONCEPT BASED ON HISTORY

Here the New Testament is read, in which insistence on Mary's virginity appears evident, based on the prophecy of Isaia (Matt. 1, 22; Luke 1, 31). The prodigious child is Christ (Matt. 4, 12; Luke 1, 32). Mary alone is the Virgin-Mother. She alone can boast this honor, just as to Christ alone can be attributed divine honors such as those mentioned.

If I am in possession of a badly-focused photograph and a well-focused one of the same subject, it is evident that the uncertainties and haziness of the former must be rendered clear by the latter. Thus the Old Testament becomes clear in the light of the New.

(c) THE PROPHETIC CONCEPT

The above comparison is excellent, but by this we do not mean to say that the first photograph, the Old Testament, is an objectively clear image. No text of the Old Testament taken by itself brings us necessarily to the conclusion of Christ's divinity, of the Holy Spirit, and the virginal maternity of Mary.

The prophetic concept, therefore, maintains that it is difficult to say whether or not Isaia intended to affirm clearly the simultaneous virginity and maternity of the mother and the humanity and divinity of the child. This is particularly true since the discovery of the Oriental literatures and of the *genus annunciationis.*

The first historical concept, that makes the prophet see everything clearly, is an exaggeration. Above all, it uproots him from his historical environment in which he promises a sign to Achaz. It seems, then, to require a contemporaneous mother who, with her child, is the symbol of the great prodigy to come later.

Let it be noted that in all four of the passages quoted it is the infant who is the sign, not the virgin-mother, who, however, forms a magnificent background for the child.

Conclusion: In the Old Testament the *genus annunciationis* [19] is well known, but in no part of it is the virginity of the mother stressed.

Does it, perhaps, appear here, in Isaia 7, 14?

It would seem that Mary was unaware of it, since she inquires: "How shall this happen, since I do not know man?"

Heaven is to reply, appealing to divine love in person, to the Holy Spirit, whose action is to furnish evident proof of the divinity and holiness of Christ.

But a further explanation from heaven is required, because in Israel the state of virginity in a woman of marriageable age was unheard of, as was also the idea that a woman be at the same time mother and virgin. This indicates that no prophecy of the Old Testament suffices to explain the New. A fresh intervention of God is necessary, which will explain that God by means of Isaia gave a clear sign of divine protection to the prophet's contemporaries, by presenting the image of the mother with her child.

This was but a pallid image of another mother and child who were the true and authentic ones symbolized, because the mother was to be at the same time a virgin, to show that the child was also God.

Isaia had some kind of intuition, but full light only appeared when Jesus began to preach. For he alone was "the light that enlightens every man who comes into the world."

All prophets, when they are dying, cry out with Goethe: "More light, more light!" (*Mehr Licht, Mehr Licht!*).

VII. GOD THE MOTHER (ISA. 65-66 AND 49)

Gradually as the centuries proceed, the light shows itself more clearly. A faithful disciple of Isaia is to meditate on the marvelous figure to come, and then to ask himself why God manifests himself thus, a child in the arms of his mother?

Thus he discovers a new heaven and a new earth:

Jerusalem joyfully caressing her children because God loves them as a mother.

It is the Hebrews, just returned from Babylonian slavery (528 B.C.), who in the midst of their difficulties in building the new Jerusalem are consoled by the supernal vision of divine tenderness.

Yet Sion is scarcely in labor when she gives birth to her children. Shall I bring a mother to the point of birth, and yet not let her child be born? says the Lord; or shall I allow her to conceive, yet close her womb? says your God.
Rejoice with Jerusalem and be glad because of her; exult, exult with her, all you who were mourning over her!
Oh, that you may suck fully of the milk of her comfort, that you may nurse with delight at her abundant breasts!
For thus says the Lord: Lo, I will spread prosperity over her like a river, and the wealth of the nations like an overflowing torrent. As nurslings, you shall be carried in her arms, and fondled in her lap; as a mother comforts her son, so will I comfort you; in Jerusalem you shall find your comfort (Isa. 66, 8-13).

In order to understand this chapter fully, we must remember that it represents the epitome of postexilic theology (536-100 B.C.) which has characteristics all its own.

In fact, whereas the Messias, son of David (Isa. 9-11), predominates in the first forty chapters of Isaia, here it is the daughter of Sion, bride of the Lord, who appears:

As a young man marries a virgin, your Builder shall marry you; and as a bridegroom rejoices in his bride so shall your God rejoice in you. . . . See, the Lord proclaims to the ends of the earth: Say to daughter Sion, your Savior comes! (Isa. 62, 5 and 11).

Whereas in the pre-exilic prophets the Word of God sounds powerfully forth, the present pages are pervaded instead by the tenderness of his Spirit:

The favors of the Lord I will recall, the glorious deeds of the Lord, because of all he has done for us; for he is good to the house of Israel, he has favored us according to his mercy and his great kindness. . . . Where is he who put his holy spirit in their midst?

. . . Like cattle going down into the plain, the spirt of the Lord guiding them. . . . Where is your zealous care and your might, your surge of pity and your mercy? (Isa. 63, 7-15).

It is precisely this atmosphere of divine tenderness, in which Jerusalem becomes a mother by the supernatural operation of the Holy Spirit of God, that the divinely natural words gush forth spontaneously: "As a mother comforts her son, so will I comfort you."

Thus this sinful people exposed to persecution and to sin, like leaves carried away by the wind (Isa. 64, 5), are to find once more the joy of forgiveness in a maternal, divine embrace!

By this time the Old Testament can terminate, for it has reached fullest maturity. Here not only are we promised the Mother (Gen. 3); not only are grace and tenderness tacitly attributed to God (Ex. 32-34); not only is it declared that the woman is the purest expression of God's tenderness (Osee-Jeremia), that she is with her child the symbol of salvation (Isaia); but also what concerns us more: it is unequivocally affirmed that God is like a mother.

Infinitely more tender, indeed, than a mother. This is what the Israelites are told as they groan in captivity because of their sins, tempted by this time to think that God has forgotten them:

Can a mother forget her infant, be without tenderness for the child of her womb?
Even should she forget, I will never forget you (Isa. 49, 15).

Thus the Old Testament opens our hearts to the fulfillment of the marvelous divine promise, preparing us for the apparition of Mary of Nazareth.

APPENDIX

THE SPOUSE AND THE MOTHER IN THE SAPIENTIAL BOOKS

The reader who passes from the prophetic to the sapiential books (Canticle of Canticles, Proverbs, Sirach, Wisdom of Solomon) is completely at sea. In the former, God predominated with his Word, whereas here he hardly appears at all, even by name, and much less does he speak. Take the Canticle of Canticles, where the name of God appears only twice.

Some are anxious to supply what is lacking by finding in every verse of Solomon's most beautiful song an implicit prophetic statement. Thus, when the spouse says "My lover to me and I to him" (2, 16), there is to be reference to the prophetic expressions "You are my people and I will be your God" (Os. 2, 25; Jer. 31, 33; Ezek. 36, 38).

Although it would be an exaggeration to deny the probability of this thesis entirely, we ourselves prefer to take the Bible without too many subtleties, recognizing already in human love itself a divine consecration.[20]

Thus when we read that the spouse browses among the lilies, it is not necessary, as Feuillet emphasizes, to see in this a direct invitation to purity, but an effusion of love between man and woman (Cant. 2, 16). Thus the Canticle of Canticles is literally the hymn of a bridegroom with his bride and consequently of each soul with her God. Just as every bride yearns continually for her spouse, so must the soul experience the longing to behold her God.

Naturally, anyone who believes that the true lover is the Mother and that maternal love is the model for all love, purifying every turbid and violent love (Alain), will then apply to Mary in the fullest sense all the passages concerning the bride, and to Jesus those regarding the bridegroom, with due respect for what has been learned in reading the New Testament.

Only thus can the myth of human love be duly appreciated, sublimated, and redeemed, with neither mystical straining nor commonplace rationalisms.

✻   ✻   ✻

Just as the "Daughter of Sion," once more the spouse of the Lord, appears as a fruitful mother, thanks to the divine Spirit, thus Wisdom in contact with God seems to appropriate the title of "mother."

The chapters which chiefly concern us are: Proverbs 8-9; Sirach 24-26; Wisdom 7-9.

In Proverbs, Divine Wisdom is manifested all clothed in divine qualities, "counsel and advice, strength and understanding" (Prov. 8, 14; Job 12, 13), which were formerly applied to the Messias, son of Jesse (Isa. 11, 1). She is not God, however, and in fact she says she has been created by him:

> The Lord begot me, the first-born of his ways, the forerunner of his prodigies of long ago; from of old I was poured forth, at the first, before the earth. When there were no depths I was brought forth (Prov. 8, 22-24).

H. Cazelles was struck by the words "he begot me, I was brought forth" which indicate the great intimacy between God and his wisdom. Indeed, God even becomes the mother who gives birth in suffering (Gen. 4, 1; Deut. 32, 18).[21]

Von Rad stresses, on the contrary, the intimacy of the colloquy between Wisdom and men, since she introduces herself as a mother to her own children.[22] "I found delight in the sons of men. So now, O children, listen to me. . . . Happy those who keep my ways" (Prov. 8, 31-32).

This entire drama is wonderful if it is accepted that the wisdom of the Hebrews is dependent on that of Egypt where it is always the father who teaches, although expressions such as the following are not lacking: "Wisdom is more rare than the famous emerald, yet it can be found in the mouths of bondswomen."

It is also true that Maat, the idea that orders the created world, may have influenced the Israelite scribes and sages. Here is a significant text in this connection: "If you are a leader who directs the affairs of a multitude, strive after every excellence until there be no fault in thy nature. Maat is good and its worth is lasting. It has not been disturbed since the day of its creator, whereas he who transgresses its ordinances is punished. It lies as a path in front even of him who knows nothing. Wrongdoing(?) has never yet brought its venture to port." [23]

Nevertheless many modern authors break away decidedly from this hypothesis of the Egyptian origin of Hebrew wisdom. [24]

Among these the more audacious have been anxious to trace the birth of Wisdom to Astarte, the goddess of love, failing to notice that the reflection of Astarte is rather to be found in the woman "folly" (Prov. 9, 13-18) who leads men to death. [25]

It is perhaps better to read Sirach, Chapter 24 in order to learn of the further development of the doctrine of wisdom in Israel. "From the mouth of the Most High I came forth, and mistlike covered the earth" (Sir. 24, 3). First among all peoples, even before time began, she is to be found beneath the same tent in which the Lord rests. Later we learn that this woman is the Mosaic law. In this chapter she is not called the bride of the Lord nor the mother of man, but she is said to offer the typically feminine gift of her grace, amid fragrance and flowers, in the trees' refreshing shade (Sir. 24, 16):

A gracious wife delights her husband, her thoughtfulness puts flesh on his bones; a gift from the Lord is her governed speech, and her firm virtue is of surpassing worth. Choicest of blessings is a modest wife, priceless her chaste person. Like the sun rising in the Lord's heavens, the beauty of a virtuous wife is the radiance of her home (Sir. 26, 13-16).

We see then how Sirach is less maternal than Proverbs, but more delicate and kind; although aware that "In woman was sin's beginning, and because of her we all die" (Sir. 25, 23), Sirach sails better with the gentle wind of grace.

A contemporary of Sirach, or rather one who died some decades later, was to write the Book of Wisdom. In Chapters 7-9 he causes us to penetrate more deeply into this doctrine. Here, however, it is no longer the mother who speaks, but the son who, although king of Jerusalem, feels himself to be a weak mortal because "in my mother's womb I was molded into flesh" (7, 1).

He is fortunate in having understood that he has another mother, namely Wisdom, from whom he can expect all good things. "She is the image of the goodness of God" (Wisd. 7, 26). This mother then becomes the bride *of whose beauty he is enamored* (8, 2). Finally, in Chapter 9, which is the closest to Proverbs 8, man assumes once more his own identity as the child of Wisdom and prays the merciful God (*eleous*) to infuse into him the spirit of his divine mother:

> Now with you is Wisdom, who knows your works and was present when you made the world; who understands what is pleasing in your eyes and what is conformable with your commands. Send her forth from your holy heavens and from your glorious throne dispatch her that she may be with me and work with me, that I may know what is pleasing to you (Wisd. 9, 9-10).

Here we have the Platonic myth of love (*Symposium*, 195-197) sublimely poetical and entering into revelation on the very threshold of the New Testament. Although it takes us far away from the prophets, this lyricism is pleasing. The luxuriant mythical boughs which surround the Wisdom of Solomon are to be stripped decidedly of their leaves by the New Testament alone, through the prosaic history of Jesus and Mary.

Without a doubt a number of the ideas found in Proverbs, in Sirach, and in Solomon's Wisdom are applied to Christ, the Wisdom of the Father. Recall the Pauline concept of Christ as the *image* of the invisible God, the *first-born of every creature* (Col. 1, 15), or as the *brightness* of God's glory (Heb. 1, 2), or lastly, as the light most clear which shines through the entire Gospel of John. One realizes that the poetry of Wisdom, already partially sublimated in the Old Testament, now finds its source which is Christ.

Has Mary any part in this sapiential world? Catholics themselves are content with an adapted application.[26] Personally I believe in going further. The Church, in applying Proverbs 8, Sirach 24, Wisdom 7, to Mary in her liturgy draws us into a Marian atmosphere.

If we consider, moreover, that to Christ are referred those divine qualities which in the Old Testament are proper to the Lord God, such as the creation (John 1, 3; Col. 1, 16),[27] a margin of maternity remains which can be applied in the fullest sense to Mary. Thus, when it is affirmed that: "The Lord begot me at the first . . . when there were no depths I was brought forth" (Prov. 8, 22), we can very well see in the Lord the countenance of Christ and in Wisdom the Immaculate Mother, so created "by intuition of the merits of Jesus."

Moreover, the concept of maternity is more in harmony with Mary than with Christ. It is always the New Testament which obliges us to focus more clearly the history of salvation in the Old Testament. Chapter 24 of Sirach is also applied to Mary by De Montfort in his *Treatise on True Devotion*.

We do not see why the following words of Sirach cannot and ought not to be taken as referring in a very deep sense to Mary:

"Then the Creator of all gave me his command and he who formed me chose the spot for my tent, saying, 'In Jacob make your dwelling, in Israel your inheritance.' Before all ages, in the beginning, he created me, and through all ages I shall not cease to be. In the holy tent I ministered before him, and in Sion I fixed my abode" (Sir. 24, 8-10). John assures us that Jesus "dwelt among us, and we saw his glory" (John 1, 14), and Luke gives us the words of the angel to Mary: "The Holy Spirit will come upon thee" (Luke 1, 35). Hence, Our Lady becomes the living tent in which the Son of God reposes, or the refreshing shade which is the resting place of the Lord who reveals himself in Christ.

In Chapters 7 and 9 of Solomon's Wisdom—where the author leaves the bosom of his mortal mother to seek the embrace of his immortal mother from whom all good proceeds—the Christian may see Mary as he reads, according to the accepted principle that every ray of maternity issues from Our Lady, the stupendous frame for the marvelous image of the Lord shown forth in Jesus Christ.

Finally, the Christian, in reading the Canticle of Canticles, can discern very well in each harmonious verse the face of the Mother, if he accepts with Alain that the first love is not between man and woman but between mother and child, an idea which Christian thought has certainly espoused.

When Mary is invoked, then, as Seat of Wisdom, or when it is asserted that she is the book in which the Word of God is written, the Catholic summarizes neatly his entire faith in God who has been pleased to insist on the figure of the Mother, manifested in Mary, before closing the Old Testament.

CONCLUSION

The entire Old Testament is no more than a divine promise. What of the reality or history which it foretells?

Let it not be forgotten that the Old Testament, although concealing in its bosom the fecund germs from which the New Testament will grow, is obstructed by an atmosphere of fear. God calls himself "He who is," the Lord, who remains at a certain distance from his creatures. He is to be loved, but above all he is to be feared; otherwise his fury will be experienced, his zeal, the zeal of the God of hosts, the fury (*'El Gibor*).

Well was it experienced by Oza who, for having touched the tottering Ark of God, was smitten by God's anger and fell dead beside the Ark (2 Kings 6, 7).

Mary, who was to be called the Ark of the Covenant, was still afar off, she who was to change the fury of God into a merciful smile, that still beams forth today over the hills of Kiriath Jearim from the countenance of *Our Lady of the Ark of the Covenant.*[28]

SUMMARY OF CHAPTER TWO:

THE essence of the forgiving God (tenderness) is manifested in three ways. 1. By the express revelation of his name (Ex. 34, 5-8; Ps. *Miserere;* Jer. 31); 2. This essence is given concrete form in woman's being (Os. 1-2; Isa. 49, 15; 65-66), as an expression of divine tenderness; 3. Finally, among women one is seen to emerge unmistakably, the woman of Genesis 3, 15, and of Isaia 7-11, where salvation appears even in the midst of sin, in the form of a son in his mother's arms.

Whereas the Jew will see here merely Eve and the wife of Isaia, the Christian will already guess that these two historical figures were but the shadow and symbol of another woman with another son.

◄{ NOTES }►

1. Cf. Albright, *Archaeology*, p. 234, in which Isa. 27 is compared with Ugarit. Cf. nevertheless our own reservations in note 10 of Chapter one.

Anyone wishing to examine more fully what follows will find excellent indications in O. Cullmann, "Geschichtesshreibung in N.T." in *RGG* (1958), III, 1501-1502, where in speaking of primeval history the author emphasizes that "the prophetical announcement of history in accounts which are not immanently historical is to be measured in conformity with revelation."

V. Hamp in *LThK* (1960), IV, 687-688, observes that no Psalm nor even the Proto-Gospel 3, 15 can be understood in a purely messianic sense, but that the true historical figure is to reveal its authentic face in the New Testament.

I. Henderson, *Der Historiker und der Theologe in Der Historische Jesus und Kerygmatische Christus*, edited by H. Ristow and K. Matthiae (Berlin: 1961): "Perhaps the action of God is written in mythical terminology. But only when the myth expresses something genuine about God as he is in himself and as he is distinct from us can it represent our history. In other words, is an existential interpretation of the myth expedient?" (p. 101).

2. From the exegetical point of view cf. G. von Rad, *Das erste Buch Moses* (Göttingen: 1956), pp. 66-68: which denies all christological and messianic sense in the text in question; Piazza-Galbiati, *Pagine difficili della Bibbia* (Milan: 1956), p. 106.

From the psychological point of view W. Kretschmer, *Psychologische Weisheit der Bibel* (Bern: 1955), pp. 144-148: "The woman remains all the time in the sphere of nature, closer to the birth of children and to the sick. The man is more inclined toward things, the woman toward persons; because the man "is" more a person, the woman more nature. Jung would have it that the woman seeks in the man chiefly the person, while the man looks for nature and spirit in the woman . . . marriage is the school of personal relations." On p. 183 this Protestant psychoanalyst leans toward the Mariological interpretation.

3. Buytendijk, *op. cit.*, p. 281, remarks discerningly: "Let us never forget that every human being has had a mother who deposited in him the germ of human possibility. Every time his existence is degraded or disorganized, the human being seeks the security of the *eternal Mother* who for each one of us is the beginning and the end."

4. Cf. note 13 of chapter one. Also *TWNT*, V, 572-575.

5. Num. 21, 4; John 3, 14.

6. In the vast literature dealing with Mary in the Proto-Gospel, cf.

A. Bea, "Maria nel Protovangelo," in *Marianum*, 15 (1953), pp. 2-5, where the author inclines toward the literal sense; J. Coppens, "Le protévangile un nouvel essai d'exégèse," in *Ephem. Theol. Lovan*, 26 (1950), p. 34: the author is inclined to favor Eve in an imperfect sense but Mary in a full and perfect sense.

7. The translations usually give *eagle*. We believe that species of kite is meant, such as we observed on the banks of the Arnon torrent. Moreover, the guide in the Harod museum also maintains that *Nshr* does not mean eagle.

8. Regarding the complexity of the text cf. M. Noth, *Das zweite Buch Moses* (Göttingen: 1961), pp. 214-215.

Observe that in Accadian to grow tender and *to have compassion* (*remu*) and grace (*remutu*) come from the same root. Cf. the discerning article "Gnade," in *LThK*, IV, 977-980. W. Eichrodt, in *Theologie des Alten Testaments* (1957), I, 162 (*Theology of the Old Testament*, Vol. I [Philadelphia: Westminster Press, 1961]), writes: "*Rhm* is appropriate to indicate love in the sense of mercy toward the needy, to express a sentiment of relationship close to the maternal sentiment toward the little child in need of assistance."

R. Bultmann, "Eleos," in *TWNT*, II, 47, distinguishes between *rahamym* and *eleos*, saying that the former term includes more affection especially that of father and mother; it is well translated by the word *love* and indicates a throbbing manifestation of it.

9. Cf. E. Weiser, *Die Psalmen* (Göttingen: 1959), II, 449, who defines it as "the most beautiful flower of biblical faith." Cf. also excellent comments in *SBJ*, *SBM*.

10. We have translated it as *benefit* but it is well to remember that the root *gml* rather signifies *pardon*. For example, in the prologue to the *Code of Hammurabi* the hero is praised for having spared the city of Larsa which was destined to be destroyed like every other enemy city; similarly the king who pardons the people of Mera and Tulul. In both cases the Accadian has the root *gml* (*gamûl, igmilu*).

11. Van der Leeuw, *op. cit.*, pp. 93-94.

12. In translations the word *tenderness* is usually generalized in *love*. But we feel that it is better to preserve in this term its original force of *maternal love* (Cf. Chap. 1, n. 23).

In Ugarit also the term *Rhmt* is well-known as applied to women. We find this tendency also in the Accadian. For instance, in the *Code of Hammurabi* we observe that this word is used preferably in reference to the love of the goddesses. Istar is called *ra-i-ma-at* and *ri-ma-am* (Epilogue XXVII, 17) or appertaining to the mother (par. 150, *i-ra-am-mu*). The terms does not appear at all in reference to the love of the gods or of the father (cf. pars. 165, 170, 180).

It is true that Psalm 102 appears to contradict our statement of the problem and seems to deny such an affirmation and shade of meaning.

But the peculiarity of Osee's text consists precisely in this, that it is a return to the primordial meaning of the word.

Regarding the interpretation of Osee from the historical point of view, cf. Albright, *The Biblical Period* (Pittsburgh: 1955), p. 35; C. Kuhl, *Prophets of Israel* (Richmond: John Knox, 1960).

From the exegetical point of view F. Buck, *Die Liebe Gottes beim Prophet Osee* (Rome: 1953), pp. 3-7; 40-41; A. Weiser in *ATD* in the chapters quoted from Osee.

13. All are aware that the Hebrew text is corrupt. We have tried to reconstruct it.

14. A. Gelin, in *Introduction à la Bible*, I, 520 ff. Those who seek a more minute and exact division of this chapter of Jeremia can consult A. Weiser, "Der Prophet Jeremia," in *ATD*, who divides it into ten parts. We have reduced it to the three essential ones.

15. Cf. the commentaries of A. Weiser and A. Pennaan on the chapters quoted.

16. Cf. C. Kuhl, *op. cit.*, pp. 64-66, in which the nature of the prophet and of the times in which he lived are clearly focused.

17. Cf. note 14 of chapter one.

18. Cf. Epilogue of the *Code of Hammurabi*, XXIV, 9-77.

19. Concerning the conception of Samuel (1 Kings, 1-2); of Samson (Judg. 13); of Isaia's son (Isa. 8).

20. Cf. *BZ*, 1964, pp. 303, 204-216.

21. H. Cazelles, *Sacra Pagina*, II, 513.

22. Von Rad, *Theologie des Alten Testaments*, I, 457 ff.

23. H. Frankfort, *Ancient Egyptian Religion* (New York: Columbia University Press, 1948), p. 62.

24. Barucq, *Les Livres des Proverbs* (Paris: 1964), pp. 95 ff.

25. H. Gese, *RGG*, 1962, IV, pp. 1578 ff.

26. Cf. G. P. Rodriguez, *Bibbia Comentada* (Madrid: 1962), p. 1191.

27. Cf. J. Schildenberger, *Opfer Christi und Opfer Kirche* (Düsseldorf: 1960), p. 94.

28. We have omitted the shining figures of Esther and Judith, already so well known. For Micheas 5, cf. R. Laurentin's excellent study, Luke I-II (Paris: 1957), p. 86. Cf. the review by Benoit in *RB*, 65, 1958, pp. 427-432, which is deep, discerning, and substantially favorable.

{3}

The History of Mary of Nazareth

I. INTRODUCTION: TRANSITION FROM THE OLD TESTAMENT TO THE HISTORY OF MARY

In passing from the Old to the New Testament we have a distinct impression that the Old looked forward all the time toward the future. The New returns continually upon a past, upon something absolutely exceptional that must have happened.

Those who think: "It was foretold, therefore it had to happen," are mistaken. If they read the Gospels without prejudice, they will be obliged to alter their perspective. The primitive Church reflected: "How did all this come to pass? Of course, because God is faithful to his promise, foretold in the Old Testament."

History is sufficient unto itself; the Old Testament is nothing more than the confirmation of it.

A further remark—while in the Old Testament the messianic announcements are vivified by a most sublime poetry, we usually find in the New Testament an unadorned and disconcerting prose.

The word of the cross, before being a unique expression of Paul's, was lived in real life particularly by Mary.

But when we speak of Mary's history the problem at once arises today as to whether it is possible to write a life of Christ notwithstanding all the goodwill in the world.[1] Not that the Gospel is not fundamentally historical, but because the Evangelists described the life of Christ by their own canons which differ from those of modern historiography and biography. These are canons proper to men who had seen Christ and believed in him, and whose main concern was that of manifesting the divine significance of Christ's life, rather than recording his history faithfully in every detail.

When they wrote their Gospels, therefore, they had a well-defined plan, which was not perfectly identical for all four. To transplant the biblical facts into other contexts then, means to lose the main idea which is the basis of an entire gospel.

It is not that more than one Christ and one Mary existed, but that there are various portraits of the single picture of the Mother with her Son. It is the same as in cinerama, where there are several projectors but a single result.

Thus the Christ of Matthew and Mark is more originally Hebrew, frank, and rather unadorned. Luke's Christ is already suffused with grace (Greek?) and tenderness. John is the contemplative. A purely Hebrew soul, he opens out to the Greek world without letting himself be carried away by enthusiasm. To him the important thing is to converse with the Father's Word of Love.

The same can be said concerning Mary.

In the Petrine catechesis the Marian atmosphere or the niche is prepared. Matthew, as an energetic man, places there the marvelous statue of the Virgin Mother, almost constrained by the evidence of the facts. Luke, the Evangelist of the woman and of tenderness, is to make this statue a living mother who *smiles*, full of *grace*. John presents her to us in vivid colors as the co-operatrix in the Church's faith and above all as the ultimate expression of the Father's Love.

Close to the Mother we are to find the Spirit who will make of her the Spouse of Eternal Love in person. By grace he is to make her the Mother of believers as he made her the Mother of Christ.

Finally, he will bring her up to heaven where, close to the immolated Lamb, the *Addolorata* is to intercede for us, as a shining symbol of the love and tenderness of the Father who willed to create the Mother so as to manifest by her smile the deepest qualities of the divine essence.

All this must now be proved.

II. PETER'S MARIOLOGY

1. The Petrine Catechesis

Today, in introductions to the New Testament, more and more emphasis is placed on the importance of Peter's doctrine.[2] It is less well developed than the Pauline or the Johannine doctrine, but precisely on this account is it the more precious, because it is closer to the life and teaching of Christ, whose words and teachings are related without too many comments.

O. Cullmann goes so far as to affirm that before speaking of a Pauline soteriology we ought to outline that of Peter which is centered in Christ as the "Servant of God."[3]

Let it not appear strange then if we venture to speak of a Petrine Mariology.

2. Peter before Pentecost

In reading the Gospel of Mark, primary source of the Petrine catechesis, we find an exposition of the relations between Christ and Peter that astonishes us by its frankness.

Jesus has just appointed Peter to be the first Pope when he begins to speak about his passion. Peter reproaches him and hears himself addressed by the title of Satan, the tempter, because he wishes to dissuade the Divine Master from following the way of the cross (Mark 8, 28-33).

It would appear that Peter, during the lifetime of Jesus, had not understood very much of the Marian mystery either. In fact, while Mark's Gospel speaks with delicacy of the Canaanite mother whose daughter was healed, of the woman afflicted with an issue of blood restored to health, of the raising of the daughter of Jairus, only the following apparently unfavorable fact is related of Mary:

And his mother and his brethren came, and standing outside, they sent to him, calling him.

Now a crowd was sitting about him, and they said to him, "Behold thy mother and thy brethren are outside, seeking thee."

And he answered and said to them, "Who are my mother and my brethren?"

And looking round on these who were sitting about him, he said, "Behold my mother and my brethren. For whoever does the will of God, he is my brother and sister and mother" (Mark 3, 31-35).

This account, narrated by all three synoptics—Luke in briefest form—allows us to affirm that Peter before Pentecost had not properly grasped the exact significance of the sorrowful life of Christ whose cross became pure humiliation for the Mother, according to the laws of human wisdom.

3. Peter after Pentecost

Undoubtedly the Pentecostal light caused Peter to discern the mystery of Christ as the Lamb immolated for our sins (Acts 3, 12-21; 1 Pet. 1, 19).

He penetrated moreover into the profound prophecy of Osee 1-2 which reveals God to us as the merciful Father:

Crave, as newborn babes, pure spiritual milk, that by it you may grow to salvation; if, indeed, you have tasted that the Lord is sweet. . . .

You, however, are a chosen race, a royal priesthood, a holy nation, a purchased people; that you may proclaim the perfections of him who has called you out of darkness into his marvelous light. You who in times past were not a people, but are now the people of God; who had not obtained mercy, but now have obtained mercy (1 Pet. 2, 2-10).

In this atmosphere of goodness and mercy, he must have penetrated also into the Marian mystery, by the power of that Spirit who "will teach you all things" (John 16, 13).

As God's word, however, does not introduce us into this wonderful Petrine discovery, we are content to conclude that Peter places the apostolic preaching entirely in an atmosphere of maternal goodness and mercy.[4] This is to be more clearly specified by John (3, 3-5) and by Luke (6, 35-36), for whom God in his essence is love and tenderness. Consequently, Mary is to appear as the expression, the maternal reflection of that infinite love and incommensurable tenderness.

In other words, Peter laid down all the premises of Mariology just as Moses laid down those of God's essence in his account of the vision of the Lord upon Sinai (Ex. 34). And just as the colloquy of Moses on Sinai is to be enlarged and clarified in the Psalms, so also the paternal sweetness and mercy indicated by Peter is to be extended in the Gospels of Luke and John, revealing itself to be truly maternal.

Thus Peter constructed a beautiful niche that could be gladdened only by the presence of the Virgin Mother full of grace, the gift of divine love.

III. MATTHEW'S MARIOLOGY

1. *Matthew, the Evangelist of God's Justice*

If it be true, as the psychological axiom has it, that justice is man's kingdom while mercy is that of the woman and the mother, then we shall understand how in Matthew 1-2, the Evangelist of God's justice, it is the man, Joseph, who always acts; whereas with the Evangelist of mercy (Luke 1-2), the actress in the forefront is Mary.

It is not difficult to demonstrate that Matthew is the Evangelist of justice. According to Matthew, Joseph is "the just one." Christ has come to save the "unjust." The last judgment is to separate for all eternity the "just and the unjust." Pilate's wife is to implore him to beware of condemning Christ, "that just man."

For us the classic text is Matthew 5, 43-48:

> You have heard that it was said, "Thou shalt love thy neighbor, and shalt hate thy enemy." But I say to you, love your enemies, do good to those who hate you, and pray for those who persecute and calumniate you, so that you may be children of your Father in heaven, who makes his sun to rise on the good and the evil, and sends rain on the just and the unjust.
>
> For if you love those that love you, what reward shall you have? Do not even the publicans do that? And if you salute your brethren only, what are you doing more than others? Do not even the Gentiles do that?
>
> You therefore are to be perfect, even as your heavenly Father is perfect.

It is to be remarked how the entire Sermon on the Mount gravitates around justice and perfection, while for Luke the center is the mercy and tenderness of the Father toward the ungrateful (6, 35-36).

These are two complementary conceptions, but they differ one from the other. Matthew's concept, like that of James, is founded on works: "You must love your enemies, otherwise your Father will not love you or pardon your offenses."

There is an admonition in the parable of the servant who having failed to show compassion for his fellow servant is cast into prison (Matt. 18, 24 ff.).

We would seek in vain such vivid colors in Luke, because he, like his master Paul, conceived Christianity as an effusion of justice that is sheer grace (Rom. 3, 21-26), pure divine mercy.

Therefore, our first step is not in a horizontal direction—help your brother, otherwise you will not be saved—but in a vertical one—receive God's grace and mercy and you will love your brother with the liberty of Christ and without worrying too much about judgment.

The line of demarcation that we have drawn between Matthew's version of the discourse on the Beatitudes and Luke's version appears very clearly also in the history of Christ's passion. In Matthew dark tints prevail—the entire Sanhedrin insults the dying Jesus who cries out, "My God, my God, why hast thou forsaken me?" In Luke, on the contrary, we have the Christ who pardons and who calls on God as "Father!" while the narrative concludes with the conversion of all those present.

Nevertheless, we should ask ourselves if we are sufficiently familiar with the theological foundation of the first Gospel which has been transmitted to us under the name of the Apostle who was a publican.

As recently as 1959, Will Marxsen maintained that, whereas monographs exist regarding the compilation of the Gospels of Mark and Luke, such a document is still lacking in regard to the Evangelist Matthew.[4a]

But in view of the monumental and exegetical work of Paul Gaechter and the eminently spiritual and theological works of Trilling—to mention only two Catholic authors—this gap would now appear to have been bridged.

For our purpose it is sufficient to mention that Matthew's Gospel can still be divided into five parts: Sermon on the Mount; sermon to the Apostles who are sent out to preach; discourse of the parables; discourse containing the indispensable conditions for belonging to the kingdom of heaven; eschatological discourse.[4b] But it must be borne in mind that through every page flows the same spirit of the new Moses, Jesus Christ, the Teacher of the New Law, very much akin to mercy, but not identical with the tenderness of which Luke speaks.

The Spirit of the Galilean Rabbi is to be revealed in the first place to his compatriots who, however, are to reject him. This rejection is to mark the beginning of the ascent to Calvary.[4c]

But if we take only the first two chapters of Matthew's Gospel, we find that whereas Luke 1-2 has already been dealt with by R. Laurentin, Matthew on the contrary still awaits a monograph.

However, Muñoz has also examined the literary style of the introduction to Matthew's Gospel. He divides it into five episodes which refer to the fulfilment of five passages of the Old Testament.

The benevolence of God toward his chosen ones occupies the leading place. In the Old Testament it is manifested toward Moses and the Chosen People who, persecuted by Pharaoh's wrath, are miraculously saved by God. In the New Testament it is manifested toward the Holy Family, delivered from the anger of Herod. In the former, God prepared the legislation of Sinai; in the latter, his Son is to legislate from the Mount of the Beatitudes and from Golgotha. Thus, in the first chapters of Exodus we are shown the great legislator of the Old Law, while in the first two chapters of Matthew we are shown the Messias and dispenser of the new justice.

Finally, we have the prologue or gateway to Matthew's

Gospel. On the frontispiece is written: "The book of the origin of Jesus Christ, the son of David, the son of Abraham." What is strange about this genealogical tree is the fact that Joseph and not Mary enters into this ramification. Moreover, the wives of the Patriarchs do not appear, while four women of doubtful reputation are mentioned.

Then we have the door itself, which opens like a diptych, on the left side of which is portrayed the scene of the virginal conception of Christ (Chap. 1), while on the right side four events are depicted, the adoration of the Magi, the flight into Egypt, the slaughter of the Holy Innocents and the return to Nazareth (Chap. 2). Remark how the latter three episodes are intimately linked with the first one, the adoration of the Magi.

As is evident, these two chapters are not just a confused mass of separate narratives, but have a well-defined center in the virginal conception of the Messias and his birth, just as in Luke 1-2 we have the annunciation and the birth of Christ, framed by the annunciation to Zachary and Jesus' three visits to the Temple.

In the manner of a good Jew, Matthew starts from King David and Abraham and bases his reasoning on explicit prophetic quotations.

In regard to Mary, the first chapter presents her as Joseph's spouse but already with child by the Holy Spirit. In the second there is mention four times of the "child with his mother."

God rules over the life of the entire Holy Family as he ruled Moses and his people in the past. Apparently he abandons his chosen ones to the brutal violence of tyrants, but he frequently reveals to the head of the family that he must act "in the dark" and without delay. Jesus and Mary are to be in his hands: ". . . take the child and his mother. . . ."

What a strange history this is, in which the tyrants

appear to move the world whereas the real actor is a poor carpenter! God himself is the producer of this drama and he appears continually on the stage; whereas Jesus the Savior and his Mother are no more than delightful playthings of his divine providence.

To anyone desirous of penetrating more deeply into the prologue of the drama written by Matthew in his Gospel, we suggest the inexhaustible mine discovered by A. Voegtle who has given us an account of it in three powerful articles published in *Biblische Zeitschrift* in 1964-1965.

From this author we have taken just a few considerations that appear fundamental to us and we have set them before the reader with our own comments.

We believe this brief introduction is sufficient to enable the reader to appreciate Mary's reserved attitude toward Joseph and the eventful history of Christ's birth. These are the two central colloquies which introduce us to the mysterious history of redemption.

2. Joseph's Dilemma [5]

Joseph is the last link in the chain which starts with Abraham and David. He is not only the man before the woman, but the Jew before Mary.

It is incredible. The virgin whom he loves carries a new life in her bosom, unknown to him! How can this be true of the woman on whose account he has remained chaste?

His hot Galilean nature was at war with the "justice" of Israel. Should he hand her over to the judges as unfaithful? The affection and esteem he bore her prevented him from doing so.

Should he marry her in that condition? Israelite justice did not permit it. What then was he to do? He chose a third course, that of flight.

Did Mary surmise something of the tragedy which had overtaken her fiancé? Why, then, did she not speak? Many things are implied in St. Matthew's first chapter which perhaps no one will ever succeed in explaining.

The poetess is not far from the truth when she breathes:

True women are quiet and desire quiet. . . . Show me the woman who writes about that which concerns her heart intimately. If it concerns her she is silent, for here silence is life, speech, death. The mystery always bears fruit, but its revelation means its end.[6]

We moderns want to know everything and see everything. We are almost irritated as we behold the Mother of the Word wishing to honor him by her silence, a silence which was depriving her of the chaste affection of her spouse and exposing her to dreadful uncertainties.[7]

But God does not forsake those who place their trust in him. He speaks and reveals to Joseph his secret, the birth of his Son Jesus of the Virgin Mother by the power of the Holy Spirit. He, Joseph, is to be the husband of Mary, but in an atmosphere of unique love such as the world has never witnessed.

In face of this fact Matthew recalls Isaia 7, 14. A virgin, while remaining so, is to become a mother. The virgin is Mary; the Emmanuel is Jesus, the Savior. Here there is no air of myth, no forcing of the prophecy of Isaia. Here there is a fact which must be observed by man, even if to this day we do not understand why Christ had a mother and not a father.[8]

The one who makes this affirmation is not a woman, whose testimony the Hebrew world rejects, nor is it a learned Hellenist, but a poor carpenter who perhaps knew nothing of the prophecy of Isaia. He only knew that he had had an unforgettable experience that still affected him deeply as he related it to a friend. An ingenuous experience for a man, and ridiculous in the telling, if it had any other explanation than that of the Evangelist.

3. The Birth of Christ

It is not the shepherds who arrive, as in Luke's Gospel, but the Magi. But as well as festive joy, the wise men from the East leave behind them the anger of a uxoricidal king outwitted by heaven.

The angel appears to Joseph ordering him to flee to Egypt. Mary is to be the Mother of the exile who crosses that Negeb desert which to this day leaves in the soul an unspeakable sadness. She is to cross the burning sands of Egypt which today are still capable of suffocating the enthusiasm of those who dash off eagerly along the road to the Pyramids.

Mary leaves behind her not only the desert but also about thirty mothers who weep despairingly at the sight of their slaughtered children.

The Evangelist then recalls the weeping of Rachel:

"A voice was heard in Rama, weeping and loud lamentation; Rachel weeping for her children, and she would not be comforted, because they are no more" (2, 18).

In vain are we tempted to add those consoling words of God which we find in the prophecy of Jeremia 31, 16:

"Thus says the Lord: Cease your cries of mourning, wipe the tears from your eyes.
The sorrow you have shown shall have its reward, says the Lord, they shall return from the enemy's land."

These mothers are never again to look into the smiling eyes of their children.

How prosaic is the history of Christ and of Mary in comparison with such sublime prophetical poetry!

✣   ✣   ✣

When the persecutor is dead, the angel again appears to Joseph commanding him to return to Palestine. We almost have the impression that heaven fears to leave its chosen ones in peace, as though in stagnant waters.

The Evangelist recalls the words of Osee, 11: "Out of Egypt I called my son" (Luke 2, 15).

How dissatisfying we find this quotation which applies symbolically to Christ in Osee's very poetical passage, coupling as it does the beloved Son with the Hebrew rebels!

The end, though, has the perfume of flowers:

And he went and settled in a town called Nazareth; that there might be fulfilled what was spoken through the prophets, "He shall be called a Nazarene" (2, 23).

Is this a quotation of Isaia 11, 1 where Christ appears as a glorious king? Or of Isaia 53, 2 where he appears as a suffering servant, growing up in arid ground, in dire poverty? Is he the good servant who now has not even the semblance of a man?

We are not far from the truth if we think of the title upon the cross, *Jesus of Nazareth*. To John that title is royal, as is the entire passion of Christ according to this Evangelist.[9] But for Matthew it is the suffering Messias who says only one word: "My God, my God, why hast thou forsaken me?"

Jesus had not yet pronounced these terrible words, but Mary already experienced the awful abandonment by God, who seemed to have forgotten that she, the beloved Daughter, clasped in her arms the only-begotten Son.

She was like a leaf at the mercy of the wind, like a drop in a stormy sea, a grain of sand in the desert storm of the Negeb.

IV. LUKE'S MARIOLOGY: MARY, THE EXPRESSION OF THE FATHER'S MERCY

The life of Mary does not end with the Gospel of St. Matthew, still less in the Negheb sandstorms. We must penetrate below the surface here to discover that God does not amuse himself by making us tremble at the unforeseen events in our lives.

1. Women in the Gospels

	Mark	Matthew	Luke	
Genealogy	—	1, 1-16	—	At least three sinful women
Widow of Naim	—	—	7, 11	Compassion for the mother
Housewife	—	13, 33	13, 21	The housewife honored
The old woman	—	—	4, 16	She is the daughter of Abraham
Herodias	6, 17	14, 3	—	Dishonest woman
The sinful woman	—	—	7, 37	Sinful woman redeemed
The Canaanite woman	7, 25	15, 22	—	Jesus treats a pagan woman harshly
The lost drachma	—	—	15, 8	Close to the Father of the prodigal son
Widow	—	—	18, 3	Defended against the judge
Mother of the sons of Zebedee	10, 35	20, 20	—	Harsh toward the mother
Foolish virgins	—	25, 1	12, 35	Luke calls them foolish menservants
On the way to Calvary	—	—	23, 27	Luke admonishes feminine compassion

We have no intention of adding other remarks to the very learned works already written on this subject.[10] One thing, though, is certain, that the reader who passes from the first two Evangelists to Luke and John finds that the attitude of the early Church toward women has changed a little. The preceding table speaks better than any number of remarks.

It is therefore to be concluded that Luke omits all the harsh meetings between Christ and women and records many others in which Jesus is compassionate toward them.

For this reason the admonition to the weeping women on the way to Calvary is particularly striking coming from Luke, the gentle Evangelist.

John continues along Luke's path. Think of the Samaritan woman who received the first revelation of Christ's Messianic character—"I who speak with thee am he,"—and is transformed into the mother of her people. Or think of the woman caught in flagrant adultery and liberated by Jesus; or of Mary Magdalen to whom he appears immediately after he rises from the dead, constituting her the first herald of his glorious resurrection.

In view of a similar panorama the colloquies between Mary and Jesus narrated by the last two Evangelists become even more enigmatic.

Mary searches for her Son for three days. She asks him why he has acted in this way and she receives the answer: "Did you not know that I must be about my Father's business?" A woman praises his mother and Jesus corrects her: "Rather, blessed are they who hear the word of God and keep it."

This reply is not for us who understand well that spiritual maternity is much more sublime than physical maternity, but for a multitude who measured a woman's worth by the number of her children.

John takes the same line. Recall the words: "What wouldst thou have me do, *woman?*" at Cana and the "*Woman*, behold thy son," a title which is not synonymous with *mother*.

This manner of acting may appear exaggerated, but we shall see that it corresponds perfectly with the designs of the Evangelists who by this time had come to understand that the Father loves the Son and sends him to the cross, that he has an immense love for the Mother and makes her the Co-Redemptrix of mankind by means of immense contradictions.

Dominic Bañez, St. Theresa's confessor, relates of the saint: "The more I humiliated her, the more she drew near to me."

We can say the same of Mary, because she had understood before Paul (2 Cor. 1, 3) that never as in times of suffering does one realize that God is "the tender Father."

"As the Child willed the cross for himself, so He willed the Sword of Sorrow for her. If He chose to be a Man of Sorrows, He also chose her to be a Mother of Sorrows! God does not always spare the good from grief. The Father spared not the Son, and the Son spared not the Mother. With his Passion there must be her compassion." [10a]

2. Grace and Tenderness, the Essence of the Father According to Luke

We have already said that the Sermon on the Mount, according to Luke, gravitates around the idea of grace and tenderness. Actually the text is as follows:

But I say to you who are listening: Love your enemies, do good to those who hate you. Bless those who curse you, pray for those who calumniate you.

And to him who strikes thee on the one cheek, offer the other also; and from him who takes away thy cloak, do not withhold thy tunic either.

Give to everyone who asks of thee, and from him who takes away thy goods, ask no return. And even as you wish men to do to you, so also do you to them.

And if you love those who love you, what merit have you? For even sinners love those who love them. And if you do good to those who do good to you, what merit have you? For even sinners do that.

And if you lend to those from whom you hope to receive in return, what merit have you? For even sinners lend to sinners that they may get back as much in return.

But love your enemies, and do good, and lend, not hoping for any return, and your reward shall be great, and you shall be children of the Most High, for he is kind toward the ungrateful and evil.

Be merciful, therefore, even as your Father is merciful (Luke 6, 27-36).

It is not our duty to investigate whether it is Matthew or Luke who reports the genuine text of Christ's sermon.[11] But for us it is important to note that in Luke we breathe a purer air than in Matthew, an air that is transformed by the merciful smile issuing from the heart of God, tender as a mother.

Tenderness and grace—which are, in fact, two synonymous concepts as we saw in Moses' colloquy with God in Ex. 33, 12-23—are most conspicuous throughout the third Gospel. As regards the concept of grace, recall the angelical salutation to Mary: "Hail, full of grace!" which is the signal for the start of Redemption. Better still, contemplate Christ in the tranquillity of Nazareth described for us as "the grace of God in him."

As regards the concept of tenderness, think of Luke's parables of the Good Samaritan (10, 33) and of the Prodigal Son (15, 20), both saturated with divine tenderness. Or consider Jesus crucified praying for his crucifiers, for those ungrateful people, so as to give expression to the mercy and tenderness of the Father who loves his ungrateful children.[12]

It is in this atmosphere that we must read the gospel of the Annunciation where the Mother full of grace appears.

* * *

Modern exegetes who have penetrated more fully into the gospel of the Annunciation to Mary (Lyonnet, Laurentin, Moraldi) strongly advise us not to separate the Nazareth colloquy between Mary and the angel from its context or literary style, which extends throughout the first two chapters of Luke's Gospel.

They generally speak of two marvelous pictures which

in their turn form a diptych. The two pictures are that of the annunciations (of the birth of St. John the Baptist and of Christ) and that of the two marvelous births (of the Precursor and of the Messias).

It seems to us, nevertheless, that we must go further if we wish to discern the essence of Luke's Mariology, which runs through the first two chapters of his Gospel.

First of all it must be stated that more than two annunciations or divine revelations are mentioned. Actually in the second chapter Luke tells of the angelic announcement to the shepherds, of Simeon's mysterious prophecy, and of Christ's enigmatic reply to Mary: "Did you not know that I must be about my Father's business?" All these are revelations which are no less important than the two famous annunciations which dominate the first chapter alone.

Moreover, a profound difference is to be observed between the atmosphere that pervades the first chapter of St. Luke and the second. The first is filled with a crescendo of *messianic joy* which explodes spontaneously in the hymns *Magnificat* and *Benedictus*. It could be defined as the synthesis of highest prophetical poetry, where the true face of the historical Christ is still veiled, hidden as it is in his mother's womb.

In the second chapter, on the contrary, the prophetic poetry vanishes and the true countenance of Christ appears, of Christ born in poverty in a stable, presented as a "sign that shall be contradicted," and who speaks in language which not even his Mother can understand.

It is true that the angelic hymn *Gloria in excelsis Deo* is also heard, but observe that the heavenly light surrounds the shepherds, not the grotto of Bethlehem. Mary hears only the account of it.

It is true that Simeon called Jesus "a light of revelation

to the Gentiles, a glory for Israel"; but for the Mother it was to be "a sword that will pierce her heart."

It is true that the doctors are amazed when they hear Jesus, Eternal Wisdom, speak; but for Mary in her distress it is a wisdom full of mystery.

Finally, in Luke's first chapter we find ourselves among the lyrics of the Old Testament prophets; in the second, on the contrary, we spontaneously recall Matthew 1-2 where the canticles of the prophets are interrupted by the real, historical life of Christ.

Indeed, in Luke the transition from the Old to the New Testament appears more strikingly than in Matthew, not alone because of the difference in atmosphere between the first and second chapters of his Gospel, but chiefly because the heavenly light that surrounds the shepherds causes the darkness of the night in which Jesus is born to appear even deeper; while the gleaming sword of which Simeon speaks appears more awful in comparison with the joy of the holy old man who has found at last the "light of the nations." Finally, the wonder of the doctors of the Temple at the revelation of Christ's wisdom clashes with the memory of Christ's incomprehensible reply to his Mother!

It is in this harmony, paradoxical as the entire theology of the cross, that we must look for the essence of Mariology according to Luke.

We shall not examine the two chapters of Luke word for word, but only a few of the more significant phrases that occur between the angelical salutation, "Hail, full of grace, the Lord is with thee!" and the entire Marian meditation on the infancy of Jesus: "The child grew and became strong. He was full of wisdom and the grace of God was upon him" (2, 40).

We shall try to adapt our style to the atmosphere

emanating from Luke's pages on the infancy of Jesus, a poetic style, that is, with a happy conclusion in commenting on the expression "Hail, full of grace, the Lord is with thee!" whereas in discerning Christ as Wisdom, crucifying the Mother, we shall adopt unadorned, incisive language that ends in the paradox: "And Mary understood nothing!"

This is the drama which, in our opinion, Luke wished to bring to our minds in the first two chapters of his Gospel, a drama of love, in perfect harmony with the theology of the cross announced by Paul: "We, for our part, preach a crucified Christ . . . the power of God and the wisdom of God" (1 Cor. 1, 23-24).

"But God commends his charity toward us, because when as yet we were sinners, Christ died for us" (Rom. 5, 8).

3. The Annunciation and the Mother Full of Grace

Now in the sixth month the angel Gabriel was sent from God to a town of Galilee called Nazareth, to a virgin betrothed to a man named Joseph, of the house of David, and the virgin's name was Mary. And when the angel had come to her, he said, "Hail, full of grace, the Lord is with thee." When she had heard him she was troubled at his word, and kept pondering what manner of greeting this might be.

And the angel said to her, "Do not be afraid, Mary, for thou hast found grace with God. Behold, thou shalt conceive in thy womb and shalt bring forth a son; and thou shalt call his name Jesus. He shall be great, and shall be called the Son of the Most High; and the Lord God will give him the throne of David his father, and he shall be king over the house of Jacob forever; and of his kingdom there shall be no end."

But Mary said to the angel, "How shall this happen, since I do not know man?"

And the angel answered and said to her, "The Holy Spirit shall come upon thee and the power of the Most High shall overshadow thee; and therefore the Holy One to be born shall be called the Son of God. And behold, Elizabeth thy kinswoman also has conceived a son in her old age, and she who was called barren is now in her sixth month; for nothing shall be impossible with God."

But Mary said, "Behold the handmaid of the Lord; be it done to me according to thy word."

And the angel departed from her (1, 26-38).

Luke has treated this chapter in a marvelous manner: his style is most refined.[13] Mary is no thirteen-year-old, ready to consent at any moment to an attractive proposal. She is greeted as "full of grace," and she wants to know why; she is told that she should accept to become a mother, and she wishes to know in what manner.

God begins the colloquy, as with Moses on Mount Sinai, and he replies to Mary's every request because she has found favor in his eyes.

Not only in the manner of Moses, but to the extent of becoming the receiver of grace in person.

In a stupendous phrase St. Bernard thus summarizes the gospel of the Annunciation: "Mary prays the Father" (*Maria orat Patrem*).

(a) THE MOTHER OF GRACE

When we speak of grace we recall at once Bernanos' phrase: "All is grace." But there is a merely human, Hellenic concept of grace and a second divine, theological, Hebrew one.

Since his style, which savors of Hellenism, leads us to believe that the Hellenic world is not extraneous to Luke who is writing for the Greeks, let us first of all analyze the humanistic aspect of Mary Immaculate.

We shall then pass on to what is more important and essential, namely, God in the heart of Mary Immaculate.

(b) HUMANISTIC FRAGRANCE OF GRACE

The term that is very frequently used signifies in general a gift granted from on high, but in a way that does not humiliate us, causing us rather to react spontaneously with joy and gratitude.

Thus the Greek would use the term grace to describe the candid view of the snows of the Alps glistening in the sunshine and stirring the human heart with joy, as happened with Voltaire who was moved to exclaim: "Truly God exists!"

But Aeschylus adds: "The grace of the most beautiful panorama disappears from man's view." Every Alpine view is soon wrapped in mist.

The little body of the newborn babe is grace to the mother's heart. Homer would say: "Athena wrapped him in a grace utterly divine." But his wailing very soon breaks the gracious enchantment.

Grace is the man who penetrates joyfully into the mysteries of nature. Homer's comment is: "Hermes grants grace and joy to the works of man."

Grace is a young woman who smilingly dances, saying:

"Oh, that I could once more take my place among the choirs as when a maiden destined to noble nuptials, not far from my dear mother I danced, rivalling the others in grace by the adornment of my hair, while many-colored veils shaded my countenance!" (Euripides, *Iphigenia in Tauris*, 1144-1150).[14]

In conclusion, the Greek grace is nothing more than the creature with all that is beautiful in it.

But all this beauty carries the germ of death, a beginning of dissolution. Who is to free us from this deadly germ! Christ, he whom Luke calls "the grace of God" in our midst. And Mary is to be filled with his grace from the first moment of her life. She is thus to become the Immaculate, that is, the virginal fulcrum of humanity, where all is grace without any germ of death.

But in order to understand this we must discern the divine perfume of grace among the Hebrews.

(c) DIVINE PERFUME OF GRACE

Luke, in speaking of grace, goes back to the Old Testament concept of *finding grace*. It is not something external; it is God with us, the Father who gives his Son, in the love of the Holy Spirit.

The much discussed expression "full of grace" probably refers to the colloquy between God and Moses.[15] As in that colloquy a sinful, ungrateful people is supposed and a person who has found favor in a special manner.

The essence of grace is God giving himself kindly to the ungrateful one out of his sheer tenderness.

The unique expression used in regard to Mary leads us to suppose, and rightly so, a special mode of donation which is very well expressed in the term *immaculate*. But the substance is in the following:

The Father bestowing: it is generally admitted that the God who speaks in the Old Testament is the Father. It is then understood at once how both the colloquy with Moses on Sinai and the colloquy with Mary begin with the Father. In him all things have their beginning; it is he who predisposes and predestines all things.

But the true gift, the grace which he gives is above all his own Son Jesus. Paul writes:

"The Father has blessed us and chosen us in Christ before the foundation of the world. He predestined us to be adopted through Jesus Christ as his sons, according to the purpose of his will. He has favored us with his grace in his beloved Son, in whom we have redemption through his blood, the remission of sins" (Eph. 1, 3-6).

Mark how all is centered in Christ and in his passion by the Father.

In the case of Mary, though, there is something quite particular. For her, "finding grace" signifies becoming the Mother of Christ, of Christ crucified. Thus Mary is completely dependent upon Christ and upon his passion. Consequently, the grace that is in her assumes an important character and renders her capable of participating in a particular way in the Redemption.

All is accomplished in the atmosphere of love appertaining to the Holy Spirit, the seal, the supreme gift of the Father. The Holy Spirit is, as it were, the personal benevolence of God toward the creature, in order that the creature may respond to divine love.[17]

Marvelous is the Annunciation scene in which the triune God reveals himself to a thirteen-year-old Jewish girl on the threshold of life! It is difficult to find in the Bible a scene in which the divine and the human are so admirably fused.

But Mary's smile was not reserved for herself alone. She was the first link in the chain of the redeemed because her Son was to bear the name Jesus, Savior, and because Christianity consists entirely in receiving in order to give.

(d) BERNADETTE'S SMILE

Plato, after having written his elevated sermon on Love, *Banquet*, falls once more into the "grace of Venus."

The poet of sensuality, Gabriele D'Annunzio, singing the praises of Venus continually, is to arrive at such a degree of nausea as to write: "Atrocious sadness of unclean flesh!"

The gospel of Mary Immaculate, precisely because it is revelation and no myth, moves upon quite another plane, that of God and his grace. A grace that is divine precisely because it appears on the face of a simple girl of thirteen, ignorant of the world but filled with God.

One day Count Bruissard went up to Lourdes determined to convince Bernadette that she was deluded in thinking that Our Lady had *smiled* at her. He found Bernadette mending stockings, and she appeared to him very ordinary. He made her tell the story of the apparitions of the beautiful Lady. At a certain stage he interrupted her and said: "Well, tell me, how did this lady smile?"

"One would need to belong to heaven to reproduce that smile," replied the girl.

"Could you not do it for me, for one who doesn't believe in your apparitions?"

"Oh, so you consider me a liar? Because you are a sinner I agree to show you the Virgin's smile."

Bruissard tells us that the girl rose slowly to her feet, joined her hands and smiled a heavenly smile such as he had never seen upon other lips. "She smiled with eyes raised to heaven, while I was on my knees before her, convinced that I had seen *the Virgin's smile on the lips* of her handmaid. . . ."

The Count ended: "I have lost my wife and my two daughters, but I do not feel that I face life alone. The *Virgin's smile* accompanies me."

This nobleman, on his knees before Mary, understood the difference between the smile of human grace and the smile of the grace of God.

These two worlds are not reciprocally exclusive, but neither can they be confused. Just as myth and history do not exclude each other, the smile of nature and the smile of God shine forth from the face of a creature who cannot but be called the *Mother of Grace.*

4. The Mother with Her Child (the Nativity)

As we proceed with the reading of Luke's Gospel, we are more and more convinced that it is impossible to contemplate the Mother apart from her Son.

(a) THE PSYCHOLOGIST

He has always delighted in describing the resemblance between the child and the woman, in voice and face and attitude.

(b) THE NOVELIST

The novelist never loses an occasion of presenting the mother with her child in her arms.

Consider Lamartine's poem *L'Humanité,* in which he describes the birth of Christ:

> "Observe the pure rays of love about to be born.
> The Virgin in her flowering at dawn,
> Unfolding like pure morning gold . . .
> It would seem as if the dawnlight
> Were playing with her,
> Or had fixed for ever its penetrating ray
> On a marble of divine contour. . . .
> Her soul is naught but tenderness,
> Her whole body a harmonious setting,
> Her whole being, caressed by the eye,
> Is naught but an anticipation of Love."

And yet, as we draw near to the Nativity, we must temper this tenderness with a quote from Manzoni:

Coming down the steps at one of the door-ways . . . he beheld a woman. . . . She carried in her arms a little child, about nine years old, now a lifeless body; but laid out and arranged, with her hair parted on her forehead, and in a white and remarkably clean dress, as if those hands had decked her out for a long-promised feast, granted as a reward. Nor was she lying there, but upheld and adjusted on one arm, with her breast reclining against her mother's like a living creature; save that a delicate little hand, as white as wax, hung from one side with a kind of inanimate weight, and the head rested upon her mother's shoulder with an abandonment deeper than that of sleep; . . . for even if their likeness to each other had not given assurance of the fact, the countenance which still depicted any feeling would have clearly revealed it.[17a]

The atmosphere in which we ought to view the Nativity emanates from the mixture of the extreme tenderness of Lamartine tempered by that of Manzoni. An atmosphere magnificently transhumanized by M. Maeterlinck in *Aglavaine and Sélisette:*

"Women never tire of being mothers: they would cradle even death should it come to sleep on their knees." Mary cradles life itself, in the shadow of the cross!

(c) SACRED SCRIPTURE

Paul, quoting a hymn of the ancient Church, already tempers the poetry of the Nativity with the memory of the cross.[18]

"For the grace of God our Savior has appeared to all men. . . . But when the goodness and kindness of God our Savior appeared, then not by reason of good works that we did ourselves, but according to his mercy, he saved us through the bath of regeneration and renewal by the Holy Spirit; whom he has abundantly poured out upon us through Jesus Christ our Savior, in order that, justified by his grace, we may be heirs in the hope of life everlasting" (Titus 2, 11; 3, 4-7).

But it is Luke especially who narrates for us the history of the Nativity, prosaic even though gladdened by the angelic hymn.

Mary must set out on a long journey, although she has reached the final days of her pregnancy. On arrival at their destination, *there is no room for them.*[19]

The babe is born. He is never described as being in Mary's arms; indeed, the angel is to give the joyful tidings to the shepherds, saying: "This shall be a sign to you: . . . an infant wrapped in swaddling clothes and lying in a manger!"

It is there that she must adore the Son foretold by the angel as successor to the throne of David.

The center and all the poetry of the Nativity with its *Gloria in excelsis Deo* is dominated by the shepherds. Mary acts merely as a witness, putting her signature to the account: "She kept in mind all these things, pondering them in her heart."

(d)   PRESENTATION IN THE TEMPLE

At the presentation of Jesus in the Temple too, the dominant note for Mary is the shadow of the cross. In fact, to Simeon the just, Christ appears as the "light of the world," to Anna he is "the redemption of Israel," to Mary the "sign of contradiction which is to pierce her heart like a sword."

At first sight we seem to be exaggerating, but let us read again Chapter 2 of Luke and we shall be convinced: for everybody *externally* there is joy but for Mary there is only sorrow which does not, however, prevent her soul from savoring an immense joy that is to explode at times in song to God and in intimate colloquy with Jesus.

❋   ❋   ❋

Thus the Annunciation ends in the *Magnificat*.

"My soul magnifies the Lord,
  and my spirit rejoices in God my Savior;
  Because he has regarded the lowliness of his handmaid;
  for, behold, henceforth all generations shall call me blessed!"

Two mothers who meet, two infants who exult in the enchanting setting of Ain-Karim: this summarizes the entire feast of the visitation which closes the cycle of the Annunciation to Mary.

But to us the finale of the Nativity is immensely more pleasing: Mary goes back to the placid tranquillity of Nazareth and contemplates her Child:

"And the child grew and became strong. He was full

of wisdom and the grace of God was upon him" (Luke 2, 40).

Here we have an entire world made up of numberless moments in which the Mother is always discovering something new in her little one who begins to take his first steps, who moves uncertainly, who grows stronger each day until he can proceed without the need of his mother's arms!

But in the midst of a fragrance of maternity, the Evangelist has something deeper to reveal: *the grace and wisdom of God in Christ.*

We already know that grace is the benevolence of God toward poor humanity crushed by sin. But what is wisdom?

Job continued to probe the mystery and the wisdom of God, but in vain. It is deep as the ocean, while man is nothing but dust and earth.

Paul sought in vain for thirty years the solution of human existence in Hebrew wisdom. In the end God was pleased to reveal the mystery to him: wisdom in Jesus crucified (1 Cor. 1-2).

Did his disciple Luke wish to place on record the same reality? In reading the account of the Nativity in Luke's edition we find several points which seem to justify us in thinking so.

But it is the last episode especially in the gospel of the Infancy which assures us: Mary entered every day more fully into the mystery of Christ, grace, and wisdom of God, days which were already darkened by mourning for the death of the Son of God.[19a]

5. *The Mother without Her Child (the Loss of Jesus)*

Two mothers are enegaged in conversation. The one, Ludomilla, has a son in Siberia; the other has her son nearby, working for the redemption of the masses. Suddenly Ludomilla exclaims: "How lucky you are. . . . It's a wonderful thing for a mother and son to stand side by side! And a rare thing. . . ." [19b]

This is the experience of Mary who must be aware that by this time Jesus is no longer a child but a youth of twelve years who must fulfill his religious duties independently of his mother.[20]

On the return journey, far into the night they await his arrival, but in vain. This lasts for three days, until at last he is found in the Temple teaching as a master. Mary can at last give vent to her feelings:

"Son, why hast thou done so to us? Behold, in sorrow thy father and I have been seeking thee."
And he said to them, "How it is that you sought me? Did you not know that I must be about my Father's business?"
And they did not understand the word that he spoke to them.

Strange! Is Jesus the wisdom, the master, the light for others only and not for these two most chosen souls?

And could they understand Jesus' wonder that his mother should have sought him?

The life of Jesus is a mystery to Mary, to this mother who fails to understand her own Son!

The usual stereotyped phrase—Mary kept all these things in her heart—attempts to re-establish the tranquillity of Nazareth in flower. But in vain. Neither the Son's habitual submission nor the memory of the grace and stature and wisdom in Christ allay the anxiety of the maternal heart.

The chapter ends: "Jesus grew and became strong. He was full of wisdom and the grace of God was upon him." The world of grace and wisdom which appeared in Christ had its impact on men. But what did men make of it? Those men who tore Mary away from the peace of Nazareth where she had prepared a cradle for her first-born, offering her in exchange a manger? Those who caused her to flee to Egypt? She had already learned to know them, with their thoughts and their secret strategical plans!

What were men going to do to her Son, every day becoming less her own and belonging ever more completely to sinners?

Farewell to the tenderness of the twenty-year-old who dreams over her child as he grows each day and develops into a graceful and sturdy boy. After the experience in the Temple, she has a foreboding in her mother's heart that life still holds many uncertainties.

But in the depths of her soul she felt happy to exist and suffer with him, the Son, and to feel, over and above all her anxieties, the loving hand of the Father, who was never so tender toward his first-born daughter as when Jesus pronounced his name, "my Father," and she understood nothing!

V. JOHN'S MARIOLOGY: MARY, THE EXPRESSION OF THE FATHER'S LOVE

Efforts to reconcile Luke and John are neither few nor futile.[21] The effort should be made.

We already saw in Osee and Jeremia how the two ideas of love and tenderness were fused.

In reading Luke, we noticed some singularly Johannine passages. Think of Jesus the light, John's central theme; recall the word *wisdom* which for John becomes the very title of the fourth Gospel: "In the beginning was the *Word*, and the *Word* was with God; and the *Word* was God." Do not forget Christ the sign of contradiction, which John is to change into *judgment* of the world (12, 31).

Yet between Luke and John there is a difference. Into the fourth Gospel the whole world of grace does not enter, except in the problematic verses of the first Chapter:

"Full of grace and truth . . . grace and truth came through Jesus Christ."

Especially it is to be noted that whereas in Luke the whole Gospel is centered around tenderness, to John it is love (*agape*).

For Luke the *agape* is not sufficient, as we saw in Chapter 6 regarding the essence of the Father; for Luke pardon begins from the Father of grace who looks once more with favor on the woman in the town who was a sinner (7, 42-47).

John, on the contrary, is never tired of telling us that God is the loving Father who manifests himself in his own Son, the Word, expressing all the Father's love.[22]

These are primordial affirmations that should always be borne in mind if one wishes to understand fully that Mary was the extreme gift of the dying Christ, speaking in the name of the Father who wished to bestow as his final gift *the Mother*.

1. Love, Essence of the Father.[23]

Beloved, let us love one another, for love is from God. And everyone who loves is born of God, and knows God. He who does not love does not know God; for God is love. In this has the love of God been shown in our case, that God has sent his only begotten Son into the world that we may live through him. In this is the love, not that we have loved God, but that he has first loved us, and sent his Son a propitiation for our sins (1 John 4, 7-10).

This passage is in excellent harmony with John 3, 5-18 where Christ is compared to the serpent lifted up, bringing salvation by his elevation.

In the two Johannine texts the undisputed lead is taken

by charity, the love of God which is always in descending order, from the Father to Christ, from Christ to us.

(a) CHRIST THE WORD

Precisely because he has received this love, Jesus has become the personification of divine love.

Strange! The title of Logos, Word, with which the fourth Gospel opens, is so sublime and yet it disappears later. Why is this?

The true reason is that the whole life of Christ, his every word, his every action, are nothing but the expressions of God. Thus the word *Logos* yields place to the other, Jesus Christ, the Word Incarnate, lifted up.

The Word was made flesh, became history, became dogma, just as mythology had vainly dreamed,[24] and as the Word he will continue to speak. It is to a woman, the Samaritan woman, that Jesus is to reveal his messianic character for the first time: "I who speak with thee am he!" (4, 26).

(b) MARY

She entered in a particular way into this colloquy with Christ. John gives us an account of only two colloquies, one more mysterious than the other, one more sublime than the other.

The first one takes place at Cana (2, 1-11):

The scene is a marriage feast, where it would seem that only joy should reign. But the wine, symbol of gaiety, runs short.

However, the Mother thinks of everything, including the happiness of the humble family who have provided the feast. She turns to Jesus:

. . . the mother of Jesus said to him, "They have no wine." And Jesus said to her, "What wouldst thou have me do, woman? My hour has not yet come." His mother said to the attendants, "Do whatever he tells you" (2, 3-5).

As in the finding in the Temple, we hear mysterious language: Woman! This title does not show any disesteem, but where is the affectionate "Mother"?

Here, too, the story ends happily: all his disciples believed in him, thanks to the miracle.

But for Mary the tension between herself and her Son increases: a tension in which she awaits his hour; that hour which Jesus himself awaited in order to pour forth his spirit (John 7, 39).[25] Who can fully understand the strain upon the heart of a mother who wishes always to remain close to her Son, close to her God, while this God and Son seems to be drawing away from her? How could she do without his person, his divine countenance?

But such is the exigency of anyone who approaches the all-holy God. As first a shudder is felt, then anguish, if one has sinned; in the end, if one persists, he will see God's true face, enchanting, full of love:

Father, the hour has come! . . . Holy Father, keep in thy name those whom thou hast given me, that they may be one. . . . Sanctify them in the truth. Thy word is truth. Even as thou hast sent me into the world, so I also have sent them into the world. And for them I sanctify myself, that they also may be sanctified in truth; . . . that the love with which thou hast loved me may be in them, and I in them" (17, 1; 11; 17; 26).

This is Jesus' last prayer, addressed to the Father, according to John. From the cross, his royal throne, he is to speak not so much to the Father as to mankind.

2. Mary and the Children of the Father
(Essence of the Mother)

Jesus' hour has come. It is also his Mother's hour. "This is the compassion." But do not think of the "Pietà" resplendent in white marble in the Vatican, but of Rondanini's "Pietà."

Here we have a symbol of crushed humanity. Jesus is a broken man, supported by the pitiful arms of the Mother, the crushed, the broken-hearted woman, the Mother of mankind.

Here we have more than the mythical Anath wallowing in the blood of slaughtered soldiers; more than the woman in Genesis crushing the head of the serpent. It would seem as if the serpent with his poison had mortally wounded mankind's prototype, the Mother with her Son. In fact:

(a) THE PSYCHOLOGY HERE IS SUMMARIZED IN A FEW
    WORDS: A FORTY-SEVEN-YEAR-OLD WIDOW
    WHO LOSES HER ONLY SON

(1) Forty-seven years:

This is not a cold historical affirmation. Whereas at fourteen the girl is full of eager anticipation of the future, which appears radiant and full of color and dreams, after forty-five the age of memories begins. By this time all is over and done. The woman feels herself condemned to a void, to nothing. It is a void which permeates her entire existence, soul and body, and the result is a disheartening depression considered to be the prelude of death.[26]

(2) The Widow:

In the Old Testament we find continually the expression: "Blessed is the man who helps the orphan and the widow." God is described as "the Father of orphans and widows" (Ps. 67, 6).

James is to write: "Religion pure and undefiled before God the Father is this: to give aid to orphans and widows in their tribulation, and to keep oneself unspotted from this world" (1, 27).

James, who was related to Jesus and Mary, cannot have forgotten that Jesus was precisely an orphan and Mary a widow.

A widow means a woman who has neither husband, nor brother, nor son to support her.[27] This was exactly the case with Mary of Nazareth. Joseph, whom she had greatly loved, was now dead. Who can fathom the conjugal love that united these two souls, who together raised their hearts to God?

On Calvary Joseph was no longer there as he had been one day in the Temple of Jerusalem, or at the finding of Jesus. John was there, but he was in the descending line, the vertical one between Mother and Son. John, though, already had a mother by his side.

(3) The Death of the Only-Begotten

Kristin, a young mother, is rocking her baby son. She thinks that perhaps God will take him from her. At the mere thought of losing her child she cries out that:

"If they were to take the child from her, she would plunge into the smoking abyss, scornfully rejecting the possibility of being saved one day along with those she loved. She would offer herself to the devil." [28]

Clare Luce, after having lost her only daughter of eighteen, was to complain to Fulton Sheen: "How can God be good if he tears children away from their mothers?"

Sin excepted, Mary, too, experienced within herself this trial. Or rather, she lived the drama of the Crucified expressed in the words "My God, my God, why has thou forsaken me?"

Mary repeated these same words, but in a personal way, as a mother. The Father had given her his Son that she might live close to him, but the Son had slowly withdrawn from her gaze to return to heaven.

Is the Father who replied to the thirteen-year-old girl
of Nazareth now to say nothing at all to that mother who
appeals to him?

(b) THE ANSWER OF SACRED SCRIPTURE
(1) Mark:

The passion of Christ, according to Mark, can be defined as the synthesis of human cruelty. Jesus is insulted
by all; the passers-by jeer at him shaking their heads, the
scribes and chief priests mock him. Even the two thieves
seem to have the right to reproach him.

Jesus calls on God and some bystanders comment sarcastically on his words, saying: "He is calling Elias." A
soldier attempts to moisten the parched lips of the dying
man and they dissuade him, saying, "Wait, let us see
whether Elias is coming to take him down." Then he
expires.

(2) Matthew:

He merely emphasizes the dark tints laid on by Mark.
The scribes and chief priests were present, but also the
elders and therefore the entire Sanhedrin. He trusted in
God—well, then, let him come down, if he can, from the
cross, this man who said: "I am the Son of God!"

When the soldier proffers an act of mercy, *all the
others* dissuade him. Mary sees all this with that feminine
psychology which easily understands by intuition, with
the heart of a mother who feels all things. She realizes
that she has brought forth a Son, that she has given men's
God to men, and that they have considered him to be a
hypocrite, a revolutionary, a blasphemer.

One day St. Paul of the Cross, founder of the Passion-
ists, asked Our Lady to reveal to him what had caused
her the greatest suffering. The Virgin replied that it was
seeing Jesus treated as a seducer and hearing it said that
she had brought him up badly.

The discernment which the Saints have of Holy Scripture is sublime!

(3) Luke:

With Luke we begin to penetrate more deeply into the passion of Christ as the expression of God's tenderness and love.

He is the only Evangelist who places the drama of Calvary between two cries of "Father!"

"Father, forgive them for they do not know what they are doing." This is the *leitmotiv* that sounds at the opening of Christ's passion according to Luke.

The tender and mild countenance of the Father therefore returns, the face of the Father who pardons because he cannot refuse the petition of his Son who knows him intimately.

"Father, into thy hands I commend my spirit." This is the final act which touches the centurion, the passers-by, and the women present. It appears that all are converted. We understand that this is Luke's optimism.

Mary must have felt something in her heart when she heard her Son pardoning his executioners. She, too, must have forgiven them.

But what was the use of her maternal pardon if none of them understood her silence, inebriated as they were that they had killed Christ? Precisely because they had killed her Son did she feel an immense compassion for them, a sentiment which could be nothing else but tenderness. And why not a maternal sentiment?

(4) John:

He assures us that the word "mother" was also pronounced. The fourth Evangelist places on the lips of Jesus two mysterious expressions: "Behold thy son, behold thy mother"; and "I thirst."

Concerning the first expression the Fathers are unanimous in affirming that this is a recommendation to John to look after the support of his Mother. The second phrase is taken as a symbol of the full humanity of Christ, who thirsts like any dying man.

But this interpretation was by no means satisfying.

Is it possible that John, who appears to treat solely of heavenly things, means to tell us merely that the dying Jesus thought of the things of earth? Such a conception is considered today to be contrary to the entire *messianic* pattern of the fourth Gospel in which Christ in his every action manifests his mission as Savior.

A further difficulty arises. All that Jesus accomplished on Calvary is but a fulfillment of Holy Scripture, of the Old Testament. Why do we have this "erratic block" (Zerwick) of words addressed to Mary which do not explicitly contain a scriptural quotation?

Yet the Church has insisted: "The profound mystery of the inexhaustible charity of Jesus Christ is splendidly revealed on the occasion of his death, when he wills to leave his Mother to the disciple John with the memorable testament: "Behold thy son." *The Church has always felt that in John, Christ designated the person of the human race,* especially of those who adhere to him in faith" (*Adjutricem Dei,* 1895).

The exegetes who shared this view with the Church investigated the matter more fully to discover the truth that Christ's faithful followers unconsciously felt and practised. The result was a deeper reading of the following text:

Now there were standing by the cross of Jesus, his mother and his mother's sister, Mary of Cleophas, and Mary Magdalene. When Jesus, therefore, saw his mother and the disciple standing by, whom he loved, he said to his mother, "Woman, behold thy son." Then he said to the disciple, "Behold, thy mother." And from that hour the disciple took her into his home. After this Jesus, knowing that all things were now accomplished, that the Scriptures might be fulfilled, said, "I thirst." When Jesus had taken the wine, he said, "It is consummated." And bowing his head, he gave up his spirit (John 19, 25-30).

The text is both clear and paradoxical. It is clear, because John continues to use the term "mother"; paradoxical, because Jesus calls his Mother "woman." It is clear that Christ had an ardent desire to fulfill Sacred Scripture. It is paradoxical if he had nothing to say except "I thirst!"

It is clear that the relationship between Mary and the beloved disciple is one of mother and son; it is paradoxical because John had there by his side his earthly mother.

It is clearly affirmed that Jesus uttered the words "Woman, behold thy son. . . ." That he was conscious of having *already* accomplished and fulfilled the prophecy of Scripture in the fullest sense and in all things. This is paradoxical because he had not yet accomplished all, for in fact he said later "I thirst."

It is superfluous to dwell further on the subject. The best way to overcome the paradoxes is to say that Jesus, according to St. John, meant to speak of another thirst and of another maternity which are always at the summit of the messianic promises. This thirst and this maternity are rendered historically concrete in *the persons of the Holy Spirit and of Mary* who, promised by God in the Old Testament, and united with Christ, were to complete the work of Jesus in those who believed in him.

These two persons are united indissolubly in John, even stylistically.

Even the word *woman* would be fully explained if it could be shown that this expression is a reference to the woman in Genesis. But this is not yet fully proved.[29]

A. Feuillet, speaking of the "maternal" love of God for his children, reminds us that Eve brought forth children in pain, but also with the help of the Lord.[30] In fact, as soon as Adam had recognized his wife as "mother of all the living," Holy Scripture continues:

"Adam knew Eve his wife and she conceived and bore Cain, saying: 'I have given birth to a man-child with the help of the Lord'" (Gen. 4, 1).

This painful maternity, always a gift of God, is also to be applied to the mother Sion: "Before she comes to labor, she gives birth; before the pains come upon her, she safely delivers a male child" (Isa. 66, 7).

John has in mind this dream of spiritual generation through acute suffering comparable to that of the woman in travail:

"Amen, amen, I say to you, that you shall weep and lament, but the world shall rejoice; and you shall be sorrowful, but your sorrow shall be turned into joy. A woman about to give birth has sorrow, because her hour has come. But when she has brought forth the child, she no longer remembers the anguish for her joy that a man is born into the world. And you therefore have sorrow now, but I will see you again, and your heart shall repoice, and your joy no one shall take from you" (John 16, 20 ff.).

In this way redemption centered in Christ's passion becomes for John "the fulfillment of the prophecies relating to the generation of the messianic people by the woman Sion."

On Calvary, Mary is called precisely "Woman" by Jesus, because by her maternal travail she must bring forth mankind to God, as was foretold of the Daughter of Sion.

Yet John's insistence on the word *woman*, addressed to the mother, is so marked as to lead us to believe that he has some precise idea in mind. Just as is evident in Chapter 12 of the Apocalypse which recalls the titanic struggle between Satan and the "woman" of Genesis 3, 16. Thus the most celebrated figure of the woman in mythology is Anath and in the Old Testament the woman of Genesis, while in history it is none other than Mary, the mother of the living.

Thus Christ represents the true man who gives his life for others and Mary is the true Mother.

＊ ＊ ＊

All is consummated!

For those who consider that Christianity is nothing but a myth, this will signify that the illusion of the mother and her Son who are to save us has vanished and we must therefore accept the harsh reality: *we shall be less happy, but more likeable* (Sartre). There is no redemption from above, they will say, so let us redeem ourselves.

But for those who accept that Christ and Mary are not suffocated by history but give it its true sense, it signifies the fulfillment of what the Father had promised to the human heart. Christ was conscious, in death, of being the expression of the will of the Father who wished to bestow the Mother as a last gift to mankind, in the loving atmosphere of the Holy Spirit himself.[31]

Sorrow had opened Mary's soul to the divine gift of maternity toward the children of the Father. This was Christ's last wish, this was his thirst, of which Mary had a first intuition on the hill of Calvary and which she understood more fully at Pentecost.

(c) THEOLOGICAL REFLECTION (THE CO-REDEMPTRIX)

The exegete willingly leaves to the theologian the task of systematizing what occurred on the hill of Calvary. Thus we enter into the celebrated problem of Marian Co-Redemption, the manner of which is still widely debated.[32]

We believe that the simplest and best way of solving the problem is to ask Mary herself who she was and what she did on the hill of Calvary.

She would have replied that she was the Mother of the Crucified, that she suffered with her Son because the heavenly Father had so willed.

She had received grace, Jesus. And with Jesus she had received all mankind. Jesus always precedes Mary, to give her grace, in forgiving, in creating her the mother of mankind.

Co-Redemption therefore signifies a continual receiving from the Son in order to bestow upon her children.

Everything begins necessarily from the Father, is expressed in the Son, and is maternalized in Mary, always in the atmosphere of the Holy Spirit.[33]

Mary, already redeemed, receives her children stained with original and actual sin; she expiates their faults with Christ and obtains in Christ the grace of divine adoption. This seems to us to be the deeper sense of the words of Pius XII:

> She it was who, immune from all sin, personal or inherited, and ever most closely united with her Son, offered Him on Golgotha to the Eternal Father together with the holocaust of her maternal rights and motherly love, like a new Eve, for all the children of Adam contaminated through his unhappy fall, and thus she, who was the mother of our Head according to the flesh, became by a new title of sorrow and glory the spiritual mother of all His members" (*Mystici Corporis*, 1943).[34]

It seems to us, for this reason, that unless one wants to give the impression of mythicizing the history of Mary, the biblical categories must be explained and not omitted.

History does not greatly favor the mention of matrimony in regard to Co-Redemption. One may speak, if so desired, of the binomial man-woman, but let it not be forgotten that history tells us that their relationship was that of Mother and Son, and moreover of a Son who gives everything to his Mother in the supernatural sphere, who creates his Mother.

The new Eve is not the wife of the new Adam, but his Mother.

The history of Mary willingly allows the idea of receiving to be developed, but does not allow categories to be introduced which obscure the word *mother*.

History does not allow of division into two parties: the Father and Christ offering, Mary and humanity receiving.

Mary, like Moses, has already entered into the sphere of grace and divine love. Thus she becomes one with Christ the Redeemer.

The division is therefore as follows: God, the kingdom of sin, the intermediate persons Christ and Mary who snatch us from the powers of darkness and bring us into the kingdom of light.

This corresponds to the division which emerges in present-day history also:

In a condensed form, we present the end of Gorky's novel *The Mother* thus:

"How happy I am! If you only knew! I shall bring them the word of my son, the word of my blood! It is almost a piece of my spirit."

In this rapture she feels herself to be the mother of all mankind redeemed by the word of her son.

The mother is surrounded by the police. She remembers the suitcase containing copies of her son's proclamation.

Hurriedly she takes these out and scatters them among the crowd, shouting: "Take them, take them all, to change this life, to free all men, so that they may rise up as I have done; men have already come, children of God, who disseminated the sacred truth secretly among the crowd . . . *it is the word of my son.*"

A gendarme pounces on her and suffocates the words

in her throat. While she gasps in her agony, the last word of the mother is heard: "Poor wretches! . . ."

Someone answers her with an outburst of sobs.[35]

Thus ends the myth of the mother and son who wished to redeem the world without God.

Very different is the history of the Mother who is constituted the Mother of mankind. Although crushed by sorrow, she does not curse, but accepts to become the Mother of her Son's crucifiers. Poor wretches, without a doubt! But by the Father's sheer tenderness and love they are transformed into his sons.

Mary's heart was overjoyed at the thought that men could now become the sons of God who, as Father, had found no better way of bringing redemption to men than in the form of a "maternal kiss."

The term Co-Redemptrix, to sum up, is the perfect flowering of the *Mother of Grace!*

LOOKING BACK

From Golgotha we can look out over the entire biblical panorama. The first biblical idea, that of the mother as the expression of God's forgiveness (Gen. 3), that had remained dormant until the era of the prophets, reawakens with Osee, Isaia and Jeremia who turn unmistakable rays of light on the woman and the mother.

In the prophets posterior to the Babylonian exile there is great progress. Recall how in the first Isaia (Chaps. 1-39) the word *love* did not even exist and Jerusalem was the fortress ruled by the Davidical Messias (Isa. 2; 7-11), whereas in the so-called second and third Isaia we have a continual blending of love and tenderness and maternity (Isa. 49, 15; 63, 7 and 15; 66, 9-14).

The sapiential books, in Proverbs 8, Sirach 24, and

Wisdom 7, give an inexhaustible lyrical and dramatic sublimity to the figure of the mother, although their historical and supernatural perspective seems to be obscured by a naturalism difficult to reconcile with the supernatural outline to which the prophets had accustomed us.

The two admirable and fundamentally historical figures of Esther and Judith contribute a little history and precision to the rich poetical vein of Israel's sages. Here, without a doubt, the woman takes the center of the stage as mediatrix of salvation for the people, as St. Alphonsus points out very well in his immortal book *The Glories of Mary*.

The New Testament, on the contrary, plunges us into a disconcerting historicity, that of the *Verbum crucis*. In the first Gospels, Mary and all mediation of the Mother with God seem to have disappeared completely. In Matthew, Mary is a mere object, not a leading figure in the drama of salvation.

But Luke and John cause the fruitful seeds planted in the heart of Mary and the Apostles to germinate under the action of the Holy Spirit. As a result the Holy Virgin appears at the summit of Redemption, thanks to the Angel Gabriel's message and to the creative expression of Jesus, the Word of the Father, who consecrates her as the universal Mother.

Her "fiat" to the Father, which becomes more perfect as her life proceeds and reaches its plenitude in Christ crucified, is to be extended to the Church when the Holy Spirit breathes upon the Chosen People a new and vital breath, causing Christ's Church to issue forth from the synagogue.

Mary, the Mother, is to be very close to the Church when it issues from Christ's pierced side, that she may make it a worthy spouse of the only-begotten Son.

SUMMARY OF CHAPTER THREE:

THE Child is to reveal his true face in Jesus of Nazareth, and the Woman divinely promised is to be called Mary, his Mother.

Here also the author is unwilling to dwell on secondary disquisitions but wishes to discover: (1) what each of the Evangelists means by the essence of God; (2) how Mary enters into the theological scheme of each Evangelist; (3) all this in relation to the Old Testament. For this reason in the third chapter there is a return to the biblical texts of the second, casting light on these by means of the historical life of Mary.

⟨ NOTES ⟩

1. Cf. our article "Gesù Crocifisso: mito o storia?" in the Italian review *Fonti Vive*, 3, 26 (1961), pp. 272-278, where we reviewed the articles "Jesus" which appeared in *RGG, LThK*.

2. Cf. E. Testa, "Le Lettere cattoliche," in *Introduzione al N.T.* (Brescia: Morcelliana, 1961), pp. 503-505.

3. *TWNT*, VI, III.

4. In commenting on the word "milk" (*gala*) Schlier prefers to take his stand on agnostic ground (*TWNT*, I, 644); we ourselves prefer to remain in the sphere of tenderness found in Osee 1-2, quoted also in 1 Pet. 2, 10. On this point P. Ambroggi's comment in *Lettere cattoliche* (p. 113), is excellent, although he fails to capture the environment of Osee.

4a. *Der Evangelist Marcus*, p. 61.

4b. S. Muñoz-Iglesias, *Sacra Pagina*, II, 146.

4c. X. L. Dufour, *Les Évangeles et l'histoire de Jésus* (Paris: 1963), p. 153.

5. On the literary style of Matt. 1-2 cf. E. Galbiati, "L'Adorazione dei Magi" in the Italian review *Bibbia e Oriente*, 4 (1962), pp. 21-24. Note that the five episodes contained in Matt. 1-2 must be viewed in the same Old Testament context so that: (a) the flight and return from Egypt recall Moses' flight into Egypt to escape being killed by the Pharoah, and his subsequent return there to save his people; (b) the virginal conception of Christ recalls the miraculous (not virginal!) con-

ception of Samson, and thus would be explained the word "Nazarite" applied to Christ, a term which reminds one of the term "Nazir," or consecrated to God, applied to Samson; (c) the coming of the Magi to adore Christ would bring to mind the visit of all the kings of the earth to Samson; (d) the quotations from Os. 11, 1 and Jer. 31, 15, expressly mentioned, already assure us of the connection between the history of the Hebrew people and the history of Christ, of whom Israel was the figure and the type.

For a psychological discernment of the text, cf. R. Laurentin, *Luc I-II*, 100: "Luke 1-2 is more intuitive, more feminine than Matt. 1-2"; J. Dupont, *Les Béatitudes* (Louvain: 1958), p. 153: "The central point which interests Matthew is the man and his behavior; his attitude is that of the moralist and the catechist. This is a characteristic trait of his version. Luke is more of a 'theologian,' not because his spirit tends that way, but merely because he is nearer to his sources."

6. Thus Ruth Schumann. Cf. G. von le Fort, *The Eternal Woman* (Milwaukee: Bruce, 1962), pp. 64-65.

7. J. Guitton, *La Vierge Marie* (Paris), p. 51 of the first edition (*Madonna* [New York: Tudor, 1962]). "The holiness (of Mary) and the silence, in which alone one can listen to Christ" (T. Merton, *Seeds of Contemplation* [London: 1950], p. 94).

8. On this question cf. St. Thomas, S. Th. III, q. 28, a. 1; M. Schmaus, *Mariologie* (Munich: 1955), pp. 138-141; K. Rahner, *Mutter des Herrn* (Freiburg: 1956), p. 66 (*Mary, Mother of the Lord* [London: Nelson, 1963]). The true reason seems to me to be that adopted by O. Semmelroth, *Maria oder Christus?* (Frankfurt: 1954), pp. 60-64: as God is jealous of his bride (Ex. 34, 14) he wishes that the Mother of his Son be entirely consecrated to him. K. Barth, *Dogmatik im Grundriss* (Stuttgart: 1947), pp. 130-131, stresses the idea of the woman as a mere potential whereas the man is the symbol of human activity. Mary would thus be the symbol of the absolute passivity of the creature before God. For us, on the contrary, she is the symbol of perfect readiness on the part of the creature to comply with God's designs, since virginity in a woman means suffering (*tapeinusis*) and every suffering accepted is an active cooperation in the plans of God.

An absolute passivity in Mary is not in harmony with the account of the Annunciation, where Mary speaks, asks for an explanation and only at the end pronounces her free and active "*fiat!*"

9. A. Wikenhauser, *Das Evangelium nach Joannes* (Regensburg: 1961), p. 133.

10. S. Garofalo, *Le donne nel Vangelo* (Assisi: 1959). J. Michl, "Frau," in *LThK*, IV, 294-297, with excellent bibliography. The article "Gune e Meter" in *TWNT* is dreadfully incomplete.

10a. Fulton Sheen, *Life of Christ* (New York: McGraw-Hill, Inc., 1958), p. 31.

11. Spicq, *Agape* (Paris: 1958), I, 98-113 (*Agape in the New*

Testament, Vol. I [St. Louis: B. Herder, 1963]), maintains that Matthew's text is more primitive; that the word *charis* not only softens the crude *misthos* of Matthew but conveys a sense of beauty, of charm, amiability, liberality, and *gratuitousness;* that *tender* (*oiktirmôn*) recalls Ex. 33, 19 and James 5, 11, and has "the meaning of most tender, that is, of maternal tenderness." In II, 381, he examines the word *xrestos* which means "manifestation of benevolence, disinterested, transfigured by kindness or mercy."

The position of Dupont (*op. cit.,* pp. 189-202), is strange when in reference to Luke 6, 27-36 he finds the passage "very superficially homogeneous" with "various interpolations and rearrangements" (p. 193) and concludes that in the text there is "a rather artificial amalgamation. . . . Luke is not merely transmitting what he receives without adding his own personal note, without lending, if necessary, a completely new form. . . . His concept of the role of an Evangelist is considerably broader than that of many of his modern commentators" (pp. 201-202).

We beg to differ somewhat: (a) because the central point of the Sermon on the Mount according to Luke: "Be merciful, even as your Father is merciful" is more genuine than that of Matthew: "You are to be perfect, even as your heavenly Father is perfect." This is not only insinuated by Dupont (p. 153) but is categorically affirmed by E. Stauffer, *Die Botschaft Jesu* (Berne: 1959), p. 133 (*Jesus and His Story* [New York: Knopf, 1960]) who refers to the text as "a genuine logion of Jesus"; (b) moreover, observe how the Letter of James, full of *teleios teleiotes,* in its final phrase defines God as "tender" (5, 11). Now, can all this be explained if not by the fact that Jesus pronounced the Lucian lesson? (c) and if the core of the Sermon on the Mount is more genuine in Luke, will not the remainder, perhaps, be more genuine than in Matthew? The solution will be found in the study of *charis* in Luke, which although it has a tinge of Hellenism, is substantially of the Old Testament, that is, identical with "tenderness and mercy" (Ex. 32-34) (cf. note 12).

12. Here a clarification of the concepts of grace and tenderness is indispensable:

(1) In Greece: (a) *tenderness* (*oiktirmôn* and the like) indicates a profound compassion toward anyone who is visibly suffering: thus Polyxena is invited to move Ulysses to compassion so that he may save her from death (Euripides, *Hecuba,* 339-341); the chorus is moved by the sufferings of Antigone and of her blind father, Oedipus (Sophocles, *Oedipus at Colonus,* 255). Nor must it be forgotten that "the woman knows the art of moving others" (Euripides, *Iphigenia in Tauris,* 1054). However, Luke's humanist contemporaries considered it unworthy of the wise man to grieve or be sad because of other people's sorrows (*Epictetus,* III, 24, 59; Seneca, *De Clementia,* II, 5-6). (b) *Grace* always immerges us in an atmosphere of joy and smiles: thus Polynestore, blinded

by the vindictive Hecuba, seeming to divine the latter's complacent smile: "Rejoice, fool, at my misfortune, thou, astute woman!" Hecuba replies: "Certainly must I rejoice that thou art punished" (Euripides, *Hecuba*, 1257-1258). Orestes fears to trouble with his gloomy memories the joy (*chairusan*) of his sister Electra (Sophocles, *Electra*, 1266).

(2) In the Old Testament the two terms correspond (cf. Ex. 33, 12-19; Ps. 103 and 50) and others already quoted by us in chapter two. Luke is very familiar with the Greek environment as appears in the accounts of the Good Samaritan, the Prodigal Son and the Widow of Naim, in which tenderness predominates. He makes of this sentiment, however, the principal attribute of God toward the ungrateful sinner (Luke 6, 35-36).

The concept of grace in the account of the Annunciation is certainly of Hebrew stamp: "for thou hast found grace with God." And in our own text, what of Luke 6, 27-36? Although granting that a Hellenic fragrance hovers here, we are convinced that fundamentally it is a Hebrew concept, that is, a giving with a smile, as God gives to the ungrateful (v. 35).

In a word, the *charis* is rather the effect, the smile of tenderness as it goes into action: "In the order of salvation the *eleos oiktirmôn* precedes the *charis,* but in the external manifestation the order is reversed and the *charis* precedes and in a certain manner prepares the way for mercy" (K. Romaniuk, *L'Amour du Père et du Fils dans la Sotériologie de Saint Paul* [Rome: 1961], p. 198).

Observe that the Septuagint usually translate *hnn* by *oiktirmô,* and *rhm* by *eleeô,* while the substantive *hn* meaning grace is softened by *charis* (cf. *DBS,* III, 745-748).

13. Cf. M. Zerwick, *Graecitas biblica* (Rome: 1955), no. 209, in order to appreciate *kecharitomene* (full of grace), that is, the lasting effect of a past action. It is vocative, to be translated therefore in: "Hail, thou who in a very special way hast received the grace of God" (cf. nos. 241, 250b).

14. Kampmann, *op. cit.,* p. 75, p. 161, observes that girls do nothing but speak of love on their first approach to womanhood. Precisely at this age Mary began to live consciously and evidently her life as the one *full of grace.*

15. For an anthology of meanings cf. A. Alastruey, *Tratado de la Virgen Santisima* (Madrid: 1952), p. 157 (*The Blessed Virgin Mary,* 2 vols. [St. Louis: B. Herder, 1963-1964]). We ourselves, though favoring from a philological point of view the translation "pardoned" (cf. Feuillet, "*la gracée*") prefer to keep in the text the traditional translation: "Hail, full of grace." For a perspicacious philological study cf. L. Moraldi in *Introduzione alla Bibbia* (Marietti, 1960), IV, 459-461.

16. Guardini, *op. cit.,* p. 81: "The Immaculate Conception of Mary

is not a grace descending from paradise, but from redemption, and thus it has a certain character which up there it did not yet have."

Everyone is aware of the endless discussion about the relation between the grace of the Immaculate Conception and the passion of Christ, which today is not yet quite clear. Practically we are advised to say: "She should have contracted original sin but in reality she did not contract it."

From Luke 1, 28 the Church logically drew the doctrine of the Immaculate Conception (Schmaus, pp. 197-198) which, however, even the best disposed among Protestants do not yet accept (H. Asmussen, *Mutter Gottes* [Stuttgart: 1951], pp. 39-40).

17. "The efficient cause is the merciful God, who freely washes and sanctifies, sealing and anointing with the Holy Spirit of the promise, who is the pledge of our inheritance. The meritorious cause is the beloved only begotten Son of God, Our Lord Jesus Christ, who when we were enemies, by reason of his very great love wherewith he has loved us, merited justification for us by his own most holy passion on the wood of the cross and made satisfaction for us to God the Father. The instrumental cause is the sacrament of baptism which is the sacrament of faith, without which no one has ever been justified. Finally, the only formal cause is the justice of God, not that justice by which he is himself just, but the justice by which he makes us just, namely the justice which we have as a gift from him and by which we are renewed in the spirit of our mind. And not only are we considered just but we are truly said to be just, and we are just, each one of us receiving his own justice according to the measure the Holy Spirit imparts to each one as he wishes and according to the disposition of each one" (Denz. n. 799 as translated in *The Church Teaches* [St. Louis: B. Herder, 1955]).

K. Rahner, *op. cit.*, p. 31, p. 46, comments: "Christianity is simply God eternal giving himself to man, who is so treated by his grace that he opens his heart freely to God, so that the entire glorious Trinitarian life may enter the heart of the feeble creature. Grace therefore signifies light, life, openness of the personal spiritual life toward God."

Thus the day of the Annunciation can be defined as the date of Christian liberty's birth certificate (H. Koester, *Alle selig Preisen* [Limburg: 1954], p. 36).

17a. A. Manzoni, *The Betrothed* (New York: P. F. Collier & Son, 1909), pp. 589-590.

18. Cf. K Romaniuk, p. 66: "The Church in using this text in the Christmas liturgy makes us think of the birth of Christ, but it must not be forgotten that this "grace" includes the entire work of salvation, that is to say, from the Incarnation to the death and resurrection of Christ, which is clearly stressed in v. 14: "He gave himself for us."

19. M. Minguens, in *Bibbia e Oriente*, 1960, pp. 193-198, affirms:

"Mary brought forth her son in the *katalyma,* which is not so much a place for animals as a little secondary house which the Arabs of today also possess beside the main house. Part of this house was used as a stable that stretched back into a cave. In short, "the manger in the *katalyma* is to be considered as a convenience offered to the guests."

We confess that this solution is attractive and that Luke's account becomes humanly more acceptable, because, after all, Joseph must have done something during the months or weeks preceding the birth of Christ when he found himself (*einai*) in Bethlehem. But we ask ourselves whether Luke for his Greek readers would have wanted to place greater emphasis on the sense of poverty and inconvenience that surrounded Christ's birth, or on the hospitable house to which was added the convenience of the manger?

19a. Being obliged to consider what is essential, we shall omit the comparison between Luke 1-2 and Sam. 1-2. Cf. the discerning article of S. Muñoz-Iglesias, "Generos literarios en los Evangelios," in *Los Generos Literarios de la Sagrada Escritura* (Barcelona: 1857), pp. 228-240.

19b. M. Gorky, *The Mother* (Moscow: Foreign Languages Publishing House, 1954), p. 374.

20. Cf. E. Galbiati in *Bibbia e Oriente,* 1960, p. 24.

21. R. Laurentin, in *Compendio di Mariologia* (Alba [Italy]: 1957), p. 57, maintains that Luke is dependent on John for written tradition. S. Muñoz-Iglesias, pp. 241-242, holds that the primary source of Luke 1-2 is John, written in more elaborate style.

A. F. Feuillet, in *Introduction à la Bible,* II, 687: "The influence upon Luke of the Johannine preaching and environment can be affirmed almost with certainty."

"An ancient proverb has it that love is born of pity: the two sentiments go hand in hand." Thus it can be said that from Luke and from the third Gospel, John is born, more mystical and not less human than Luke.

22. Here the bibliography is vast. Cf. finally the three volumes of C. Spicq, *Agape in the New Testament,* Vol. I (St. Louis: B. Herder, 1963); A. Moraldi, *Dio è amore* (Alba [Italy]: 1954), pp. 95-109. On the question of Christ as the Father's Word of Love, cf. E. Fuchs, in *RGG* (1960), IV, 439-440.

There is, however, no comparative study on the essence of the Johannine God-agape and the essence of the Lucian God-tenderness. Similarly we do not yet know of a comparative study of grace and tenderness in Luke. It can be considered that in Luke 1-2 grace ordinarily appears. On the contrary, from Chapter 6 onward it is almost always tenderness. *Eleos* in the first two chapters of Luke does not necessarily include pardon, except in 1, 77-78, magnificently translated by Msgr. S. Garofalo in *SBM:* "remission of sins the work of the depths of God's mercy." G. Saldarini, in *Introduzione alla Bibbia* (Marietti, 1960), IV,

485, stresses discerningly: "Verse 78 should be translated *by the maternal tenderness* (sic) of which our God gives us testimony."

23. Cf. E. Fuchs, *op. cit.*, p. 439; C. Spicq, *op. cit.*, III, 278-279, comment on 1 John 4, 7-70.

24. Cf. the deep reflections of Kittel, *TWNT*, IV, 132.

25. M. E. Boismard, in *Du Baptême à Cana* (Paris, 1956), p. 158, affirms that the Fathers almost unanimously had no difficulty in admitting that Jesus' words imply a reproof addressed to his mother, whatever may have been the reason. F. M. Braun, *La Mère des Fidèles* (Paris: 1954), p. 74: the words of Christ divide the life of Mary into two periods, that of the separation from Christ and that of their coming together again.

P. Gaechter, in *Maria im Erdenleben* (Munich: 1953), p. 198, speaks of a law of separation which was to be annulled in Jesus' hour.

This separation was most painful for the mother in whom "the desire to live in close intimacy with her child is deep" (H. Deutsch, *op .cit.*, II, 272).

26. "Truly this is a very critical age. The physiological decline is considered to be *a prelude of death,* when life begins to be colorless and aimless . . ." (H. Deutsch, *op. cit.*, II, 439, 456, 460).

"Elasticity and vigor diminish, the movement of the spirit no longer gushes forth in the infinite range of its possibilities, indeed in its essential lines it appears stationary; *weariness is a daily experience*" (Alice Scherer, in *Die Frau* [Herder, 1954], p. 7). Cf. also *Sarò Madre* (Milan: 1960), p. 85.

27. P. G. Duncker, ". . . Quae vere viduae sunt" (1 Tim. 5, 3) in *Angelicum*, 35 (1958), 121-138.

28. S. Undset, *Kristin Figlia di Lawrans* (Turin: 1942), p. 400 (*Kristin, Lavransdatter* [New York: Knopf, 1935]).

29. On this question we have not quoted any book. The best two remain always those of P. Gaechter and F. M. Braun already mentioned.

30. A. Feuillet, *NRTh* (1964), 174-188.

31. For the relation between the Holy Spirit and the Mother, cf. Braun, *op. cit.*, pp. 118-124. Alexander Kerrigan, "John 19, 25-27, in the Light of Johannine Theology and the Old Testament," in *Antonianum*, 35 (1960), 391. We found this article to be one of the most interesting on biblical Mariology. We are happy to agree with the author on many points, although our own investigations were carried on independently.

In order to appreciate our thesis, *Mary, final gift of the Father,* it is necessary to recall that *teleioun* indicates the fulfillment of Sacred Scripture, *as the will of the Father.* Cf. Gaechter, *op. cit.*, pp. 207-208 and also *TWNT*, VI, 294-296.

32. Among the best works which we have found are: O. Semmelroth, *Mary, Archetype of the Church* (New York: Sheed and Ward, 1963) and by the same author *Maria oder Christus?* (Frankfurt: 1954), pp. 85-89. These pages show singular discernment; the concept of Mary

as prototype of the Church and her sense of receiving is developed, but the maternity is rather blurred.

H. M. Koester, *Die Magd des Herrn* (Limburg: 1954), pp. 158-178, opens up immense visions, sometimes using a nomenclature which is not clear. It seems to us not quite exact to place Mary along with sinful humanity and on the other hand Christ with the Father, proceeding then to play on the matrimonial character of the New Alliance. Christ is Mediator precisely because he is just (Isa. 53; I Pet.) and Mary is Mediatrix because she is full of grace, like Moses in Ex. 32-34. And her grace is Jesus, the Savior, within her.

C. Dillenschneider, *Le Mystère de la Corédemption Mariale* (Paris: 1951). For the moment this is the most welcome work (cf. Schmaus, *op. cit.*, pp. 331 ff.; D. Bertetto, *Maria Corredentrice*, 1951).

We do not yet accept the New Alliance presented on the lines of bridegroom and bride, in which Mary is the spouse of the Word (cf. p. 147). To us *Mary is the Mother of the Word*. She appears thus in history, from which theology must spring, as it did in the early Church and as it does in St. Thomas (cf. Grillmeier, *LThK*, II, 1158-1159). We like G. Roschini's treatment (*Mariologia* [Milan: 1942], II, 426). He bases the question on the concept of the new Eve who, although associate and participant in the life of the new Adam, is not the wife but the mother. By a fuller development of this concept we get away from the dangers mentioned by M. Schmaus, *op. cit.*, p. 329.

33. Cf. Schmaus, *op. cit.*, pp. 298-302; Koester, p. 315; Dillenschneider, p. 114. The concept of matrimony is nevertheless too widespread to permit the acceptance of our own theory. Cf. Dillenschneider, p. 132; Koester, p. 309; Schmaus, p. 318; R. Laurentin, *Marie l'Eglise et le Sacerdoce* (Paris: 1953), II, 117. At all events, our theory is in line with our concept of proceeding from history to dogma.

34. Denz. n. 2314, cf. excellent comment in M. Bover, *Soteriologia Mariana* (Madrid: 1946), pp. 495 ff.

35. M. Gorky, *The Mother* (Moscow: Foreign Languages Publishing House, 1954), pp. 392-395.

{4}

The Commemoration of Mary's History

I. THE SPIRIT AND THE MOTHER
OF THE CRUCIFIED

1. *The Promise of the Holy Spirit*

True history comes to an end with the death of Christ, and we enter on a period of commemoration through the operation of the Holy Spirit, a period in which we advance continually in the knowledge and love of Christ, now returned to the Father (John 14, 26).

Memory (*anamnesis*) is one of those keywords without which it is impossible to understand the Bible.

The Greek world, with Plato (*Menone, Fedone*), is full of the charm of this word. According to the great master, knowing consists in remembering.

In the Hebrew world we also find predominent the memory (*zikkaron*) of the great historic events operated by the Lord, the plagues of Egypt, the miraculous crossing of the Red Sea and of the Jordan, and so on, relived in the magnificent liturgy of the Jews.

The apostolic Church lives essentially on the words of Christ: "Do this in remembrance of me." That is to say, in memory of his passion and resurrection. This is not a nostalgic memory of a reality which has already passed away, of a period which is no more. No indeed. It is a question of establishing mystical and real contact with the risen Christ, plunging into the waters of his death to be purified from our sins and continually renewed in Jesus Christ.

The liturgy is like the living space in which souls are born again to God in an ever more perfect way.

The Spirit and the Mother, proceeding from the mouth and heart of Jesus crucified, have precisely this catalytic function among men upon earth to unite them in their risen Lord.

This action that leads us to live again in our times the eternalized history of the Lord is synthetized in the commemoration of the word.

Thus we reach the colloquy between Mary and the Holy Spirit, which is later to become an intimate conversation between the mother and children.

This colloquy, already suggested by the prophets, who speak to us particularly in Isaia 11 and Joel 2 of a special effusion of the Spirit upon Christ and upon us, and colored by the insistence with which an outpouring of tenderness and maternity is foretold, is vividly present to Christ.

In Chapter 2 of John's Gospel, at Cana, we have a presentiment of something concerning the Mother when his *hour* is mentioned. Already in Chapter 3 there is mention of being born again through water and the Holy Spirit, thanks to Christ who has been lifted up like the serpent in the desert.

In Chapter 4 we hear of water springing up, of divine life offered by Christ to the Samaritan woman to whom he had introduced himself as a thirsty man. This new water permits one to adore the Father in the Spirit.

In Chapter 7 Jesus says explicitly that the water is the Holy Spirit that he will pour out upon the faithful when he shall be *lifted up*.

Finally, Christ on the cross did no more than fulfill the promises uttered by both himself and his prophets.

He did nothing more than prepare that Pentecost in which Mary really becomes the mother of believers by the operation of the Holy Spirit.

2. Pentecost

While Mary feels herself, toward the Father, to be the first-born daughter, and toward the Son the Mother, her relation to the Divine Spirit is eminently that of spouse.[1]

(a) PSYCHOLOGY

Psychology has something to say here also: if woman by her personality is in a special way donation and love by reason of her motherhood; if all this has been sublimated in Mary, will not this knowledge introduce us naturally to the theology of the Holy Spirit who is Donation and Love in person?[2] Here, too, it would seem that nature and myth are purified and elevated to the level of history; that is, they indicate redemption in Christ and in his Spirit.

(b) THE CHURCH'S VIEW

The Church appears to favor the description of bride and bridegroom to express the relation between Mary and the Holy Spirit.

Leo XIII, the Pope of the Holy Spirit, writes:

You are well aware of her marvellous and intimate relations with the Holy Spirit: so that she can properly be called his Immaculate Spouse. The prayer of the Virgin was very powerful in regard to the mystery of the Incarnation and to the descent of the Holy Spirit upon the assembly of the Apostles.[3]

In May 1945 the Sacred Congregation of Rites summarized the Marian prerogatives as follows:

The Fathers and theologians are almost unanimous in illustrating the magnificent gifts with which God designed to adorn his Daughter, his Mother, and his Spouse.[4]

Naturally, the Christian must not draw from these words the conclusion of paternity of the Holy Spirit toward Christ and toward us. One alone is the Father, one alone is the Son, and one alone is the Spirit, the gift, the pledge of the active love of the Father who in the same love generates ourselves and the only begotten Son.[5]

(c) MEDIATRIX OF ALL GRACES

What do Mediatrix of all Graces, Mother of "fair love," Mother of Grace, and our Mother, mean in the most concrete sense of the terms, in their real, practical significance?

Here also theologians are still very far from agreeing as to the modality.[6] Perhaps the exegetes can offer some assistance toward the solution of the problem.

The path leading to a solution is found in the concepts of *prayer* and *mother*.

Prayer is the deepest idea of mediation. Consider Moses on Sinai (Ex. 32-34), the Servant of God (Isa. 53, 12), the passion of Christ according to St. Luke (23, 24). It is a loving colloquy with God, an affirmative reply to all that he asks.

Mary is no exception to this rule. In the Annunciation she utters her "fiat" to the Father. It is a colloquy between Father and daughter, reminding us of the wonderful one between Jesus and the Father on the mountain:

Yes, Father, for such was thy good pleasure. All things have been delivered to me by my Father; and no one knows the Son except the Father; nor does anyone know the Father except the Son, and him to whom the Son chooses to reveal him (Matt. 11, 26 ff.).

On Calvary she repeats the same "fiat" in Christ crucified, the Word who speaks in the Father's name saying: "Woman, behold thy son!"

At Pentecost we have the realization of Mary's Golgotha assent, all pervaded by the Divine Spirit who teaches her to pray to the Father (Rom. 8, 15-23; Gal. 4, 7).

Her "fiat" to the Father includes the acceptance of salvation in order to pour it out upon his children.

Her assent to God is changed into a *colloquy between mother and children*. It would seem, that is, that the Triune God penetrates into the mind and will of Mary who, deified by the grace poured out on her by the Holy Spirit, knows and desires that the crucified Word and his Spirit be infused into us by the Father.

Not only does the Father receive the desire which he himself has aroused, but through her maternal heart he penetrates the soul, intellect, and will of his children.

The children approach the Father and confide in him, thanks to the maternal smile of Mary.

(d) THE ROSE OF GRACE

If, therefore, we pluck the petals from the rose of grace which is God in us, not only do we find the divine nature in Three Persons, but also the humanity of Christ, who has suffered for us, and the maternal tenderness of Mary.

Grace is now draped in mourning by reason of Christ's death and is perfumed by the tenderness of Mary.

If the cross of Christ were lacking it would no longer be possible to understand how the Spirit carries us by grace to Calvary and imprints in our hearts the longing to suffer with Jesus.

If Mary were to be missing from the psychology of grace we could not be her true children, nor could the filial supernatural attraction of the human heart toward the Mother be explained.

From this point of view the conversion of Francis Budenz is significant. In vain did Fulton Sheen endeavor to convince the communist leader that the only authentic redemption flows from Calvary.

Suddenly he began to speak to him of Mary. "Immediately," confesses Budenz, "my conscience was flooded with light and I saw the filthiness of the life I was leading. The peace emanating from the Virgin and which had been mine in early years flooded my mind with increasing clarity. For a moment the praise which the angel addressed to Mary sounded in my ears: *Ave, gratia plena . . .*'

"Down through the years I have met with a number of malicious men and women, I have conferred with government ministers and senators, twenty times have I heard in court the final word in lawsuits in which I was involved, awaiting the verdict with bated breath and experiencing each time the triumphant joy of acquittal, but never was my soul gripped by a sense of love and reverence as it was that evening in April." [7]

During the *"Peregrinatio Mariae"* a person was assailed by a doubt: "All this flocking of crowds, is it sentimentalism or religion?"

He was answered: "In general it is the call of the blood!"

The reply is exact if by blood is meant the blood of Christ bringing divine grace, set in motion by the tears of Mary.

All this is enveloped by the same Divine Spirit of Love.

II. MARY'S SMILE UPON THE CHURCH MILITANT

1. The Church as Love

The best name that can be given the Church today is that of mother. The early Christians, on the contrary, preferred the word love (*agape*). The two ideas are admirably blended, since a mother in her tenderness is the prototype of love.

But the ancient denomination, which is less humanistic, placed the emphasis better upon the action of God.

St. Ignatius, Martyr, writes: "Ignatius, called Theophorus, to the Church which is the object of mercy (*eleemene*) and of the munificence of the most high Father, and of Jesus Christ, his only Son; beloved (*egapemene*) by will of the one who wills all things that are, according to the love (*agape*) of Jesus Christ, our Lord, our God, which in Rome presides holy, venerable, worthy to be called blessed, meriting praise and joyful progress, adorned with the candor of love (*agape*), depositary of the law of Christ and honored with the name of the Father:

"I greet this Church in the name of Jesus Christ, Son of the Father. To the faithful united in body and soul in the observance of every precept, filled with inexhaustible grace (*pepleromenois charitos*) and far from every alien blemish, many greetings, wishing them the purest joy in Jesus Christ, our God." [8]

The Church is always she who receives love, light, mercy and grace. We ask ourselves now what relation is there between Mary and the Church, between these two mothers?

2. Mary, Mother of the Church (Apocalypse, Chapter 12)

Sacred Scripture closes with the Apocalypse of John. The Church is being persecuted by Domitian, who wishes to be adored as God. The Christians feel discouraged. The author of the Apocalypse consoles them, presenting for their consideration two refulgent figures, *the Divine Lamb and the Woman clothed with the sun.* The Divine Lamb dominates the fifth chapter in which it is revealed that precisely because *he has been slain* for us he has obtained the power to open the book of history: it is

Jesus who by his passion has redeemed us and who gives us strength to resist Satan who is persecuting the Christions through the Roman emperor.

In Chapter 12, the center of the Apocalypse, our eyes are gladdened by a heavenly vision:

And a great sign appeared in heaven: a woman clothed with the sun, and the moon was under her feet, and upon her head a crown of twelve stars. And being with child, she cried out in her travail and was in anguish of delivery.

And another sign was seen in heaven, and behold, a great red dragon having seven heads and ten horns, and upon his head seven diadems. And his tail was dragging along the third part of the stars of heaven, and it dashed them to the earth; *and the dragon stood before the woman who was about to bring forth, that he might devour her son.* And she brought forth a male child, who is to rule all nations with a rod of iron; and her child was caught up to God and to his throne. And the woman fled into the wilderness, where she has a place prepared by God, that there they may nourish her a thousand two hundred and sixty days.

And there was a battle in heaven; Michael and his angels battled with the dragon, and the dragon fought and his angels. And they did not prevail, neither was their place found any more in heaven. And that great dragon was cast down, the ancient serpent, he who is called the devil and Satan, who leads astray the whole world; and he was cast down to earth. And I heard a loud voice in heaven, saying. . . .

And when the dragon saw that he was cast down to the earth, he pursued the woman who had brought forth the male child. And there were given to the woman the two wings of the great eagle, that she might fly into the wilderness where she is nourished for a time away from the serpent. And the serpent cast out of his mouth after the woman water like a river, that he might cause her to be carried away by the river. And the earth helped the woman, and the earth opened her mouth and swallowed up the river that the dragon had cast out of his mouth.

And the dragon was angered at the woman, and went away to wage war with the rest of her offspring, who keep the commandments of God, and hold fast the testimony of Jesus.

Who is this sublime woman?[9]

(a) OPINIONS

Here too we have the usual triple conception, mythicizing, prophesying, historicizing.

The first group maintains that we have here returned
to the myth. The Patmos visionary forgets human reality
and plunges into the realm of fables and myths. And they
quote 1 Qumran 3, 6-18, that we mentioned in the first
chapter, on page 17.

The second group says: Children, wife, mother are
synonyms as in the Old Testament. The woman is therefore the Church, at least prevalently. This group too willingly appeals to the Hebrew apocalypse, to Qumran.[10]

Here is a recent text discovered in the Qumran grottoes,
which is the object of much discussion among present-day
exegetes. We give Millar Burrows' translation:

> . . . they made my life like a ship on the deep,
> and like a fortified city before them.
> I am in distress
> like a woman in travail with her firstborn,
> when her pangs come,
> and grievous pain on her birth-stool,
> causing torture in the crucible of the pregnant one;
> for sons have come to the waves of death,
> and she who conceived a man suffers in her pains;
> for in the waves of death she gives birth to a man-child;
> with pains of Sheol he bursts forth
> from the crucible of the pregnant one,
> a wonderful counselor with his power;
> Yes, a man comes forth from the waves.
> In her who conceived him, all the waves came quickly,
> swift pains also when they were born
> and horror for those who conceived them.
> When he was born all the pangs came in the crucible of the
>   pregnant one.
> She who conceived nought had grievous pain,
> and waves of the pit with all horrors.
> The foundation of the wall are broken

like a ship on the face of the waters;
the clouds sound with a noise of tumult,
the dwellers on earth are like those who go down to the seas,
terrified by the noise of the waters.
All their wise men are like sailors on the deep,
for all their wisdom is confounded by the noise of the seas,
when the depths boil above the springs of water (Selections
from the Thanksgiving Psalms, V [iii. 6-15]).[10a]

This text undoubtedly assumes exceptional importance.
In the first place it has demolished the rationalistic theory
that Apocalypse 12 stems from the Greek myth of Apollo,
his mother Leto, and the Pytheon.

But now we must ask ourselves what is the connection
between the Qumran psalm and Apocalypse 12. M. Delcor
not only sees a close link between the two texts but ends
by maintaining their mutual dependence. He reproves A.
Feuillet who urges prudence regarding relations between
Qumranic and Johannine spirituality.[10b]

J. Carmignac and P. Guilbert conclude with greater
prudence: [10c]

The allegory developed in this verse from certain points of view
reminds us of the vision of the woman in travail in the Apocalypse
(12, 1-6 and 13, 18). We have the same fundamental comparison,
the same quotation from Isaia 66, 7, the same diabolical intervention. But when we study the question more closely we realize that
these parallel elements have their origin in the Old Testament,
whereas the elements proper to the hymns are not found in the
Apocalypse where the symbolism is considerably more complicated;
in the hymns the male child is a collectivity, whereas in the Apocalypse he is clearly individualized (12, 5); in the hymns the struggle
is waged especially between two pregnant women, whereas in the
Apocalypse it is the male child in particular who defeats the dragon
(12, 4); in the hymns the powers of evil are swallowed up at once
(lines 17-18), whereas in the Apocalypse they invade the earth for
a short time (12, 12) which is then prolonged considerably (12,
14-17); above all, in the hymns it is merely a question of the personal trials of the author, while in the Apocalypse there is a synop-

sis of universal history and of the drama which involves the entire world.

All will see the difficulties obstructing a sure solution to the problem. We do not go so far as to deny all probability to the hypothesis which finds in Apocalypse 12 a reflection of the literary style shared by the apocalyptic writings of the Old Testament and Judaism contemporary to Christianity, rather than the history of Mary reflected in purely apocalyptic style.

Nevertheless, our opinion is that the safest hypothesis is that which follows here.

The supporters of the historical conception maintain that the entire Apocalypse is dominated by an eminently historical fact, namely, the death of Christ, the *immolated Lamb,* around whom rotates the whole of human history reflected in the Apocalypse. The other figures then must also have an eminently historical character, something which is lacking both in myth and in the confused prophecy of the Old Testament, which are insufficient to explain the Christian apocalypse.

The Judaic apocalypse is entirely projected into the future, whereas the Christian one does nothing but return upon the past, recalling the history which contains the future in embryo. To our mind this latter opinion appears to be the correct one.

(b) OUR CLARIFICATION

The text states that the woman in question is *eminently a mother, that her maternity is from heaven, and that she has cooperated in it through suffering.*

Explanation of terms: (1) that the woman is eminently a mother appears clear: she is represented in the act of giving birth to a male child; the serpent persecutes her because he can do nothing against the male child. Finally, he persecutes the rest of the woman's offspring, because he could not harm the woman herself;

(2) that this maternity is received from heaven appears from the symbols: the sun, the moon and stars, the wings, etc.;

(3) that she has cooperated in this maternity appears from the unspeakable suffering that belongs to her nature as a woman.

To us these qualities are excellently applied to Mary, but only with difficulty can they be perfectly applied to the Church.

Proof: the quality of mother is never applied elsewhere to the Church by the author of the Apocalypse, who prefers the concept of spouse.

It is true that the Gospels (Luke 8, 19-21 and parallels) and St. Paul (Gal. 4, 26) are familiar with the quality of mother as applied to the Church. But the historical soundness of the two accounts should be noted: they always pass from real mothers to mothers in the spiritual sense.

Would the historical foundation which is so evident in the vivid apocalyptic description be lacking precisely at this point?

Moreover, history teaches us that the male Child is Jesus Christ, persecuted by Satan even up to the time of his ascension into heaven; that Mary his Mother is persecuted for a further period, until her corporal assumption; and that we, the Church, "the rest" of her offspring, are persecuted for the entire duration of the Church militant on earth. History reflected in St. John's Apocalypse explains this fully without any recourse to the fantastic Hebrew apocalypse.

Maternity received from heaven: here John is in agreement with Luke 1-2 and Matthew 1-2, where the birth of

Christ of the Virgin Mary is described as a heavenly work. John himself assures us that Mary's spiritual maternity is derived from the Crucified.

It is true that the Church has also received this, but would the author of the Apocalypse have had the courage to describe it as clothed with the sun, with God, after the reproaches of Chapters 1-4 in which each church appears contaminated?

Nor is the woman clothed with the sun in Chapter 12 to be confused with the magnificent bride of the Lamb in Chapter 21, 11, where we have perfect eschatology, in heaven; whereas in Chapter 12 she is still struggling as Church militant against the serpent (cf. v. 17).

Cooperation in suffering embraces the entire life of Mary. It is not so much a question of the physical suffering of maternity as of the intimate sorrows of her maternal heart which was ever yearning for her Son.

The Church suffers too from the devil's assaults; but this suffering appears in verse 17 as quite distinct from that of the woman. These are the sufferings of "the rest of the woman's offspring."

(c) CONCLUSION

The mother cannot therefore be confused with the bride of the Lamb, nor with the rest of her offspring. We feel that this would be to confuse what is clear with what is vague, to confuse history with prophecy and myth, and the New Testament with the Old.

To us the expression "the rest of her offspring" signifies the members of Mary's Son. The first account of this is the entire Pauline theology on the Mystical Body, the substance of which is known to John (John 15). The second account is specifically that of Luke and John.

We therefore believe that when the Supreme Pontiffs

affirm that the woman clothed with the sun is Mary assumed into heaven, they are merely extracting a dogma from a historical fact recorded in Apocalypse 12.[11]

The exegete who believes in the Church is more and more convinced as time goes on that the Church alone knows how to read Holy Scripture fully.

The most obvious historical exegesis is that Mary, thanks to the sufferings that she bore with Christ for us, has gone up to heaven with the immolated Lamb, to intercede as Mother of sorrows on behalf of the Church which is still battling with Satan, the ancient serpent, her mortal enemy.

It is precisely the Mother who smiles on the Church because the latter continues, in time, to be the perfect image of Mary.

The author of the Apocalypse places the Mother of God right in the center of his work in order to console those persecuted by the Emperor Domitian (A.D. 81-96) who sorely need to contemplate the smiling countenance of Mary.

III. MARY AND THE HISTORY OF
THE CHURCH

It is common knowledge that young people are anything but enthusiastic about history as taught in the schools today. Is the true reason for this the fact that such history is something very remote from our own lives? Or is it because the history they are taught is merely an account of facts and of wars, without the *afflatus* of the Holy Spirit?

1. Real History

Anyone who wishes to examine the history of our time, without taking into account the observations that we have

ventured to bring forward, will be dissecting a corpse
rather than history made by persons who are free with the
freedom of the Son of God. How can one speak, for instance, of Peron, Mussolini, or Hitler without considering
how they were influenced by women?

Professor Raddmond writes regarding Hitler: "I fear
that it was not Eva Braun who gave herself to Hitler but
at times Hitler to her. Probably many things would have
taken a different course if this woman had not been there.
In my opinion she had such a strong influence over the
dictator that his inflexibility, his political and military in-
capacity, particularly in the years immediately preceding
his death, were not brought about solely by his own
decision." [11a]

There is something which goes even deeper: the influence of a mother over a human life.

A Spanish proverb presents the mother thus: "The
hand that rocks the cradle rules the world!" Napoleon put
his signature to this when he said: "All that I am, I owe to
my mother."

2. Mary in the History of Christ

Modern historiography generally forgets this figure.[12]
Hence the Catholic protest which conceives salvation all
the time in the light of the union between Christ and
Mary.

In this it does not consider that it is yielding too much
to phantasy if, from Genesis 3 to Apocalypse 12, the whole
of human history appears under the sign of the Mother
with her Son.

There is an even more positive aspect. During the
lifetime of Salomé, the maiden who tempted Herod by
her extravagant dance [13] and of the queens Poppaea,
Messalina, and Agrippina whose fine feats are related by

Tacitus,[14] there lived in a despised Galilean village a poor unknown woman named Mary.

This maiden became the pivot on which the whole of human history turns. Through the operation of the Divine Spirit, she became the connecting link between the divine and the human.[15]

Without her Christ becomes merely an idea, a myth. The historical picture of Christ fades into a fable if it has not Mary as its frame.[16]

But the Virgin Mother has a name, Mary, and a hometown, Nazareth. Above all has she suffered too much to be confused with the myth. She has, in particular, a heart, that heart which is the symbol of woman and of love, that heart which is lacking in our technicized world.[17]

3. *Mary after Pentecost in the History of the Church*

The atheistic woman when she passes forty-five years of age feels herself to be useless and therefore passes her time in a continual round of social visits, boring others and being bored herself.[18]

The woman who indulges in psychoanalysis deceives herself that she has found a second maternity in the affection of her nieces and nephews.[19]

The psychologists console her, maintaining that the beauty of an older woman goes much deeper than juvenile beauty, being much more gracious and seasoned, like the fruit in comparison with its flower, like fulfillment compared with the promise of it.[20]

It is true that advanced age deprives a woman of *eros*, but it permits her to be really *agape*, with a love that is unselfish, discerning, and spiritual.

This is the atmosphere that surrounds Mary after the descent of the Holy Spirit.

During the lifetime of Jesus upon earth, when she interrogated her son and when she spoke to the angel Gabriel, she appeared very human; when she stood by the dying Christ she diffused a fragrance of incredible tenderness; but never before did she appear to be all love, as now that she is transfigured by the Spirit.

With a love that no one saw but which all felt, she filled the early Church with grace, with the Holy Spirit. She carried the bride of Christ to Calvary, because it is only there that the Spirit of the Crucified is received.

Thus Christianity learned from its Mother that its kingdom is not of this world, nor its policy that of worldly armies. Its realm is that of inner life and of love. Thus the Church became the soul of the world.

Mary was its queen, sharing the royalty of Christ crucified. Nobody saw it, but if the Church was set in motion, it must surely have had a driving power, a heart.

The heart of the Church was Mary.

4. Holy Mary and the Holy Spirit (Mary in the History of Each Individual)

Léon Bloy's lament is popular: *"There is only one misery. . . . and that is—NOT TO BE SAINTS."* [21]

People continue to write about the Church's failings, but sanctity is precisely the irradiation of Christ's power in the midst of human misery (2 Cor. 12, 9).

Bernanos writes: "Note that this man of letters Claudel is a genius. I do not deny it, but these literary men are all the same: as soon as they begin to treat of sanctity, they smear themselves with the sublime, they bring the sublime into everything! Sanctity is not sublime." [22]

Thus we forget that Theresa and Athanasius, before being saints, were children of the pilgrim Church. The picture of Maria Goretti is rejected because she is represented as a little peasant girl.[23]

The mysticism of theatre and television and marriage are interwoven, but we do not sufficiently bear in mind that Eva Lavallière, when she wanted to give herself totally to God, gave up the theatre to devote herself to a life of sacrifice at the icy baths of Lourdes.

But the Church loves history in which she has been founded. Therefore she will continue to say that Maria Goretti is a peasant girl of the Roman countryside, one of the poor girls who fill those rugged moors with groans and sighs and grace even if they are unaware of it.

Especially will the Church continue to say that Mary of Nazareth is one of those "wretched, poverty-stricken" ones who fill the entire Bible and the whole of human history with their sighs and who know how to keep their place. Mary is their representative, their prototype.

She, the Mother of God, did not pose. She kept the last place for herself, she who was the first among women, the Mother.

Nor did she change when she was greeted as "full of grace," the Mother of that Christ who had "become poor" in order to enrich us with his heavenly gifts. The poverty of her Son soon becomes her rule of action, the death of Jesus the center of her life.

As she recalled the life of her Son, eternal love in person caused her to recognize clearly the most delicate nuances of Christ's life. *Nuances,* these, which could only be grasped by a woman's sensitiveness, by the spotlessness of an immaculate mother.

Papini writes: "The poet full of passion, the saint all sacrifice, have something of the woman in them. A woman is hardly content one day with what is too much, while another day she regards even the least things as superfluous. She can be obedient as the tool in the hands of a smith or indocile as the wind upon the sea."

But in Mary's case the wind was the Divine Spirit and the sea in which she navigated was the infinite love of God to whom she offered filial obedience.

She did not launch forth into daring adventures, but was happy to entrust herself to the current of existence. Her daily embroidery consisted in reproducing in her soul the image of her Son. She sensed that every moment was a golden thread. Only at the end is Christ to appear in his ravishing beauty, but he is to have a special charm which only the soul of Mary Immaculate can impart to him.

Here it would be necessary to go into the psychology of the tiny momentary things of which the feminine soul is made up.[24] We should hear melodious notes not yet sung: He advanced in grace . . . Jesus looked at her and said: "Woman, ..."

All this is a world which only the Spirit can reveal to us, as he did to Luke and John. But the Spirit who weaves the sublime tissue of Christ in Mary, the Spirit who, like a divine rainbow of the Father and the Son, casts divinely colored rays upon Mary, reserves for us this intuition in the silence of prayer close to the Eucharistic Christ.

On the wild heaths of Numidia an enchanting spectacle can be enjoyed. The sun rises beyond the Nile. Its first rays penetrate like a lance into the age-old caverns, cross the rocky chamber and arrive directly and precisely as far as the statue of the god Abu. Illuminating the statue, the sunlight endows it with an enchanted life.

Mary is precisely this divine ray that appears to be created for the purpose of vivifying the temple of the Eucharistic Christ.

Her earthly life and her heavenly life perpetuated in her liturgy and feasts have no other purpose than that of enabling us to discern the nuances of Christ's soul.

All this is sublime and may appear even mythical. But this is not the case, because we have passed by way of the history of Christ, after which we have its inebriating echo and a life which renders us blessed.

The *echo* is Mary, the *life* is Eternal Love in person. It is the irradiation of Christ in the midst of our wretchedness, in our humdrum daily life.

Here lies true sanctity.

IV. THE APOTHEOSIS OF THE ASSUMPTION
(*Maria in Sinu Patris*)

The woman clothed with the sun is therefore Mary assumed into heaven. What is the meaning of this feast, of this dogma?

1. *Vision of The Essence of God* (*Mary Ascending*)

One day Paul was overcome by unspeakable sorrow. He knew that his suffering was the suffering of Christ, Nevertheless, he felt so brokenhearted as to wish for death. It was then that the Apostle had one of the most wonderful experiences of God as the tender Father who stoops down to us in our suffering. Paul is to reveal his discovery to the disciples in Corinth in the most personal of his letters:

"Blessed be the God and Father of our Lord Jesus Christ, the Father of mercies and the God of all comfort" (2 Cor. 1, 3).[25]

Yet Paul was aware that this vision of the Father was as it were in a mirror, in a partial and indistinct manner.

What will it be when the Father is seen face to face? When we shall know who we are and who he is—the Father?

Herein lies the whole meaning of the Assumption, the passage from a life full of suffering to an eternity full of bliss. It is the very instant of death which lived in Christ becomes eternal life.

The Church assures us that "the Immaculate Mother of God, Mary ever virgin, at the end of her life was elevated to heavenly glory in soul and body." [26]

In the historical moment of her Assumption into heaven, Mary recognized the essence of God, an eternal recognition that renders her soul forever blessed.

(a) OBEDIENCE TO THE FATHER

Mary then understood that he who knows how to *obey the will of the Father* can cast himself into his paternal bosom, indeed, into his ever fruitful maternal bosom, from which she came forth by being created a woman rendered sublime by the infusion of grace.

In this consisted the true motive of her being as woman, as virgin, as mother and free from all stain of sin. She was a woman made of love, a virgin reserved to the Father all-holy, a mother who received her Son from the bosom of the Father (Rom. 8, 28-30).

Mary experienced what the essence of the Father really is; she who was adorned as a woman with a deep intuitive sense. She who was clothed in a virginal body, could experience what the tenderness of a mother signifies.

This was no vague tenderness, not even for an instant; it was the very source of tenderness, forever, in the plenitude of vision.

All this is summed up in the colloquy between the Father and his first-born Daughter.[27]

(b) LISTENING TO THE SON

The Father is a marvelous being, not motionless or mute as a statue. He speaks, but he utters one Word alone, the Son, the *Verbum*.

Mary who had always listened to this Word now hears it as if it were new, although it is not new.

In fact, in Mary we find the whole tender and loving Father, but we also have the humanity that sprang forth from her virginal womb.

Strange to say, the humanity of Christ, which is the echo of the Word, does not disappear before him, the reality, but forms a frame for him, a frame that is made eternal by the Eternal Son. *Ecce Agnus Dei!* (Apoc. 5).

Mary had already looked beyond Christ's humanity. His wounds on Golgotha appeared to her to be the natural rays leading into the heart of Christ, into his divinity.

As time went by, the veil had become more and more transparent. But it was only on the day of the Assumption that this marvelous picture on which the Word of the Father is written appeared to her maternal eyes.

Her heart exulted, asking "Was this my Son?" And the question was lost in the hymns of the angels while there remained the historical reality: My Son! Son of the Father!

Mary uttered only the first of these invocations in which she expressed all her gratitude to the Father; the second invocation was pronounced by the Son for her, the Son who in uttering the word "Father" caused the historic word "Mother" to re-echo in her mind.

"We shall be like him, for we shall see him just as he is" (1 John 3, 2).

Here we have the eternal colloquy between Mother and Son.

(c) DOCILE TO THE ATTRACTION OF THE HOLY SPIRIT

There are no further words in heaven. But there is another deep reality that permeates the whole of paradise and without which the very reason and foundation of the colloquy between the Father and the Son would be lacking. It is *the Holy Spirit, Love in person.*

Mary had never failed the Holy Spirit even when he drew her to Golgotha. The Spirit had animated Christ and caused him to rise from the dry earth of Gethsemane, to climb the hill of Calvary so as to utter the word "Mother!" which synthesizes all the Father's tenderness. This Spirit had sustained Mary also. It was precisely Mary's assent that rendered her the spouse of that love which flows only from the wounds of Christ (Heb. 9, 14).

The Spirit sprang forth from the eyes of the Father as he looked on the Son who returned that gaze: the meeting of their eyes, of their gaze constitutes or sends forth the Holy Spirit.

She who as a mother understood what it was to love found herself naturally in the arms of Love and she loved in a blessed manner.

In loving Love she did not detach herself by any means from the Father and the Son. Indeed, the more she was immersed in Love, the more affectionately did she clasp to her heart the Son who alone could say in full: Abba, Father!

This word of the Son re-echoed in her heart as if she had uttered it herself. Because of her nearness to Love, she felt that all heaven consists in answering the Father in Christ and in the joy of loving the Holy Spirit.

It would appear as if we had yielded to the temptation to mythicize, a temptation that is innate in every human being. Yet, if the Bible is history, then what we have said is substantially reality.

2. Mary Assumed into Heaven and
Ourselves (Mary Descending)

Up to the present we have spoken in the past tense. But, with death, time comes to an end and eternity begins. The historical moment of Mary's death has been stripped of what is transient, to become eternal.

From the mountain of eternity Mary follows us every-where.

Roschini in concluding his thesis on Mary, Mediatrix of all Graces, invites us to go to her with confidence because she "can help us; she knows us and she wishes to help us." [28]

An excellent synthesis which, in the setting of Trinitarian theology, is translated as follows:

(a) SHE CAN DO ALL THINGS

Mary can do all things as the first-begotten daughter of the omnipotent Father (Luke 1, 19), the Father, supreme power ceaselessly operating. Mary, who in herself has the mere power of a woman, but because of her obedience to the Father feels herself to be associated with him in bestowing the power of becoming sons of God (John 1, 12).

God did not destine man to be born again without a mother. "When the Catholic speaks of his Heavenly Mother, his heart is full of all the strength of feeling that is contained in that word. Mary is as it were a gracious revelation of certain ineffable and ultimate traits in the nature of God, which are too fine and too delicate to be grasped otherwise than as reflected in the mirror of a mother." [29]

(b) SHE KNOWS US PERFECTLY

Does not what we have said above obscure the Son, as if he were incapable of reflecting in created things the most delicate expression of love, which is tenderness?

No, because all that Mary is, she is in the Son. Son and Mother, new Adam and new Eve, form but one reality. She feels herself "known" by the Father in the Son, without whom her life has neither meaning nor consistency.

In contact with the Son she knows us also, children of the Father, irradiation of Christ, forming one body with him.

Christ said: "I am the Good Shepherd, and I know mine and mine know me, even as the Father knows me and I know the Father" (John 10, 14-15). Observe how the knowledge of the individual members of the flock comes from the Father. Mary also knows them.[30]

Thus I can say that Mary knows me at every moment by her mother love.

"The notion of the mother (let us say it with Plato and Goethe), implies a practical solicitude that considers the existence of the individual alone. It does not offer the possibility of thinking of the child's day or of his sorrow in a vague, abstract, global manner. A day in the life of her child, marked by various needs, full of little surprises and little catastrophes, is made up for the mother not of continuous time but of a succession of little eternities. The sorrow of her child is composed of weeping, of insistence, of sighs, each of which has a particular nuance in the order of suffering.

"Moreover, when we are free from the limits imposed by space and time and by what is social and general, we no longer have recourse to abstraction nor, as a result, to its language. It is our limitations and our necessities which oblige us to see things wholesale. Already to the extent to which we love we correct this generality which dims our view. Beyond the grave, humanity will become for us what it is for God, namely, a collection of individual destinies.

"If this is true of us, it is even more true of the creature who has been constituted mother of all men according to grace. Understand well the word *all*, which can be very ambiguous and which signifies here each one in particular." [31]

Thus not a sigh nor a smile nor a sin exists in our lives

which Mary does not follow with maternal concern. I mention sin here also, because all things cooperate toward good, even sin, adds St. Augustine. And St. Thomas Aquinas is to have it enter into the order of predestination.

In Christianity the word *chance*, or unforeseen event, does not exist. Everything is foreseen by the Father of mercies and by the maternal heart of Mary, by a Father and a Mother who, precisely because of their tenderness, search for the stray sheep, the lost drachma, the prodigal son.

(c) SHE LOVES US

But the one who urges her to turn toward us is always Love in person, the Holy Spirit.

St. Thomas says: "The Father and the Son love one another reciprocally in the Holy Spirit, or Love who proceeds: not themselves alone, therefore, but also us."

This means that the Holy Spirit is sent to us precisely because we are loved by the Father and the Son; and thus Mary comes to us, because, brought by this same Love, she is the spouse of the Holy Spirit. She opens the way, as it were, for the entry into us of the Triune God. Along with the Three Divine Persons she tastes heaven in our hearts. So will it be until faith is changed into vision and the seed of grace blossoms into eternal life.

Thus does the gift of the Father reach us, perfumed by the humanity of Christ crucified and fragrant with the tenderness of Mary.

SUMMARY OF CHAPTER FOUR:

THE life of Christ with his death and resurrection is eternalized. Having become the "Lord of glory," he permeates with his Spirit the entire Church whose office is that of "bringing to mind" what Christ has said.

Thus the Church is found united with Mary at Pentecost, experiencing that maternal assistance which is made eternal in the apotheosis of the Assumption.

❦ NOTES ❧

1. This title is attributed to Mary particularly by De Montfort. Scheeben does not like it (Koester, *op. cit.,* p. 461), nor does K. Wittkember, "Braut," in *Lexicon Marienkunde,* coll. 898-910, for fear of precipitation into the paternity of the Holy Ghost in relation to Jesus.

Nevertheless we consider this title to be very suitable, according to the mentality of Leo XIII and the Congregation of Rites, to indicate the relations between Mary and the Holy Spirit. Cf. also L. Colomber, "Relaciones de Maria con la Santisima Trinidad" in *Estudios Marianos,* 8 (1949), 129-131: for the author it is the best name since it indicates the intimate union between Mary the spiritual mother of men and the Holy Spirit who bestows on them this divine life.

2. St. Thomas, *Summa Theol.* Ia, q. 37-38: "The name Love in God . . . if taken personally it is the proper name of the Holy Spirit" (Ia, q. 37, a. 1); "Gift, taken personally in God, is the proper name of the Holy Ghost" Ia, q. 38, a. 2).

For the concept of woman as love and donation, cf. notes 23-24 of chapter one. Consider, moreover, the doctrine of Sister Elizabeth of the Most Holy Trinity, or better still, Elena Guerra advising Leo XIII to write the famous encyclical on the Holy Spirit, *Divinum Illud* (May 9, 1897), and something will be understood of the relation existing between the woman who loves and the Holy Spirit, Eternal Love in person.

3. Cf. H. Marin, *Documentos Marianos* (Madrid: 1954), pp. 325 ff.

4. *Ibid.,* p. 575.

5. It is to be recognized, however, that *Mystici Corporis* does not use our language.

6. In synthesis, here are the modern positions:

1. *Nomenclature: Moral cause:* she is limited to praying to obtain grace. *Psychological diposition:* she disposes our intellect and will psychologically, but does not infuse grace; she merely prepares the soul to receive it. *Instrumental physical cause:* grace passes through the psychology of Mary, the mother, and thus reaches us maternalized, Marianized.

2. Opinions: R. Laurentin, *Marie l'Eglise et le Sacerdote,* II, 196: "Mary prepares the soul to receive the grace which the sacraments confer." Alastruey, *op. cit.,* pp. 647-688: Based on the *Adjutorium Simile Sui* of St. Albert the Great, rejecting the instrumental physical cause; Mary as coagent "has a real influence on the effect, in dependence on the principal cause, Christ." Roschini, II, 557: with excellent *status quaes-*

tionis, affirms: "there is really solid probability in favor of the instrumental physical cause." Schmaus, after eighteen pages on prayer, prefers the moral cause, but does not reject the instrumental physical one, as in the sacraments (pp. 365-367).

It seems to us superfluous to proceed further.

7. Here we let the mystics speak. *Marie De Sainte Thérèse, Union mystique à Marie* (Paris: Editions du Cerf, p. 96): "When the sweet mother was constantly by your side to guide you in the path of virtue it was in order to prepare you for the spiritual nuptials with her most dear Son. Now that these nuptials have been celebrated, she stands aside and allows the bride to converse alone with her Spouse, as is fitting."

8. Cf. "Introduzione alla Lettera ai Rom.," by G. Bosio, *Padri Apostolici* (Turin: 1942), II, 100.

9. A return to myth is seen here by R. Bultmann, *RGG* (1960), IV, 1281; and even by his opponent Staehlin, *ibid.,* col. 748.

Pre-eminence of the Church almost exclusively, gradually supported: M. Boisard, *Introduction à la Bible,* II, 737-738; A. Dassing, *Die Kirche und Maria* (Düsseldorf: 1958), p. 163; Schmaus, pp. 58, 78.

Pre-eminence of Mary: Braun, p. 143; H. Rahner, *Maria und die Kirch* (Innsbruck: 1951), p. 115 (*Our Lady and the Church* [New York: Pantheon, 1961]); B. J. Le Frois, *The Woman Clothed With the Sun* (Rome: 1954), pp. 269-271; A. Romeo in *SBM.*

Nevertheless, not a few seek equidistance between Mary and the Church, inextricably mingled. Cf. A. Mueller, *Ecclesia-Maria* (Fribourg, Switzerland: 1955), pp. 234-235.

10. Cf. Kassing, p. 138, where the text of Qumran is quoted, 1 QH 3; E. Lohse, *Die Offenbarung Johannes* (Göttingen: 1960), pp. 62-63, rejects the immediate parallel between Apoc. 12 and I QH 3 and is inclined toward a Marian interpretation, but finds a stumbling block in vs. 17.

10a. From *The Dead Sea Scrolls* by Millar Burrows. Copyright © 1955 by Millar Burrows. Reprinted by permission of the Viking Press, Inc.

10b. M. Delcor, *Les Hymns de Qumran* (Paris: 1962), p. 124.

10c. J. Carmignac and P. Guilbert, *Les Texts de Qumran* (Paris: 1961), p. 197.

11. Pius X in the encyclical *Ad diem illum;* Pius XII in *Munificentissimus Deus.* The entire liturgy of the Assumption.

11a. *Neue Weltschau,* IV: 7 (1958).

12. Cf. the classical works of R. Bultmann, *History and Eschatology* (New York: Harper, 1962). O. Cullman, *Christ and Time* (Philadelphia: Westminster Press, 1964). Mary does not appear at all, but still they focus well the question of Christ as the center of history. These are Protestants. It is displeasing when this essential aspect of history is seen to be lacking in Catholic literature.

13. E. Stauffer, *Jerusalem und Rom* (Bern: 1957), pp. 94-95.

14. *Annali* II (Rome: Rizzoli Editions), 253 ff.

15. Schmaus, pp. 157, 182, 175: "Christ is not an idea, Christianity is not an ideology. Christ is deeply rooted in history, the figure of Mary is grafted onto history. In Christology and soteriology the historicity of Mary has an *essential* function in salvation. Otherwise the idea of redemption would collapse. . . . Mary is not just the symbol of maternity, of fruitful virginity, nor is she merely the symbol of the Church. She is a living, real and personal historical fact. Her concrete historical reality and insertion into history are expressed in the fact that she bears a name: Mary!"

16. H. Asmussen, *Mutter Gottes*, pp. 9, 12, 60: "Mary is a well-defined figure, not a myth . . . she is the central point of all history. The historical fact is Christ, but in virtue of this historical fact come a whole series of other historical facts. First of all, Mary."

17. Cf. R. Guardini, in *Hochland*, October (1953), 64. A. Scherer, in *Frau*, p. 164. H. Rondet, in *NRTh*, 79 (1957), 940.

In order to estimate the interior action of history proper to woman, it is necessary to remember that not only actions but also reactions, interior sentiments, make history. R. Bultmann, *Geschichte*, p. 162 (*History and Eschatology* [New York: Harper, 1962]).

18. Cf. the sadistic description of Beauvoir, II, 417: "She knows herself to be useless. . . ."

19. H. Deutsch, *op. cit.*, II, 456 ff.

20. Kampmann, I, 231-232; Buytendijk, p. 279.

21. L. Bloy, *The Woman Who Was Poor* (New York: Sheed & Ward 1947), p. 356.

22. Cf. *Civiltà Cattolica* (Italian Jesuits) (1948), p. 503.

23. Y. Congar, *Le Christ Marie et l'Eglise* (Desclée), p. 88.

24. G. von Le Fort, *The Eternal Woman*, p. 108; *Leben spricht zu Leben*, G. Ehrle (Freiburg), p. 197.

25. Cf. Bonaventura Rinaldi, "Il Padre di Gesù Crocifisso," in the Italian review *Fonti vive* (1961), pp. 20-21. Cf. Romaniuk, *op. cit.*, p. 188.

26. Denz., n. 2332.

27. Observe that the whole of theology is based on the colloquy between God and us. K. Barth, *L'Humanité de Dieu* (Geneva: 1956), pp. 37-41 (*The Humanity of God* [Richmond: John Knox Press, 1960]); M. Schmaus, *The Essence of Christianity* (Scepter, 1962); O. Semmelroth, *Incontro personale con Dio*, (Alba [Italy]: 1955). In heaven the Triune God of the theologian appears precisely as he is. Cf. G. Lagrange, *De Gratia* (Turin: 1950), pp. 317-326.

28. *Mariologia*, II, 557.

29. Karl Adam, *The Spirit of Catholicism* (New York: Image Books, 1954), p. 120. It seems to me that P. Congar, pp. 47 and 83, fears this approach too much.

30. In order to understand properly the technics of Marian knowledge and love, the words of St. Thomas must always be remembered: ". . . we must say that since in God *to love* is taken in two ways, essentially and notionally, when it is taken essentially it means that the Father and the Son love each other not by the Holy Ghost but by their essence. . . . But when the term Love is taken in a notional sense it means nothing else than *to spirate love;* just as to speak is to produce a word and to flower is to produce flowers. As therefore we say that a tree flowers by its flower, so do we say that the Father, by the Word or the Son, speaks Himself, and His creatures; and that the Father and the Son love each other and us, by the Holy Ghost, or by Love proceeding" (*Summa Theol.* Ia, q. 37, a. 2. Translation by Dominican Fathers of the English Province [New York: Benzinger, 1947]).

31. J. Guitton, *op. cit.,* p. 165.

{5}

Mary's Problems and Ours

I. INTRODUCTION

After having dealt with the essence of Mariology in rapid fashion, we should have liked to have come to a full stop, while patiently awaiting the criticism of specialists before going further and explaining more fully the ideas already expressed.

However, we considered it advisable to fill in some of the more evident gaps by means of this final chapter which might be entitled "the accidents," or the accidental part of Mariology, since it treats of less-important questions about which Catholic theologians are still very uncertain. Moreover, in using the term "accidents" we mean what are ordinarily classified as accidental happenings—the unforeseen events and problems of daily life.

We shall, therefore, seek to solve these modern problems and difficulties in Mariology without presuming to say the last word on the subject.

Note, therefore, the title "Mary's problems." There is question here of probing the heart and intelligence of Mary in her earthly life to see how faith and knowledge, sorrow and joy, virginity and maternity can be harmonized in that life.

Our problems. We deal, first of all, with two rather speculative difficulties: Mary, the new Eve, and our Mother; Christ, Mary, and the Church; then with two practical themes: Mary's tears and Mary's smile as expressions of the presence of God in our modern history.

We hope in this way to fill in any gaps which may have remained of necessity in the main part of this work.

II. FAITH AND KNOWLEDGE IN MARY

1. *Statement of the Problem*

Anyone who reads the first two chapters of Luke's Gospel will be astonished by the insistence with which the hagiographer presents the principal actress in the drama, Mary of Nazareth, as the one who "ponders" (2, 19; 2, 51), who "is astonished"; indeed, as the Mother who "did not understand the words of Jesus!" (2, 50).[1]

When we consider that these words were written after decades of reflection on Mary's part, when she had come to understand Christ's mysterious manner of acting and speaking, we are naturally plunged into the whole problem of faith and knowledge; a faith whose object does not appear with convincing evidence, but which is nevertheless reasonable, because Christ has said so, Christ who is God and who cannot err or deceive.

The whole problem lies here: the problem of wishing to see clearly and having to be content, on the contrary, with a confused intuition; hearing the human voice of Christ and not seeing clearly his beautiful divine countenance, although every gesture and word of the Son raised her to the sphere of the divine and holy.[2]

In reality the object of her faith is prevalently Christ. John leaves us no room for doubt: "But to as many as received him (faith in Christ) he gave the power of becoming sons of God, to those who believe in his name" (Prologue).

Therefore, the question of Mary's faith is reduced to her gradual penetration into the mystery of Christ, without arriving at the full splendor of perfect or beatific vision.

We may divide the subject in the following manner: (1) modern extremism regarding Mary's knowledge; (2) an attempt at a solution beginning with the *Magnificat,* so as to investigate the object and inquire into the manner of Mary's knowing.

2. Modern Extremism

Modern extremists in this field fall into two classes: those who suppose that Mary enjoyed the beatific vision at least at times, and those who insist with Guardini that "during the lifetime of Jesus, Mary certainly did not understand that Jesus was the Son of God." [3]

The first opinion is not impossible, but for the present there are no grounds which render it probable, first of all, because it has not been fully proved that Moses and Paul had the beatific vision, so that every analogy with other saints falls to the ground. Nor must the phrase *seeing God face to face* be exaggerated. Otherwise several other saints could be said to have had the beatific vision. [4]

Moreover, let us take the account of the Annunciation. The biblical text does not point to intuitive or beatific vision in which the soul sees in an instant the entire reality. Indeed, Mary is enlightened by degrees as to the purpose of the angelic apparation, as to the harmonious blending of virginity and maternity.

These are not, it is true, insurmountable difficulties, but today such a hypothesis is merely a possibility.

Every theologian, moreover, knows how difficult it is to find biblical texts which prove in an evident manner the beatific vision in Christ. It is only his sense of the teaching Church, whose office is that of ascertaining exactly the true meaning of a bibilical verse, that can set the mind of the believer at rest.[5]

Guardini's too extreme opinion is mitigated by Dillenschneider who says "nothing has more support from the psychological point of view than the fact that Mary was unaware of the full meaning of the mystery of her Son's divinity. From the beginning she must have been dimly aware of this mystery and have accepted it in implicit faith. It was at Pentecost that she entered into it fully."[6]

In face of the great prudence shown by the best modern mariologists we would be tempted to leave the matter as it stands.

3. Attempt at a Solution

We venture, on the contrary, to add some remarks. If, instead of entering the realm of psychology, we read the Gospel, what do we find? Elizabeth exclaims: "Blessed art thou among women and blessed is the fruit of thy womb! And how have I deserved that the mother of my Lord should come to me? For behold, the moment that the sound of thy greeting came to my ears, the babe in my womb leapt for joy. And blessed is she who has believed because the things promised her by the Lord shall be accomplished" (Luke 1, 42-45).

The shepherds affirm that the angel has announced to them: "A Savior has been born to you, who is Christ the Lord" (Luke 2, 11).

Peter, enlightened by the Father, recognizes in Jesus "the Son of the living God" (Matt. 16, 16).

John the Baptist testifies: "And I have seen and borne witness that this is the Son of God" (John 1, 34). This is a reading which tends to disappear in modern translations as in Peter's discourses after Pentecost (Acts 1-5). To us, however, this does not seem exact since the fourth Gospel is entirely built upon the divinity of Christ and since Peter declares: "Therefore, let all the house of Israel know most assuredly that God has made both Lord and Christ, this Jesus whom you crucified" (Acts 2, 36).

In view of these statements we ask ourselves if it is possible that before Pentecost, Elizabeth, the shepherds, Peter, and John the Baptist were all aware of the divinity of Christ, while Mary knew nothing of it? [6a]

It is true that *form-criticism* (*Formgeschichte*) leaves us a little perplexed regarding the Gospel statements. It is well to remark, though, that when it states that the divinity of Christ has been created by the Church, it is absolutely false; if it teaches us that the Apostles understood Christ's life more fully from certain circumstances, especially from the light they received at Pentecost, then we can welcome it.[7] At least a nucleus of history of Christ's life must be accepted. Otherwise the entire Gospel would be reduced to a myth.

But certainly Luke had no intention of writing a myth when he wrote:"The Holy Spirit shall come upon thee and the power of the Most High shall overshadow thee; and therefore the Holy One to be born shall be called the Son of God" (Luke 1, 35).

4. The Magnificat

If we pause for a moment at this point to examine the *Magnificat*, the hymn of the early Church, modeled from the point of view of style on the hymn of Anna (1 Kings 2), but which relates substantially Mary's experience during the days of the Visitation, we perceive the following:

(a) The object of the *Magnificat* is "God my Savior." Mary centers her attention on God as the Savior who uses the "despised" and the "things that are not" (1 Cor. 1, 28) to be the principal actors in his history.[8]

She recognizes in herself the classic example of divine logic: "henceforth all generations shall call me blessed."

The fact that Christ has so little place in the *Magnificat* and that Mary chants in Old Testament language may surprise us.

In the *Magnificat*, the Father, the God who saves, has the leading place. Later on, Mary is to understand more fully that Jesus is the Lord and Savior (Luke 2, 11). Thus we find that the first chapter of Luke is entirely centered round the Father of mercy, while in the second chapter this mercy is given concrete expression in Christ the Savior.

But Mary's knowledge is to alternate between light and shadow: after the contemplation of her little boy-charis, comes the loss of the Son for three days; her meditation on the young man Jesus is to be followed by the period of his preaching, during which she is abandoned.

Finally, the object of Mary's human or infused knowledge is, first of all, God the Savior who becomes human in Christ crucified. It is only through the unforeseen historical events, particularly the death of her Son, that she is to penetrate into the mystery of the divine essence.

(b) The subject of the *Magnificat* is a girl of thirteen who confesses that she is the "handmaid" of God, "the Mighty," who has regarded her. A very deep gaze for a thirteen-year-old on the threshold of life; the gaze of the merciful Father who, like a mother, "has given help to Israel his servant, mindful of his mercy."

Mary's manner of chanting is that of the believer [8a] who, filled with joy, contemplates God the Savior. Even the second part of the *Magnificat*, the development and application to the Church of the Marian destiny, expresses no other ideas than those enunciated in the first part. It merely wishes to say that what has taken place in her is nothing more than the fulfillment of the Old Testament promises; just as Peter is later to explain the Pentecostal event by recalling Joel 3, 1-5.

What pleases most in the *Magnificat* is the preponderance of that logic that characterizes the intuition of the contemplative soul. The soul of a woman who, precisely because of her spotlessness, could understand so well the things of God, as if she were the producer of the history of salvation, making all things move through Christ.

To us Mary is not a visionary like the angels, but the *pilgrim* who penetrates humbly and perseveringly into the mystery of Christ until the day in which she sees God as he is, no longer by human reasoning but by the evidence of the beatific vision.

III. SORROW AND JOY IN MARY

1. Mary's Sorrow

(a) A WOMAN'S SORROW

Sorrow is the paradox of human life. The vertical line of the human heart's ascent toward happiness appears to be broken by the horizontal one of actual human life in which tears are an ingredient.

We are aware that in a woman sorrow is particularly striking, since she who is the harmony of creation appears to have power to rise above the nauseating heaviness of this earthly life.

But the woman's longing to abase herself so as to subsist and attain salvation seems a vain one; a dream revealing a lively desire for life.[9]

The divine malediction comes down implacably: "In pain shall you bring forth children," indicating something deeper than the physical and mental pain of maternity.[10] It is the active participation of the woman in the procreation of the children of God, who permits this pain because he wishes the creature to be aware of sharing in the gift of life extending into new areas.[11]

Léon Bloy has expressed the same truth in a practical way: while Clotilde is reading the acts of the martyrs, suddenly her eyes fill with tears and she exclaims: "No— she has not changed. Still the same 'autumn sky' as of old, with the beginning of twilight, a sky of rain and a dying sun. But she is more *like herself*. By dint of suffering she has so conquered her *identity* that, sometimes, in the street, very small children and young babies will stretch out their arms to her, as if they recognized her as somebody they knew. . . ." [12]

Anyone who draws near to a suffering woman must discover precisely the true woman who caused Jesus to groan at Naim (Luke 7, 11), who caused the Son of God to burst into tears when he saw Mary the sister of Lazarus weeping (John 11, 33-35).

(b) OUR LADY OF SORROWS

Thus the *Mater Dolorosa* has a greater fascination for us than the radiant *Aurora Consurgens* of the Immaculate Conception, than the *Ancilla Domini* of the Annunciation.[13] Without doubt the picture of the Mother of Sorrows has given greater consolation to the faithful than any fine human invention.[14]

Sorrow is not a momentary thing in the life of Mary, but a tide flowing toward the day of her Son's death, an ocean of tears and sighs of which Mary reminds Jesus in the Temple: ". . . in sorrow thy father and I have been seeking thee."

Without indulging too much in wordy lyricism, we can identify the sorrows of Mary in a few key episodes:

(1) *Real Sorrows.* When he appeared to St. Margaret Mary Alacoque, Jesus complained that while many praised and celebrated the glories of his cross, there were few who embraced its rough wood.

Mary was truly among those few, permanently overshadowed by the cross.

There is something disconcerting in the concreteness of her sorrows: the sorrows of the betrothed who is misunderstood, of the poverty-stricken mother, of the exile crossing the exhausting desert of Negeb, of the mother who experiences every day the animosity between Christ and his cousins who come to the point of declaring that he is beside himself, that he is crazy!

Finally, Mary sees her sister contemplate a glorious kingdom for her sons James and John, whereas she herself is now fully aware that the kingdom of her Son is very different from that of which Mary of Salome dreams!

(2) *The Suffering Subject.* Every sorrow in Mary must be meditated in the psychology of the woman of deep intuition who knew how to weigh things and who was silent all the time, the immaculate woman who understood that sin was the first and greatest sorrow. If St. Gemma Galgani sweat blood at the mere sound of blasphemy, what must Mary not have experienced on seeing the people of her own Nazareth cast Jesus off, on seeing him betrayed by the kiss of Judas? On witnessing the refusal of Jerusalem and the Jewish people to believe in him?

If Paul (Rom. 9-11) and John (Chap. 9) are aghast on seeing Christ rejected by the Jews, what must not Mary have suffered?

We can glimpse only occasionally the sinister gleam of the sword of sorrow that pierced Mary's heart, whereas the deepest reality is hidden in the unfathomable mystery of divine predestination.

(3) *The Object of Her Sorrow*. It was not so much men as Christ crucified. This affirmation can be proved historically, psychologically, and theologically.

Historically. Jesus said to St. Paul of the Cross: "Son, he who draws near to me draws near to the cross." It was thus with Mary. Jesus is still within her bosom when he creates the famous drama with St. Joseph. The joy of her infant Son's first wailing cry is experienced in the darkness of a cave. The Child is hardly born when he forces his mother to flee into Egypt. Not even the festival days are happy ones for Mary. She presents Jesus in the Temple and hears that a sword will pierce her heart. In that same Temple Jesus is to be lost during the Pasch, a foreshadowing of that other Pasch during which she is to see him nailed to the cross.

Psychologically. The life of the mother is like a circumference that projects all the rays of her maternal affection upon her child. Every thought, every heartbeat is colored with maternal tenderness for the Son.[15]

It is not just the woman of modern times who suffers this conflict between her body working in the factory and her affection that goes out to her child at home. Already Mary, who felt herself made to live at her Son's side as a mother who could adore her own Son, was to be separated from him for three days, for three years, and later for the remainder of her earthly life.

This pain in Mary was not a mere conflict between her body and soul, but a tearing apart of the Mother from the Son who departed from her.

More than any other mere creature, Mary had known the two faces of the thrice holy God: a countenance that attracted to the point of ecstasy and that was terrible to the point of inspiring the desire to be annihilated.

Theologically. Christianity is a paradoxical harmony because it is made up of joy and sorrow, of rationality and mystery. It is the scandal of the cross, wisdom and foolishness, light that can be blinding.

Here are the paradoxes of Mary's life: her Child is foretold as a king and born in a stable; Simeon speaks of Christ as "light" and "glory," then calls him a sign to be contradicted; and it is for her to prepare the Victim for his sacrifice.

If Simeon's prediction is to be so awful, what of the realization of the prophecy on the day on which Christ taken down from the cross is to be laid, a bloodless corpse, on the knees of his Mother? [16]

In that moment she understood fully the import of the words chanted to the "God and Savior," who had so loved the world as to spare not even his own Son!

Mary, through her very sorrow, understood something else, namely, that "a woman does not truly exist unless she is without bread, without comfort, without friends or spouse or children: only thus can she oblige her Savior to come down." [17]

2. Mary's Joy

(a) CHRISTIANITY, A RELIGION OF JOY

It is sorrow itself that affords woman the deepest joy of being herself. This is particularly true of the Mother of Sorrows.

Christianity is the religion of joy. Rightly does François Mauriac reproach the men of modern times for having filled the world with anguish. It was believed that Christianity rendered life sad, so the men of this century rejected it. As a consequence the world is more afflicted than ever.

The Gospel, on the contrary, announces "great joy"

(Luke 2, 10), a joy already present in this life: "These things have I spoken to you that my joy may be in you, and that your joy may be made full" (John 15, 11).

This is not the noisy joy of the world that reigns in the midst of luxury and frenzied dancing, but that deep interior joy which consists in praying to the Father: "Amen, amen, I say to you, if you ask the Father anything in my name, he will give it to you. Hitherto you have not asked anything in my name. Ask and you shall receive, that your joy may be full" (John 16, 23-24). "But now, Father, I am coming to thee and these things I speak in the world, in order that they may have my joy made full in themselves" (John 17, 13).

But Christian joy springs from sorrow. It is sufficient to read the Beatitudes proclaimed by Christ in order to be convinced that only through tears can our eyes smile.

The Apostle of love writes: "You shall be sorrowful, but your sorrow shall be turned into joy. A woman about to give birth has sorrow because her hour has come. But when she has brought forth the child, she no longer remembers the anguish for her joy that a man is born into the world" (John 16, 20-22).

This paradox of sorrow which is turned into joy is the daily experience of the Christian woman.

While Eva Lavallière lay on her bed racked with pain, she had a visit from her friend Robert de Fleurs who asked her:

"Are you in pain?"

"In atrocious pain! the doctors cannot understand how I am still alive."

"But can they not relieve your pain?"

"Perhaps they can, but I hope they will not succeed. I am so happy! You cannot imagine how happy I am!"

"In the midst of such suffering?"

"Yes, indeed, precisely because of this suffering!" [18]

(b) MARY, MOTHER OF JOY

It is not easy to pass from the happiness of Eva Lavall-ière to Mary's joy. Nevertheless, it is evident from the Gospel that her life is all perfumed by the angelic annunciation: "Hail, full of grace! The Lord is with thee!"

The most harmonious lyric of Marian joy is the *Magnificat:* "My soul magnifies the Lord, and my spirit rejoices in God my Savior!"

Here is the creature giving back to her God, in gratitude, her whole self. Anna, the mother of Samuel, also chanted:

> My heart hath rejoiced in the Lord and my horn is exalted
>   in my God!
> My mouth is enlarged over my enemies,
> because I have joyed in this salvation (1 Kings, 2, 1).

The Greek chorus also sang:

> But behold, Niche arrives glorious (*megalonumos*),
> She smiles (*antichareisa*) at Thebes, the warrior!
> After these wars, to rejoice in oblivion.
> Let us go dancing at night to all the temples of the gods.
> May Bacchus lead us, who set Thebes in motion
>   (Sophocles, *Antigone*, 148-153).

But the Marian hymn, immortalized by the Church's liturgy, does not stoop to nocturnal orgies; nor does it hurl itself violently at its enemies. Rather it is an extension of self to God, in his mercy.

Thus while Anna concludes her hymn with the recollection that "the adversaries of the Lord shall fear him and upon them shall he thunder from heaven," Mary ends with the memory of "his mercies and experiences," an inner happiness which is spiritual and unmistakable in comparison with the Greek and Old Testament joy.

It was on Calvary, where the extreme struggle between Satan and Christ took place, that Mary experienced the joy of feeling herself completely the Mother of God and of men. Suffering opened her soul to the vocation of universal motherhood. When Jesus addressed her as "Mother," "Woman," he imparted to her the immense joy of spiritual maternity. This joy was wrapped, it is true, in untold sufferings, but it was, nonetheless, real, even if it is true that the Spirit, her Spouse, was interceding for her in her sufferings (Rom. 8, 14-27); even if it is true that sorrow does not crush the woman, but enables her to find her true identity.

Thus, upon Calvary Jesus experienced the profound joy of being the Son of God, and Mary that of being his Mother and ours.

It is ever the paradox of Christianity that it causes innermost joy to spring from deepest sorrow. Supreme sorrow brings supreme joy!

And it makes the Sorrowful Mother Mary, the Mother of Joy.

IV. VIRGINITY AND MATERNITY IN MARY

1. *The Belief of the Church*

Boris L. Pasternak writes with deep perception: "It has always seemed to me that every conception is immaculate, that in this dogma regarding Our Lady the universal idea of maternity is expressed."

On the contrary, we almost have the impression that today the coexistence of maternity with perfect virginity is considered impossible. Full maternity is therefore preferred and the myth of perfect virginity is tacitly abandoned.[19]

But insufficient attention has been paid to the fact that the virgin birth appertains to one of the pivots of the

Catholic faith which professes: "He was born of the Virgin Mary." [20]

The Fathers of the Lateran Council (A.D. 649) already affirmed: "If anyone does not hold that Mary Immaculate, ever Virgin and Mother of God, conceived by the Holy Ghost and gave birth without corruption, preserving her indissoluble virginity even after the birth, let him be anathema."

The Fathers of the Church were so convinced as to compare the passage of Christ from the maternal womb to the resurrection of Jesus from the sepulchre.

2. The Non-Christian View of Virginity

In the case of other fundamental truths (the resurrection of Christ, the conversion of Paul, etc.) attempts were made, in all good faith, to place them in the myth category.

On Mary's virginity there were extreme views, commencing with the virgin birth. But Mary's perpetual virginity is not to be confused with the myths.

(a) THE JEW

Among the Jews permanent virginity in a woman was inconceivable. Read the history of Jephte's daughter who, although accepting the role of victim of God, asked her father:

" 'Let me have this favor. Spare me for two months, that I may go off down the mountains to mourn my virginity with my companions.' It then became a custom in Israel for Israelite women to go yearly to mourn the daughter of Jephte" (Judg. 11, 37-40).

At the time of Christ the same mentality persisted: celibacy in men was contemplated (the Essenes), but the woman who continued in virginity after having reached marriageable age was a shameful paradox.

(b) THE GREEK

In Greece the same idea was to prevail: to go down to the grave a virgin was the greatest torture. Sophocles has Antigone speak thus: "And now I drag myself around with my hands in chains, without nuptials, without the wedding chant, without having known the joy of the bride and mother! Thus abandoned, friendless and unhappy, I go down alive to the tombs of the dead. What divine law have I violated?" (Sophocles, *Antigone*, 917).[21]

(c) THE ROMAN

In Rome, on the contrary, temporary virginity on the part of a woman was not unknown. Plutarch writes thus of the Vestal Virgins:

It was decided by the King (Numa) that these sacred virgins must remain inviolate for the space of thirty years. During the first decade they learn the things appertaining to their ministry; in the second decade they put them into practice; in the third, they teach them to others, At the end of this time they are set free and those who so desire may marry; but it is said that not many have willingly availed of this faculty, and that those who did so did not prosper but spent the rest of their lives in regret and deep melancholy. They therefore occasioned in the others such a superstitious fear that these remained unwed until old age and death (*Life of Numa*).

It is not necessary to underestimate this affirmation of Plutarch in order to exalt Mary's perpetual virginity, since Seneca, too, has spoken with veneration of "most noble virgins, awakened in the heart of the night to offer sacrifice to Vesta" (*De Providentia*, v. 3). I consider it right, though, to remark that it was the king's will that obliged them to temporary virginity, whereas Mary without any imposition whatsoever says: "I do not wish to know man," she who appeared bound to live an ordinary life, by reason of the existing Jewish mentality and indeed by reason of what the angel himself had told her: "Thou shalt conceive and bring forth a son."

Finally, the Vestal Virgins preserved their virginity under the protection of divine vengeance, whereas Mary did so because she found joy in pleasing God without reserve (1 Cor. 7, 32-34). Moreover, the Holy Spirit imbued her with instincts very different from those of the flesh, of the wife and mother, and this during her entire life.

3. Conclusion: Natus Ex Muliere

Epictetus writes: "In this order of things as they are at present, as if he were on the battlefield, the cynic must be free from worry (concerning a wife and children), entirely dedicated to the divine service, free to go among men, not bound by any private human interests, nor involved in human relations which he cannot violate, but must observe as a good and respectable man, thus destroying his vocation as a messenger and herald of God. As regards marriage, we do not find that in the present situation it is a thing to be overestimated by the cynic . . . we are not surprised if the cynic does not marry and does not have children. As a man the cynic has generated all men, he has all men for his sons and all women for his daughters: thus he approaches all, in this spirit he cares for all" (*Discourses III*, 69, 76, 81).

These texts have the honor of resembling the Pauline texts on virginity (1 Cor. 7) even by reason of a certain lexical affinity.

Nevertheless, the state of perfect chastity was a mere myth to the ancients, an unrealizable aspiration. Epictetus himself, after having sung the praises of chastity, preferred in his old age to take a wife so as to be helped with the education of a little foundling boy.

It is useless to build castles in the air. The flesh continues to have carnal tastes until God by his Spirit infuses divine tastes into it. Only thus can a woman desire to remain a virgin. Only in this way can the perpetual virginity of Mary be understood.

Oldfather begins the life of Epictetus by quoting a Pyxidian inscription: "Epictetus was born of a bond-woman and was himself a slave for many years." In the end he returned to the slavery of that flesh that he wished to forget.

Paul, in the only Marian reference to be found in his letters, writes: ". . . born of a woman, born under the Law, that he might redeem those who were under the Law, that we might receive the adoption of sons" (Gal. 4, 4-5).

Whether or not the virginal maternity of Our Lady is contained in the phrase, "born of a woman," is not clear to the exegete and the theologian.[22] However, it is an evident fact that the Church has declared it explicitly and clarified it in the other phrase: *Natus ex Maria virgine*.

It is precisely because she remained ever a virgin that we ceased to be slaves of the flesh and of the law so as to live as children of God for all time!

V. MARY, THE NEW EVE, MOTHER OF THE LIVING

1. Mary, The New Eve

(a) PATRISTIC CONCEPT

In passing from Sacred Scripture to tradition we are amazed to find that prior to the Council of Ephesus (A.D.

431) Mariology is not centered around the title *Theotokos*, Mother of God, but in the concept of the new Eve who by her faith in the angel of the Annunciation brings us life, just as the first Eve generated death for us by listening to the serpent.[23]

From Justin, Irenaeus, Tertullian, Gregory the Wonder-worker, Cyril of Jerusalem, and John Chrysostom to Ambrose, Augustine, and Jerome, there is a continuous litany that refers to Mary as the new Eve. Epiphanius is to go so far as to say that in Mary alone is fulfilled the prophecy in regard to Eve as the "mother of the living." [24]

After Ephesus, for five centuries the title of Mother of God is to predominate and it is only in the early Middle Ages, with the Marian treatise attributed to St. Albert the Great, that we are to have the exact formulation of Mary Co-Redemptrix and spiritual mother of mankind, as the new Eve: "representative of Christ, associate in his passion, helper in redemption and mother of regeneration."

We ask ourselves at this point how it is that the Fathers know almost nothing of Mary's immediate cooperation in Redemption or even of her spiritual maternity according to John 19, 26.[25]

How is it that, with a few exceptions,[26] Mary's cooperation in Redemption stops short at the Annunciation?

(b) EXPLANATION OF THIS MENTALITY

Reading the Bible, we easily perceive that one does not pass from Christ's divinity to his redemptive work, but that it is from his work of Redemption that his divine sonship springs.

We give just three examples. In the Gospel of the Annunciation the name Jesus, Savior, appears first, then Son of the Most High. In the Apocalypse, appearing not so much as God but as redeemer, Christ has the right to open the book containing the secrets of human history.[27]

In Peter's sermons after Pentecost (Acts 1-5) the saving work of Christ is to predominate to such an extent as to give weight to the rationalistic objection which holds that at the beginning of the apostolic preaching the divinity of Christ did not exist.[28]

While guarding against all exaggeration, we must admit that the same holds in the case of Mariology. To the Fathers of the first centuries Mary appeared above all as the one who had brought forth the Savior, the new Adam.

Even in the Middle Ages there was to be insistence upon her "most firm faith." [29] Nor must it be forgotten that in Thomas' time, as it had been for Paul, faith was the only saving virtue. Not, of course, the Lutheran *sola fides* considered as a blind trust in God that would save without works, but in the sense of a complete giving of oneself to God.

With Pius XII we have made a happy return to the first patristic concept.

In addition to the extract from the *Mystici Corporis* already quoted on page 131, we find another passage in the Encyclical *Ad Caeli Reginam:*

"From these considerations the proof develops on these lines: if Mary in taking an active part in the spiritual salvation of souls, was, by God's design, associated with Jesus Christ, the source of salvation itself, and in a manner comparable to that in which Eve was associated with Adam, the source of death, so that it may be stated that the work of our salvation was accomplished by a kind of 'recapitulation,' (Irenaeus, PG7, 1175B), in which a virgin is instrumental in the salvation of the human race, just as a virgin had been closely associated with its death; if, moreover, it can likewise be stated that this glorious Lady had been chosen Mother of Christ 'in order that she might become a partner in the redemption of the human race,' (Pius XI, A.A.S. 25 [1933], 80) . . . then it may be legitimately concluded that as Christ, the new Adam, must be called a King not merely because He is Son of God, but also because He is our Redeemer; so analogously, the Most Blessed Virgin is Queen not only because she is Mother of God, but also because, as the new Eve, she was associated with the new Adam" (Unofficial translation, published by the Vatican Press, 1954).

Cardinal Billot goes so far as to maintain that the title *new Eve* would constitute a first principle of Mariology.

While seeking to clarify the question a little more, we ourselves, convinced that the foundation of Mariology is the title Mother of the Crucified,[30] wish to emphasize the importance of the title of new Eve as applied to Mary.

It means that both patristic and biblical tradition (John 19; Apoc. 12) have always been pleased to return to the Proto-gospel and to the primeval history of mankind.

The Annunciation also (Luke 1, 26) is developed from this soteriological point of view.

Conclusion: The Bible and tradition prefer to place more emphasis on Mary's cooperation in salvation than on her divine maternity. Beneath the guidance of the Holy Spirit, Redemption is conceived as being a return to the origin, to the first mother, Eve, and not so much to a creation out of nothing. This is an evident sign that between nature and grace there is a certain continuity in the divine designs.

2. Mother of the Living

But if we read the history of Adam in the light of Romans 5-6 we find that whereas Adam introduces into the world the kingdom of sin (original) and death, Christ, the second Adam, introduces the kingdom of grace and life.

If the new Eve enters indissolubly into Redemption side by side with the new Adam, she, too, must cooperate in some manner in the irradiation of grace and the infusion of new life.

Logically, therefore, the idea of the new Eve has been followed by that of Mary, Mother of all men.

One has passed logically from the scene of the Annunciation to Calvary, because according to Paul Redemption is completed through the blood of Christ (Rom. 5, 5-9). And for John, Calvary marks the hour of salvation.

However, the clear vision of Mary's spiritual maternity is reserved to our own times, although it remains true, as Leo XIII remarks, that "the Church always felt that supernatural maternity, more or less consciously"; she is our Mother, because she is the Mother of Christ! This is the most exact title in which to summarize the entire modern mariological trend which finds in the new Eve the mother of the living.

St. Theresa of the Child Jesus is to write to her sister Céline: "In regard to the Blessed Virgin, I must confide to you one of my foolish dealings with her. Sometimes I find myself saying to her: My good, holy Virgin, I find that I am happier than you because I have you for mother, whereas you have no Holy Virgin to love. . . . It is true that you are the Mother of Jesus, but you have given this Jesus entirely to me . . . and he, on the cross, gave you to us as mother; thus we are richer than you, because we possess both Jesus and you! Long ago, in your humility, you wished to be one day the servant of the Blessed Virgin who would have the honor to be the Mother of God, while I, on the contrary, a poor little creature, am not your servant but your child and you are the Mother of Jesus and my Mother" (Letter of October 19, 1892).

If we read attentively each expression in the foregoing we shall readily recognize the sound theological and spiritual pointers given by the saint to the soul of our times who thirsts for Mary and for Christ.

We shall discover especially that Mary alone, in the fullest sense, is the Mother of the living, God's children, precisely because God is essentially the Living Being (Apoc. 4, 10; Matt. 16, 17).

VI. CHRIST, MARY, AND OURSELVES
(Christology, Mariology, and Ecclesiology)

1. Christ and Mary

"To her child the mother stands for all that is good, providence, the law; in a word she is the divinity in tangible form." [30a]

Henry Amiel's affirmation is in keeping with the entire mariological line which we have traced and developed in this work.

But a difficulty at once arises. What then is the position of Christ if Mary is already the perfect mirror of the divine essence of love and tenderness? Moreover, is it really necessary to assign to Mary a place that is distinct from ours and from that of Christ?

Anyone who is abreast of developments in the mariological field knows that these objections are very widespread. [31]

The enlightened Christian knows that Christ is the Son of God. His incarnation is but the echo of the Eternal Word (St. Augustine).

This echo is to become the grace-charis to Luke, it is to be the speaker par excellence to John, or else the way, the truth and the life.

Mary, on the other hand, is always the "one who receives grace," she who listens, is enlightened, directed and vivified.

Finally, we have in Christ the God who gives himself through his Son; in Mary the woman who receives in order to give. Here the psychological axiom is eminently valid: the Son creates the Mother!

Thus the Son of God who possesses the entire marvelous essence of the Father, reflects it only partially in his human nature. Mary gives better expression to certain virtualities than Christ as man can claim.[32]

By divine will the Incarnation has its limits and its laws: whereas one drop of blood of the Son of God was sufficient to redeem the world, all the blood of the Son of Man was required. Naturally, the dignity of Christ is by no means diminished by this, because if "in him were created all things, through him and unto him, and in him all things hold together" (Col. 1, 15-18), we do not see how Mary can escape this law.

It follows that recourse to Mary, rather than to Christ, must not scandalize, but must be considered as a law of divine psychology that has full understanding of the human heart, which finds it easier to pass from the Mother to the Father, from Mary to God.

These truths have already been well expressed by Catholic theologians:

"If therefore a Christian turns with particular confidence to Mary, he does not do so because he hopes to find there greater love than in Jesus Christ. He acts thus because he feels drawn toward Mary in a different way than toward Jesus Christ. It is because she shares with him the character of creature and the need of Redemption. Moreover, human sentiment toward the mother can play a special role. But he who prays to Mary knows and desires that his prayer, through Christ, may reach God."[33]

2. Mary and Ourselves, the Body of Christ

It is not easy to keep the proper distance between Mary and ourselves. Nevertheless, we do not admire the efforts of those who seek to give Mary a special place and a grace essentially different from ours.

Certainly, the privileges of divine maternity, the Immaculate Conception, perpetual virginity and corporal assumption into heaven are worthy of our attention.

But we prefer to think of Christ's reply to the woman who attached primary importance to maternity: "Rather blessed are they who hear the word of God and keep it" (Luke 11, 28).

I believe for this reason that the entire problem lies in determining Mary's exact place in the Mystical Body.

The image of the neck is openly preferred, since the neck unites the head with the members.

Personally I should prefer that of the heart, since the woman is the heart of the family and of society and since this image conveys in a better way the idea of a vital instrument bringing blood and life.[34]

However, it is better not to enter too deeply into a discussion of terms, but rather to consider all the time the reality, namely, that Mary is the Mother of believers.

Thus, if the Christian recites the *Pater noster* close to the *Ave Maria*, he will find that the *Ave Maria* has no other object than that of introducing him to the devout recitation of the Lord's Prayer:

". . . Mary possesses not only a personal relation to the Son of God and her personal salvation, but also a relation to the 'many' who are redeemed by her son. She is mother not of the Redeemer alone, but also of the redeemed; and so she is the mother of the faithful. The Catholic acknowledges in heaven not only a Father, but also a mother. Though by her human nature she is infinitely distant from the Father, yet her special graces have raised her to a wonderful nearness to God, and as mother of the Redeemer she reflects God's goodness and bounty with an inwardness and a truth that are possible to no other creature. When the Catholic speaks of his Heavenly Mother, his heart is full of all the strength of feeling that is contained in that word. Mary is as it were a gracious revelation of certain ineffable and ultimate traits in the nature of God, which are too fine and too delicate to be grasped otherwise than as reflected in the mirror of a mother. *Ave Maria!*" [35]

VII. MARY'S TEARS

1. Mary Calls Us to Penance

In speaking to the Jews, Paul locates their sin "in their contempt for the riches of his goodness and patience and long-suffering, not knowing that the goodness of God is meant to lead them to repentance" (Rom. 2, 4).

Mary's sweetness also, the expression of divine goodness, can give rise to the illusion that God will save us without our living an earnest Christian life.

Mary frees us from this illusion. When she appeared at Lourdes she asked for: "Penance! Penance! Penance!"

At Fatima she even disturbed the quiet life of three little shepherds, speaking to them of sinners and of penance, showing them hell into which a great many souls are plunged because there is nobody to offer sacrifices for them.

At Syracuse (Sicily) she does not even speak. She weeps!

Behind those tears which descend from eternity into time there is something which tells us that Christian life has become too soft and that this troubles Most Holy Mary.

One of our Protestant brethren, on the contrary, is indignant in face of Mary's sadness. Speaking at Fatima he defines is as *the most perfect illusion in Marian devotion*. His reasons are: that there is no mention of the

Father, the center of revelation, nor of the name of Jesus, nor of the Holy Spirit and the commandment of love; that the Mother of God dwells on the description of hell and sin, not on love, nor on the parable of the Good Samaritan, nor on the sacerdotal prayer of Jesus. "She has no word, no compassionate glance for the world's numberless poor and oppressed. Fatima's Christianity is *completely arid, dried up, devoid of joy and spirit and poetry; it is a Christianity without the Gospel, without the cross, without love.*" [36]

What reply are we to make to such an indictment, which is really rather exaggerated, even though its author signs it with the name of Bernardus?

2. *The Importance of Penance among the Jews*

We believe that Mary has not come to teach us something new by her words and her tears.

The word "penance" runs through the entire Old Testament.[37] Here is a passage from the prophet Jeremia which illustrates its importance. In Chapter 3 there is an excellent call for a return to God, that is, to do penance!

> If a man sends away his wife and, after leaving him she marries another man, does the first husband come back to her? . . . yet you would return to me, says the Lord. . . . And I thought, after she has done all this she will return to me. But she did not return; . . . Juda did not return to me wholeheartedly, but insincerely, . . . says the Lord. Go, proclaim these words toward the north, and say Return, rebel Israel, I will not remain angry with you; for I am merciful, says the Lord, I will not continue my wrath for ever. . . . Return, rebellious children, says the Lord. . . . Yet you did not return. (Jer. 3, 1; 7; 10; 12; 14).

Penance or return to God has become so important as to be placed by the rabbis among the seven things that existed before the creation of the world, side by side with the Law.

Philo of Alexandria, at the end of a treatise on divine blessings and maledictions, is to write: "If, all confused, they are converted in their whole soul, reproaching themselves for their error, avowing and confessing with loud voice all their failings, with a pure intention, with the clear and honest eye of conscience, they shall obtain favor with the saving and merciful God, who has conferred on the human race the elect and most high gift of relationship with the divine Logos, whence, as from an archetype, human intelligence is born" (*De Exsecrationibus,* 163).

3. *Luke's Double Call to Penance*

The New Testament opens with the cry of the Baptist: "Do penance, for even now the axe is laid at the root of the trees: every tree, therefore, that is not bringing forth fruit is to be cut down."

Luke speaks of two kinds of penance. His cry is directed first of all toward people who are willing to do penance. It is a happy cry, full of exultation.

We are reminded of the parable of the sheep that was lost and found, which concludes with the refrain: "There will be joy in heaven over one sinner who repents, more than over ninety-nine just who have no need of repentance" (15, 7).

The parable of the lost drachma is also to be gladdened by the same exceeding joy (Luke 15).

Then, in Luke there is another species of penance, and here a desperate cry, as of one desirous to save at all costs from an impending danger, is directed toward persons who do not even deign to listen to him.

(a) LUKE 10, 13: "WOE TO THEE, CAPHARNAUM!"

Jesus groans over the town which has become his second home, because at the day of judgment it will be judged more severely than Tyre and Sidon, who would have done penance if Christ had performed there the miracles worked in Capharnaum.

(b) LUKE 11, 32: AGAINST THE EVIL GENERATION!

The Jews are continually asking for prodigious signs, but they never do penance. On the contrary, Nineveh is converted at the preaching of Jonas. For this reason the men of Nineveh will judge and condemn the Jews.

(c) LUKE 13, 1-7: PILATE, THE MURDERER!

The Roman procurator has killed some of the Jews. At the announcement Jesus is not moved, but adds: "Unless you repent, you will all perish in the same manner." And he continues: "Do you remember the eighteen men who perished beneath the tower of Siloe? Well, unless you repent, you will all perish in the same manner."

Let us note the contrast between the description of great joy and the anger of the divine Judge, much more terrible than seismic and political disasters. More terrible to those who have witnessed his miracles and heard his divine words.

These passages are indeed striking because they are reported by the gentle Luke, the Marian Evangelist, who had accustomed us to mild and soft-hued descriptions of Christ.

In the face of these Gospel passages how can it be said that Mary exaggerates when she calls us to penance and to the thought of hell or when she sheds tears?

Let us hope that her weeping will recall us to the life of grace and save us from that place where there is nothing but weeping and gnashing of teeth!

VIII. MARY'S SMILE

1. *Divine Grace Transfigured by Mary's Smile*

The discouraged soul in modern times can never be told enough about divine grace which alone gives us the strength to do penance and to live as children of God.

Paul's lament, "unhappy man that I am," can always be applied to us, men of the present day, until we feel the grace of Christ within us.

Non-Catholics accuse us of having reduced divine grace to a mere cold accident and of having forgotten the loving relation between God and the creature.[38]

But Catholic life is not what is found in books. It is the life of prayer and interior activity lived with Mary. Grace is then no longer a mere accident, but the maternal smile of Mary who opens our hearts to the gift of the Triune God who wishes to come to us, to dwell within us permanently and to converse with us.

2. *The Pagan "Be Ye Happy" and the Marian One*

The pagan world wished all the time for grace, for the happiness of life, but with infinite bitterness it was forced to conclude that happiness is an illusion whether in death or in life.

The colloquy between the mother Hecuba and her daughter Polyxena, who is to be sacrificed on the altar, is a terrible irony in regard to all human illusion:

Polyxena: I shall see no more the radiant sun. To him I address my greeting for the last time. O mother, to whom I owe my life, farewell! I am going toward the darkness beneath the earth.

Hecuba: O daughter, and I remain a slave in the light . . .

Polyxena: Be happy, mother, and may Cassandra be happy.

Hecuba: May the others be happy, your mother can no longer be so!

(Euripides, *Hecuba*, 411-426)

How different is the "be happy" of the angel to Mary. It is the whole world of divine tenderness that reaches out to sinful humanity languishing in sin and in the shadow of death.

It is useless and even impossible for us to try to rise up again of our own accord. The divine hand alone, outstretched maternally toward us, can raise us up into an atmosphere where there is nothing but light and grace and life.

St. Theresa of the Child Jesus relates how Mary's smile circumfused her with the joy of living. She lay seriously ill and all those around her were praying for her.

". . . I too turned to my Heavenly Mother, asking her with all my heart to take pity on me now. . . . Suddenly the statue came to life, and Mary appeared utterly lovely, with a divine beauty I could not possibly describe. There was a wonderful sweetness and goodness about her face, and her expression was infinitely tender, but what went right to my heart was her smile. Then, all my pain was gone. Silently two big tears trickled down my cheeks, tears of complete and heavenly happiness. Our Lady had come to me! 'How happy I am . . .'" [38a]

3. *Praying in Order to Face the Future with a Smile*

Léon Bloy concludes his book *The Woman Who Was Poor* with the well-known plaint:

There is only one misery . . . and that is—NOT TO BE SAINTS [38b]

We often recall, on the other hand, a phrase pronounced by Garrigou-Lagrange in a classroom at the Roman Angelicum: "There is but one affliction, one sorrow, that of no longer being able to pray."

Modern life would appear to be entirely arranged so as to prevent us from hearing the voice of the Holy Spirit inviting us to prayer (Rom. 8, 14-27).

For this reason the pagan proverb is continually repeated—life is grief!

But the Christian who remembers his Mother sighs and laments in another way: "To thee do we cry, mourning and weeping in the this valley of tears. Turn then thine eyes of mercy toward us . . . O clement, O loving, O sweet Virgin Mary."

This is not only the voice of the Einsiedeln monks, but the voice of every soul who, even though far from God, has perceived within itself the smile of Mary.

This is the experience of Douglas Hyde, former editor of the English Communist paper *The Daily Worker*.

Having lost faith in communism, he wandered gloomily through the London streets until he found refuge in a Catholic church. But he did not know how to pray.

Then a young woman of about twenty, evidently very upset, came into the church. She put a coin in a box and lit a candle, then she began to finger her Rosary beads. Superstition?

But when the girl passed by him again she was calm. "Whereas I," he writes, "had been carrying my heavy burden for months and years!"

Then, almost convinced that he was doing something disgraceful, he drew near to the statue of Our Lady, but how was he to pray? He had no idea. He racked his brains to remember a prayer of Chesterton and Belloc, but in vain!

"At last I heard myself mumbling something which seemed appropriate enough when it began but which petered out, becoming miserably inappropriate. But it did not matter. I knew my search was at an end. I had not talked to nothing.

Outside the church I tried to remember the words I had said and almost laughed as I recalled them. They were those of a dance tune of the nineteen-twenties, of a gramaphone record which I had bought in my adolescence:

> O sweet and lovely lady be good
> O lady be good to me." [39]

This is humanity crying out, but still hoping, because it has found its Mother. And it commences to smile. "Begin, little one, to know your mother by her smile!" (*Pastoral Poems*, IV, 60).

Never was a more harmonious verse sung in pagan mythical poetry to express the loving response of the child who commences to know the mother who has suffered so much for him.

But it has been granted to no other century than our own, filled as it is with distress and atheism, to perceive behind Mary's tears her maternal smile inviting us to pray.

We are still able to smile at life and at the future, full of gratitude to the Father of all grace who has created us for happiness.

SUMMARY OF CHAPTER FIVE:

THIS is not a discussion chapter—*date veniam stylo*—but a penetration into the problems of Mary and into our own problems, because by seeing how she solved them, we too shall have light and strength to solve our own.

If God causes Mary to reappear in our times so that her tears may remind us of Jesus' exhortation to "do penance," it means that God wills to save and pardon us through her.

❴ NOTES ❵

1. R. Laurentin, in *Luc I-II* (Paris: 1957), pp. 99-100, remarks with perception: "There is question here of a history which is elaborated on a basis of memories whose first kernel at least goes back to Mary, the principal witness of the whole, the only witness of the Annunciation. These memories were preserved and observed with attention, that is to say, they were meditated upon. Such meditation is indicated precisely by the word *sumbalousa*. This word, which is Luke's own in the New Testament, signifies in other cases intense reflection on a problem whose solution presents difficulty. It is a question of interior religious reflection, *in cardia* (in the heart) on the infancy of Christ, full of mystery in its human obscurity. Luke 1-2 is more intuitive, more feminine than Matt. 1-2."

2. Regarding faith as an intellectual and loving penetration into the mystery of Christ, cf. R. Aubert, "Questioni attuali intorno all'atto di Fede," in the Italian review *Problemi e Orientamenti di Teologia Dommatica* (Milan: 1957), II, pp. 697-700. For faith centered in Christ, cf. J. Mouroux *I Believe* (New York: Sheed & Ward, 1959), pp. 33-34, who writes:

"These words point to the most real and personal characteristic of faith, considered objectively. Our faith is Christian and is defined entirely in relation to Christ. . . . Thus our faith is Christological and, because of this, it is also Trinitarian." All can appreciate the importance of faith understood in this fuller and perhaps more biblical sense of complete personal surrender of man to God. The germ of this statement is found in St. Thomas (IIa-IIae, q. 11, a. 1). It will be well, however, to point out at once the intellectual character intended by the Church's doctrine. Cf. Denz. n. 1789, in which, before a definition of faith is given, it is stated that "the entire man must offer perfect homage of intellect and will to God by means of faith."

The centering of faith in Christ gives a much more historical and solid value to revelation as a whole. It appears to me that these specifications have a particular value with reference to knowledge and faith in Mary.

3. R. Guardini, *Die Mutter des Herrn* (Würzburg: 1955), p. 49: "During Jesus' lifetime Mary did not yet fully recognize in him the Son of God in the complete sense of Christian revelation." This thesis is favored by M. Schmaus, *Mariologie* (1955), p. 76; also by O. Semmelroth, in a review of Guardini's work in *Scholastik*, 31 (1956), p. 435. We do not feel inclined to welcome Guardini's thesis when he maintains that Mary became aware of the divinity of Christ only at Pentecost, because this lends itself to the rationalistic equivocation, namely, that Pentecost created the divinity in Christ who had never revealed himself

as the Son of God during his lifetime. Cf. on the contrary, the reasons given in our reply.

4. If the phrase "seeing God face to face" were to indicate the Beatific Vision, then Jacob (Gen. 32, 30) and not Moses (Ex. 33, 23) ought to be the prototype of the seer (cf. John 1, 51). But all are aware of God's reluctance to reveal his name (cf. comments of E. Galbiati in *SBM* on Gen. 18, 1; 32, 25-31).

As regards Paul (2 Cor. 12, 2), certainly the third heaven according to the rabbis is the heaven in which God resides; but in this vague text can it really be affirmed that there is no question of the Beatific Vision? St. Thomas makes this statement—as also in regard to Moses—on the authority of St. Augustine IIa-IIa, q. 175, a. 3. Modern exegetes are inclined to deny it (cf. R. Schnackenburg, *LThK*, I (1957), pp. 583-584). To us the proof of the Beatific Vision in Christ and the not yet proved Beatific Vision in Mary consists in the fact that Christ appears in a singular way as the Seer (Matt. 11, 25-27; Luke 10, 21-22; John 14, 4-10), whereas Mary is the reflection and the interrogator even in the Annunciation. What biblical texts can be brought forward in favor of the Beatific Vision in Mary? We are not familiar with them.

5. P. Parente, *De Verbo Incarnato* (Turin: 1953), pp. 187-188. I. Solano, *De Verbo Incarnato* (Madrid: 1953), pp. 129-130.

6. C. Dillenschneider, *Le principe premier d'une Théologie Mariale organique* (Paris: 1955), p. 148; R. Laurentin, *op. cit.*, pp. 165, 175, finds it sufficient to answer: "That Mary may have known the divinity of Christ is presented from the exegetical point of view as being most probable, and not as a certainty."

6a. Cf. note 8a of the present chapter.

7. As the most powerful modern work on this question we indicate H. Ristow and K. Matthiae, *Der historische Jesus und der kerygmatische Christus* (Berlin: 1961). The twenty-four collaborators, among whom are some celebrated Catholic exegetes, treat from a great variety of standpoints the question of the historical Christ and the post-Pentecostal Christ. We indicate for preference the article by the Catholic H. Schurmann on "Die voroesterlichen Anfaenge der Logiontradition," in which the author does not accept the *form-criticism* that limits its field of investigation to the time after Easter and Pentecost, the new faith being considered to be a creation of the assembly. "A tradition founded exclusively on the facts of Easter and Pentecost, which cannot go back to the historical Christ (1 Cor. 11, 23) and to the disciples before the Resurrection, loses its historical value and in final analysis is not to be distinguished from the Gnosis" (370). O. Cullmann even maintains that the present generation must once more face the problem of the Christ of history as opposed to Bultmann's exaggerations which hold that the early Church created the new belief. Insofar as the Bultmann method is cor-

rupted by existentialistic philosophy, it has given us an existentialistic Jesus, but not the Jesus of the Gospel (pp. 268, 271, 280). This is why we do not accept Guardini's Madonna, too humbly and naturally psychological, but not revealed.

8. Hence, the assertion of Gaechter who places the *Magnificat* after the birth of Christ appears to us inexact. We prefer the traditional opinion followed by M. Schmaus and P. Laurintin, *et al.*

8a. It will not be useless to recall the relation between Abraham, *father* of our faith, and Mary, *Mother* of our faith, since the verb *"pisteno"* and the tense (*aoristo*) which Paul and Philo adopt in reference to Abraham are applied by Luke to Mary (*pisteusasa*) and in an emphatic way (cf. Rom. 4, 17; *De Praemiis*, pp. 28-30; Luke 1, 45, in the comments of M. Zerwick, *Graecitas Biblica*, no. 23).

9. Simone De Beauvoir, *op. cit.*, II, 467, 514-515, 481. H. Deutsch, on the contrary, speaks of masochism, the joy of being tormented, as an essential component of feminine psychology, *op. cit.*, I, 239 ff.

10. We are aware that the Hebrew term *'sb* indicates suffering in general, all the more so since in the verse that follows (Gen. 3, 17) it is applied to man's suffering. Moreover, we cannot see that the Oriental author wished to indicate in a particular way physical suffering, since Oriental women give birth to their children without excessive pain. Cf. W. Kretschmer, *op. cit.*, p. 184. For the moral aspect cf. the discourse of Pope Pius XII on *Painless Childbirth* (Jan. 8, 1956).

11. F. J. J. Buytendijk, *Il Dolore* (Brescia: 1957), pp. 148-149; M. Scheler, *Liebe und Erkenntnis* (Bern: 1955), pp. 64-69, in which among other things it is stressed that communion in suffering with Christ is born of loving communion with him and not vice versa (p. 66).

12. L. Bloy, *op. cit.*, p. 221.

13. T. Kampmann, *Die Psychologie des Frauenwesens* (1947), II, 189. H. Deutsch, II, 153: "The woman, turned inward, groaning under the cross of pregnancy and yet happy in this condition, exceeds the normal bounds of feminine masochism and even during pregnancy distorts her maternal function too much in the *Mater dolorosa* direction."

14. H. Volk, *Christus und Maria in Catholica* (1955), p. 103.

15. "Objectively the mother is a vital emotional necessity for the child, and her knowledge of this fact places the child between the mother and the rest of the world as a kind of screen that acts to intercept her other emotional and intellectual interests. Moreover, outside all cultural influence there are the mother's deep longing for a more intimate relationship with her child, her justified concern about his emotional development . . ." (H. Deutsch, *op. cit.*, II, 283).

16. Cf. A. Feuillet, *L'épreuve predite à Marie par le veillard Siméon*, in *Verbum Domini*, 40 (1962), pp. 37-38.

17. L. Bloy, *op. cit.*, p. 229.

18. M. Sticco, *Lavallière* (Milan: 1949), p. 264.

19. A. Mitterer, *Dogma und Biologie der Heiligen Familie* (Vienna: 1952), pp. 113-128. J. Galot, "La Viginité de Marie et la naissance de Jésus," in *NRTh*, 82 (1960), 449-469. These two Catholic authors have a tendency to place the birth of Jesus on the same plane as any human birth. J. Galot writes: "It would be erroneous to think that by such childbirth the maternity of Mary would obliterate her virginity. If a distinguishing mark is to remain in Mary's body and to persist at present in her glorified body, it is the mark of her virginal maternity, the sign of the opening by Jesus of her maternal womb, a womb which was closed to men and yielded freely to none but God himself" (p. 467). Cf. R. Laurentin, *Compendio di Mariologia*, p. 157, who rejects the thesis of Mitterer.

20. Cf. "The Apostle's Creed," Denz. n. 2. Cf., moreover, the warning of the Holy Office.

20a. Denz. n. 256.

21. The attempt to bring the birth of Christ through the supernatural action of the Holy Spirit in Mary onto the plane of the myth in which a god fecundates the woman by his spirit, now seems to be quite untenable, since in classical Greek the expression *pneuma agion* is nowhere to be found; nor is the myth of conception and generation of the son of a god through the divine spirit to be found at all in the Hellenistic age, so that "a direct relation with the birth of Christ by means of the Spirit is automatically excluded" (*TWNT*, VI, 336, 340).

22. Cf. R. Laurentin, *op. cit.*, p. 28.

23. F. M. Schueth, *Mediatrix* (Innsbruck: 1925), p. 73.

24. A. Mueller, *Ecclesia-Maria* (Freiburg: 1955), p. 214, in which he summarizes his study of the Fathers who deal with the subject in question, indicating the pages of his book in which the patristic texts are to be found.

25. Cf. M. Schmaus, *op. cit.*, pp. 332-333; D. Bertetto, *Maria Corredentrice* (Cuneo, Italy: 1951), pp. 41-45; C. Dillenschneider, *Le Mystère de la Corédemption Mariale*, p. 138. In order to avoid misunderstanding let us state precisely that the texts quoted speak rather of the absence of explicit statements regarding Mary's cooperation in Redemption which for us is equivalent to spiritual maternity in its first phase or potentially. For the nomenclature, cf. G. Roschini, *Mariologia*, II, 296. On the other hand, as regards spiritual maternity in its second phase, we have the classical Augustinian expression: "Spiritual mother, not indeed of our head of whom she was spiritually born, but of all his members" (*De Sancta Virginitate*, 6, PL 40, 399).

26. Thus Ambrose says: "From the woman came foolishness, from the Virgin, wisdom. From the tree came death, from the cross, life" (*PL* 15, 1614).

K. Rahner, in *ZKTh*, 74 (1952), p. 233, explains the evolution from the "fiat!" of the Annunciation to that of Calvary by the same process whereby the acorn becomes an oak.

27. A. Wikenhauser, *L'Apocalisse di Giovanni* (Brescia, Italy: 1960), p. 83: "Christ has the right and sufficient dignity to open the book, although neither by his unique relationship with God nor by the perfection of his life on earth, but by his victory over Satan and the world which is subject to him, which victory he obtained by his death on the cross."

28. J. Dupont, *Les discours missionaries des Actes des Apôtres d'après un ouvrage récent*, RB, 69 (1962), pp. 52-56.

29. Cf. texts of St. Thomas, St. Bonaventure, St. Albert the Great, *et al.* in C. Dillenschneider, *Le Mystère*, pp. 156-157. For the concept of faith as a complete surrender of self cf. S. Zedda, *Prima lettura di S. Paolo* (Turin: 1961), II, 239: "In the greater number of texts faith is used in the subjective sense. It is man's fundamental disposition toward redemption by Christ, through which the preaching of Christ is accepted, and in personal adherence to him one's entire behavior is committed in obedience to God, thus coming into possession of the salvation which God has operated in Christ."

30. Cf. our article "La Madre del Crocifisso," in the Italian review *Fonti vive*, 29 (1962), where we have summarized this whole work of ours. On pp. 67-68, we remarked how the word "mother" indicates the maternal element of Mariology, formal element of the Crucified since it indicates the particular divine light which lights up all theology and Mariology. Certainly, those who do not admit that Christ is the formal object of theology cannot accept our statement of the question. They must confess, however, that the *Deitas in ipsa* (God as he is in himself), as the formal object of theology, is an expression so vague as to give the impression that Catholic theology is an evanescent speculation (Cf. Denz. n. 2314).

30a. Henry Amiel, *Journal Intime*.

31. Cf. Yves Congar, *Christ, Our Lady and the Church* (Westminster: The Newman Press, 1957).

32. A. Grillmeier, *Christology*, in LThK (1958), p. 1165, remarks discerningly: "Christ is 'a man.' He is a man and not a woman, he is unmarried, capable of suffering, he is in the midst of history and not at its beginning. . . ."

33. M. Schmaus, *op. cit.*, p. 360

34. For the concept of the woman as heart, cf. the autobiography *St. Theresa of the Child Jesus*, in which she bursts forth in immense joy when she has discovered her vocation of being "love in the heart of the Church, my mother." Kampmann, *op. cit.*, II, 188, writes: "Just as the woman is the center of the human family, more exactly can it be said that her heart is the center of this center. And as the heart, she is the physiological point in which the whole man is concentrated, just

as she is also psychologically related to all that goes on in man." Gertrude Von Le Fort tells of the gracious medieval custom of anointing the queen over the heart, whereas the king was consecrated by anointing of the forehead.

35. K. Adam, *The Spirit of Catholicism* (New York: Image Books, 1954), pp. 119-120.

36. P. Bernardus, "Fatima Wahrheit oder Tauschung," in *Des Neue Mariendogma*, 1952, no. 3, pp. 265-266.

37. Cf. *TWNT*, IV, 99. This is a true mine on our subject. Nevertheless the double aspect of penance in Luke is lacking in it. We remark, in parenthesis, that the term in John is changed into "new birth," by which John, according to the text quoted from Philo also, considers Christians to be already in the ideal state of grace and children of God.

38. P. Althaus, *Der Brief an die Römer* (Göttingen: 1959), p. 51.

38a. *The Story of a Soul* (Westminster: The Newman Press, 1964), p. 34.

38b. L. Bloy, *loc. cit.*, p. 356.

39. Douglas Hyde, *I Believed* (New York: G. P. Putnam's Sons, 1950), p. 267.

General Conclusions

Everyone, including Catholics, feels the need for a more profound Mariology, neither perfumed nor flowery, but adhering to the true history of Mary. In a word they wish to see the science of Mary entirely separated from myth and illusion; they wish it to be historical and biblical.

Myth and Psychology (Marian Humanism)

In the first place we must remark that the myth is no mere illusion but the intuitive expression of deepest human needs (God, the Mother, love, etc.) that every man must respect. The myths with which we are concerned are those that speak of the woman with her child and the serpent (Anath, Nikkal, Isis, Tiamat, Siduri), of which we found a powerful echo in the Bible.

But the modern world despises myths and prefers to speak of psychology which, after all, takes the place of the myth. Such investigation leads us to the definition of woman as grace, love, and tenderness. Thus we have a Marian humanism according to the ancient myth-making mentality and according to that of modern psychology. Is all this to find a place in revelation and in modern Mariology?

The Old Testament (Promise of Mary)

We note how God quite frequently appears in a sinful environment as the God of grace, tenderness, and love (Ex. 33-34; Os. 1-3; Jer. 30-31). In other texts we find salvation appearing in the form of the woman with her child (Gen. 3; Isa. 7). Strange to say, in these latter passages the words grace, tenderness, and love never appear; on the contrary, we easily find here a similarity to the Ugaritic Anath and Nikkal. Does all this not indicate that the Mother with her Son is synonymous with the God of grace, tenderness, and love and that what is divine in the myth is saved? Those texts in which the woman becomes the mirror of divine tenderness lead us to this conclusion (Os. 2, 25; Isa. 49, 66). To sum up, *God is tender as a Mother.*

The New Testament (History of Mary)

Mary appears in her historical reality as a woman of natural grace and tenderness and love, while the Lord and Savior takes flesh in Jesus. What is the relation between them? Luke tells us that Mary has found grace with God and that Jesus is the "charis" of God. To John, Jesus is the Logos of the Father's love, and Mary is the one to whom he spoke, creating her the mother of love (Cana, Calvary). Luke, therefore, presents us with a relation between Christ who bestows grace and Mary who receives it. Why? Because Christ, full of grace, "of whose fullness we have all received," shared his fullness with her so as to proclaim her the Mother of mankind (Calvary).

Thus through myth and divine promise we arrive at Christology, of which Mariology is the most human expression.

Conclusion

God in Christ bestows true grace, tenderness, and love upon the soul best disposed to receive this gift. Mary is the purest mirror of the Blessed Trinity. From Calvary we pass to Pentecost and the Assumption. Thus Mary achieves in our times what she lived during her own lifetime, bestowing what she has received. Her problems become ours; receiving through her we all become children of the same tender and merciful Father, and from Mary's maternal bosom we pass into the arms of God.

As our history proceeds, we have the impression of having returned to the myth. This is the impression of K. Barth, who considers Mariology to be a mere appendage to Christology.[1]

We feel we can understand his affirmation because, as he himself admits, he had not yet discerned the essence of God, the tender and loving Father.[2]

We feel we can also understand Bultmann's typically rationalistic statement that if the Bible contains but human words, as a consequence the divine tenderness mentioned in it is a merely human expression. But if that is so, how is the faith in only one God to be explained, a belief that is absent from all literature contemporary with the Old Testament? Above all, how does the rationalist explain the immovable faith of Christianity in the divinity of Christ and in the virginal maternity of Mary, which appear quite abruptly in the New Testament (Matt. 1, 18-25; Luke 1, 34-36)?

Those who accept the Bible as being the Word of God centered in the love and tenderness of God are no longer surprised that Mary is the word, apparently most mythical but in reality most historical, since she is the divine utterance pronounced by the Word in the Father's name, the utterance which responds to the deepest desire of the human heart, the Mother.[3]

This is the first word that springs to the lips of the tiny baby. It is the word with which the Bible opens: in the beginning God promised us the Mother. The final word of the dying Son of God is: "Behold thy mother."

Lourdes, Fatima, and Syracuse cannot easily be labeled illusion; they lead us to reflect upon the deepest biblical truths, sin, and God's tenderness, which veil the Mother with sorrow and with tears.[4]

The Lutheran theologians saw clearly when they wrote in the Dresden Manifesto in regard to the cures of Lourdes: ". . . today, in some countries, the existence of Christianity is in danger. It would be utterly rash to ignore God's voice which, through the intercession of Mary, is speaking to the world. Silence cannot be maintained for much longer concerning this fact. We must examine it thoroughly, without prejudice, because the catastrophe is close at hand. It could be, too, that by refusing or ignoring the message God sends us through Mary, we are rejecting the grace which offers us the last chance of salvation."

We still have a moment, the moment of our present life, in which our eternal salvation is hidden.[5] It is given us that we may free ourselves from the obsession of technology, from the giddy dance around the golden calf, and delirious from the sting of the ancient serpent. Who is to save us?

One day a young man who had been possessed for five years was brought to the tomb of St. Francis de Sales. The sufferer was subjected to a stream of questions. At one of these questions, an eyewitness affirms, the devil uttered furious shrieks, crying: "Why must I come out?"

Thereupon, the mother of Chaugy, with the promptitude natural to her, implored: "Holy Mother of God, pray for us! Mary, Mother of Jesus, help us!"

At these words the infernal spirit redoubled his cries, yelling: "Mary, Mary! Ah, there is no Mary for me! Do not utter that name which makes me tremble. If I had a Mary as you have, I would not be what I am!"

All were weeping at this stage. The evil spirit continued: "If I had even one of the moments that are wasted by you, a single moment and a single Mary, I would no longer be a devil." [6]

All this has the semblance of myth, but it is history, the eternal struggle between the Woman and the Serpent, between Mary and Satan. Blessed are those who know how to live the moment of their present life in Mary! Their febrile activity will be turned into ecstasy in the contemplation of the utterly tender Father.

{ NOTES }

1. K. Barth, *Dogmatique* (Geneva: 1954), 1-2, pp. 128-129 (*Church Dogmatics* [Edinburgh: Clark, 1958-1962]).

2. K. Barth, *L'Humanité* (Geneva: 1956), pp. 15, 17-20 (*The Humanity of God* [Richmond: John Knox Press, 1960]): "Properly understood, the *divinity* of God includes his *humanity*."

3. Cf. J. Levie, *La Bible parole humaine et message de Dieu* (Paris: 1958), pp. 332-336. (*The Bible: Word of God in Words of Men* [New York: P. J. Kenedy & Sons, 1961]).

4. Cf. "Mary's tears" in our fifth chapter.

5. R. Bultmann, in *History and Echatology* (Edinburgh: The University Press, 1957), p. 155, ends his book by writing: ". . . *the meaning in history lies always in the present,* and when the present is conceived as the eschatological present by Christian faith the meaning in history is realized. Man who complains: 'I cannot see meaning in history, and therefore my life, interwoven in history, is meaningless,' is to be admonished; do not look around yourself into universal history, you must look into your own personal history. Always in your present lies the meaning in history, and you cannot see it as a spectator, but only in your responsible decisions. In every moment slumbers the possibility of being the eschatological moment. You must awaken it."

Personally I prefer Schiller's verses in *The Death of Wallenstein:*

> "Gordon: Oh, time is a marvellous god.
> In an hour many thousand grains of sand slip by.
> Swift as these do men's thoughts travel.
> In just one hour your heart may change.
> Tidings may arrive, a joyous event, decisive and saving,
> Can descend unexpected from heaven.
> Oh, what can an hour not do?
> Buttler: You remind me how precious the minutes are!"

(Act 5, Scene 6)

6. P. G. Tissot, *L'Arte di utilizzare le proprie colpe* (Alba, Italy: 1944), pp. 78-79. For the biblical background other than Gen. 3, 15 and Apoc. 12, cf. H. Schlier, *Mächte und Gewalten im N.T.* (Freiburg: 1958), pp. 31, 45: "The final ratio is: boycotting, persecution, imprisonment, war and death. Because one of his names is 'destroyer' (1 Cor. 10, 10), or rather, as John says (John 8, 44): 'He was a murderer from the beginning.'"

Short Linguistic Theological Vocabulary

Essence (Name): This term is not taken in its static, philosophical sense (*id quo res est id quod est*) but in its phenomenological meaning, that is, in the apparition of the innermost part of a being. In this way the essence of the woman appears in the tender caressing hand that gently strokes the infant's little head as he imbibes the maternal milk (Buytendijk); the essence of God appears in his pardoning the sinful Hebrew race and leading them into the Promised Land (Exodus 34). Better still, it is to appear as *love* in Christ who died for us (1 John 4, 7-10); while the essence of Mary appears in the act of receiving us, miserable wretches and murderers of her Son, as her children on the hill of Calvary.

Thus, essence is not merely an *ens rationis cum fundamento in re,* but a most real, historical thing of which are born a faith and a philosophy that can never adequately contain the reality until faith will have given place to vision of the essence of God and of his *Logos.* It is easy to understand what historical concreteness Christianity receives from this precise statement which, without denying the metaphysical value of essences, emphasizes their phenomenological, historical, and biblical aspect.

Girl: This corresponds to the Hebrew *alma,* to the Ugaritic *galmat,* to the Greek *neanis.* Although it is sometimes a synonym for virgin, it has a more ample meaning. In Babylonian *almatta* signifies widow.

Goodness: This is the Hebrew *tob,* the Ugaritic *tb,* the Babylonian *damatqu,* the Egyptian *nfr.* Generally it means what is good, beautiful, well, but we must be careful not to form an abstract idea of it, which would be alien to Oriental mentality. Thus the Egyptian does not say *beauty,* but *beautiful things (neferut),* the Hebrew has no concept of life in general, but of vital moments in life (*hayym*).

Grace: This is the Hebrew-Ugaritic root *hnn,* the Babylonian *enenu,* the Egyptian *iam* or *ima,* the Greek *charis.* Especially in the Greek term is there an inherent nuance of gratuitousness, spontaneity, smile, and joy. In the etymon a certain sweetness and charm is expressed. Its meaning is very close to tenderness. Compare the Hebrew Ex. 33, 19 and the Babylonian *remutu,* which is also translated grace, derived from *remu, to move to pity.* In the New Testament we also have an admirable union between grace and tenderness: Luke is precisely the Evangelist who, drawing from Hebrew sources, has kept the two words most perfectly. When it is said of Jesus that "the grace of God is in him," it should be understood to mean that Christ is kindness or grace personified, while Mary, called by the angel "she who has found grace" or the "full of grace," is, as it were, the first smile of Christ.

History: Here we mean the *history of salvation,* which appeared in Christ the "fullness of time," the history running from the Annunciation to the death of Christ and which is supported by some documentary evidence in the history of mankind, surpassing the latter, however, in time and extension as well as in its outlook. After Christ's death we have merely a dilatation of true history. Thus, the title *history of Mary* is reserved to the Virgin's life during the earthly life of Christ. Subsequently, it is to be more a *commemoration* and penetration of the mystery of Christ who appeared in the history of man.

Love: This is the term reserved for the Hebrew word *'ahab,* the Ugaritic, *'hb,* the Babylonian, *ramu,* the Egyptian, *meri,* the Greek, *agapao.* It includes the idea of *reciprocal affection,* especially between man and woman. Thus it is used to indicate the affection between God and Israel his spouse, and here, too, a powerful affective link is understood. The New Testament does not deny this sentimental interpretation (Eph. 5) but sublimates it in a mystical transport between the soul and God (1 John 4, 8 ff.). Let it never be forgotten that *agape* is derived from *agamai,* which means to marvel, to be astonished. The greatest marvel of the New Testament is to be God's sacrifice of his Son for us sinners (Rom. 5).

The Egyptian *meri* is worthy of particular attention. It means *to wish, to like, to love,* from which is derived Mary, *loved.* In fact, one can see in the Egyptian Museum in Turin the tomb of Meri or Mary (*merit*), the noble wife of a government official who lived in the fourteenth century B.C.

Mercy: This is the Hebrew *hesed,* the Ugaritic, *dpd.* El is called the "God of mercy" (*dpd*). The hesed expressed the bond established on Sinai between God and the Hebrew people. When the Jews remind God of it they always mean to refer to the historic event on Sinai. However, it became later on a synonym of tenderness (Isa. 63, 7; Os. 2, 21; Ps. 103, 4).

Cf. the discerning remarks of Wuerthwein in *RGG* (1958), II, 1633, and the excellent articles of F. Ascensio, *Misericordia et Veritas* (Rome: 1949), 65.

Myth: For a complete view cf. N. Turchi in the *Enciclo-*

pedia Cattolica, where myth is defined in a broad sense as "animation of nature and life phenomena, due to that primordial and intuitive perception by which man projects himself into things, that is, animates and personifies them, endowing them with a character and attitudes suggested by the imagination; it is, in short, *an imaginary representation of reality, spontaneously outlined by the mental apparatus.*"

By myth we ourselves simply mean personification of the deepest human needs sometimes to the extent of divinization, in the attempt to answer and satisfy the heart of man. Although it is a mistaken answer, being prevalently imaginative and subjective, the myth reminds us of man's deepest needs. In the present case it is the yearning for tenderness and for the essence of the mother.

Tenderness: This corresponds to the Hebrew-Ugaritic root *rhm,* the Babylonian *remu,* the Egyptian *hrn having hmt* (woman), the Greek *oichteiro* and *splanxna.* Fundamentally it means the maternal bosom or womb and for this reason becomes the characteristic of mother-love. In the Bible it is applied to God who is moved and pardons. We must be careful, though, not to form a vague idea of tenderness. In Hebrew *rahamym* appears all the time to indicate thirty-eight different sentiments of tenderness. In regard to the peoples living on the eastern basin of the Mediterranean, what Lily Abegg (*Ostasien denkt anders* [Zürich: 1949]) says of the peoples of the Far East can never be repeated too often, namely, that they think not with their head but with their heart and stomach (recall Buddha) and that they feel and love with their entrails!

Virgin: This corresponds to the Hebrew *betula,* the Ugaritic, *betulatu,* the Greek *parthenos.* Perhaps to the Babylonian *naditu,* which is derived from the verb *nadu, to give* or even *to throw away* and would therefore indicate a woman who, obliged as a priestess of high rank to remain childless, appears like an abandoned field which bears no fruit, or better still like a field offered and given to what is divine. Cf., however, chapter one, note 8. Does it necessarily include the idea of physical integrity? Gordon (Glossary, No. 375) denies this decidedly. The Catholic Rehm, in *BZ*, 1964, pages 88-101, accepts that outside the New Testament virginity is synonymous with the unmarried state. Thus the Babylonian goddess Baba, as well as Astarte and Anath according to the Egyptian and Ugaritic texts, and Demeter, Artemis, and Aphrodite, are called virgins and mothers since they gave birth to children without man's intervention. If we read the context attentively we recognize that we have pure myth, with its many and changing faces, whereas Mary is a virgin by a virginity which exists not alone in her heart but which is authenticated by divine consecration through the Holy Spirit (Luke 1, 34) and to which man testifies historically (Matt. 1, 18-23).

Index

A NOTE ON THE TYPE

IN WHICH THIS BOOK WAS SET

This book is set in Caledonia, a Linotype face created in 1939 by W. A. Dwiggins, which is by far one of the best book types created in the last 50 years. It has a simple, hard-working, feet-on-the-ground quality and can be classed as a modern type face with excellent color and good readability. The designer claims Caledonia was created by putting a little of each of Scotch Roman, Bulmer, Baskerville and Bodoni together and producing a lively crisp-like book type. This book was composed and printed by the Wickersham Printing Company, of Lancaster, Pa., and bound by Moore and Company of Baltimore. The typography and design of this book are by Howard N. King.